GW00371188

REVELATION: VISION A.

Ian Boxall has been Tutor in New Testament at St Stephen's House, Oxford, since 1994, having previously taught New Testament at Chichester Theological College. A lay Roman Catholic, he studied Theology at the Franciscan Study Centre, Canterbury, and Oriel College, Oxford, before embarking on his teaching career in Anglican theological colleges. He developed his particular interest in the Apocalypse as a graduate student, and has written several articles on the subject. He is a member of the Theology Faculty in the University of Oxford.

REVELATION: VISION AND INSIGHT

An Introduction to the Apocalypse

Ian Boxall

Published in Great Britain in 2002 by
Society for Promoting Christian Knowledge
Holy Trinity Church
Marylebone Road
London NW1 4DU

Copyright © Ian Boxall 2002

All rights reserved. No part of this book may be reproduced or
transmitted in any form or by any means, electronic or mechanical,
including photocopying, recording, or by any information storage and
retrieval system, without permission in writing from the publisher.

Scripture quotations are from the New Revised Standard Version, © 1989,
by the Division of Christian Education of the National Council of the
Churches of Christ in the USA. Used by permission. All rights reserved.

Cover image: 'Apostle John on the Isle of Patmos', from *Revelation
Illustrated*, a series of 35 illustrations by Pat Marvenko Smith © 1982,
1992. Used by permission. Available as art prints and teaching materials.
For ordering information contact Revelation Productions, 1740 Ridgeview
Drive, North Huntingdon, PA 15642, USA. Tel: 1-800-327-7330.
Website: www.revelationillustrated.com.

British Library Cataloguing-in-Publication Data

A catalogue record for this book is available from the British Library

ISBN 0-281-05362-6

Typeset by Trinity Typing, Wark-on-Tweed
Printed in Great Britain by
The Cromwell Press, Trowbridge, Wiltshire

Contents

Abbreviations	vi
Acknowledgements	vii
Introduction	ix
1 Beginning to Read	1
2 What Did John See?	27
3 Viewing the Whole Tapestry	48
4 Looking across the Aegean	83
5 Looking into the Future	106
6 Looking into the Heart of the World	128
7 Revelation in the Life of the Church	146
Further Reading	159
Index	163

Abbreviations

1 Clem., 1 Clement
1QM (Qumran document), *War Scroll*
2 Bar., 2 (Syriac) Baruch [= Apocalypse of Baruch]
Adv. Haer. (Irenaeus), *Adversus Haereses*
Adv. Marc. (Tertullian), *Adversus Marcionem*
Apoc. Abr., Apocalypse of Abraham
Asc. Isa., Ascension of Isaiah
Carm. Saec. (Horace), *Carmen Saeculare*
Cat. (Cyril of Jerusalem), *Catecheses*
Ep. (Jerome), *Epistles*
Georg. (Virgil), *Georgics*
H.E. (Eusebius), *Historia Ecclesiastica*
Hist. (Tacitus), *Histories*
In Apoc. (Victorinus), *In Apocalypsin Johannis*
Mart. Pol., Martyrdom of Polycarp
Or. (Dio Chrysostom), *Orationes*
Pss. Sol., Psalms of Solomon
Sib. Or., Sibylline Oracles
Silv. (Statius), *Silvae*
Smyrn. (Ignatius of Antioch), *Letter to the Smyrnaeans*
Trist. (Ovid), *Tristes*
War (Josephus), *The Jewish War*

Acknowledgements

Many might think the book of Revelation of at best marginal interest to a scholar of the Bible, and a desire to write about it a sign of madness. Yet, madness or not, this is the New Testament book which, above all others, has fascinated and enthused me over the past decade. But my specific interest in matters apocalyptic springs from my passion for New Testament studies, which has been nurtured over many years. First of all, therefore, I must express my gratitude to those who taught me the New Testament and, in their diverse ways, inspired me to make their subject my own: Tony Cassidy CSSR, Tony Hodgetts CSSR, John Fenton, Eric Franklin, John Ashton, and Bob Morgan. Colleagues of the Graduate New Testament Seminar in Oxford during the early 1990s were also sources of insight and encouragement, especially that informal extension of the Seminar which retired regularly to the Eagle and Child! Of these, Mark Goodacre and Barbara Shellard have been particularly inspirational. Mark was kind enough to read a draft of this book, as was my Oxford colleague, Henry Wansbrough OSB; I am grateful to them both.

My teaching colleagues at Chichester Theological College and St Stephen's House, Oxford, have put up with my eccentric fascination with Revelation, and encouraged me in many ways. The students of both colleges have been the guinea pigs for many of the ideas espoused in the following pages; without their patience, frankness and insight this book would have been very different. My greatest debt, however, is to Chris Rowland, with whom as a graduate student I first explored the riches of John's fascinating book, and who more than any other has taught me that the Apocalypse is a text worth grappling with. His comments on the typescript of this book were characteristically incisive, insightful and generous. My debt to him is immense.

The initial stages of my writing were greatly enhanced by a visit to Patmos during sabbatical leave in the Trinity Term of 2000. I would like to thank the House Council of St Stephen's House, particularly its Finance and General Purposes Committee, for financial support which made this trip possible. By a happy coincidence, I had the privilege of leading a St Stephen's House pilgrimage to the Seven Churches of Asia just weeks before submitting my manuscript. The experience of reading the Apocalypse *in situ*, assisted by an able band of pilgrims, helped clarify many thoughts in time for the final deadline. During the whole writing process, Ruth McCurry of SPCK has been an indispensable guide through the unfamiliar terrain of publishing; I am most appreciative of her help and encouragement.

Finally, I wish to express my profound gratitude to the many friends and family who have supported me in this work: in particular, to William Whittaker, a constant source of encouragement, and to my mother, who along with my father first nurtured me in the ways of the Lamb. This book is dedicated to her with love.

I am grateful to the following for permission to reproduce pictures within this book: the Tate Gallery, London, and the Bodleian Library, University of Oxford. Unless otherwise stated, biblical quotations are from the New Revised Standard Version of the Bible, © 1989, by the Division of Christian Education of the National Council of the Churches of Christ in the USA.

Introduction

Just over nineteen hundred years ago, on an insignificant island off the coast of Asia Minor, a man named John had a vision. Who precisely he was, what he was doing there, and what he actually saw are questions which have exercised the minds and imaginations of great and small ever since. For this John wrote what he had seen in a book. This book, known as the Apocalypse of John (following its Greek title) or the Revelation to John (following the Latin), has profoundly marked the history and culture of Christendom and Western civilization. Tapestries, mosaics and frescoes portraying what John saw survive in virtually every corner of Europe. Medieval cathedrals and castles were modelled upon Revelation's description of the heavenly Jerusalem. Over the centuries, Christians were confronted with its vivid scenes in their prayerbooks at home, and over the altar at Mass. John's book was one of the first to be illustrated with the advent of printing, and woodcuts portraying crucial scenes were to play a fundamental role in subsequent Reformation polemics. Nor has the book of Revelation lost its hold on the popular imagination in the present day. Its vision of the Four Horsemen and its connection of the last great battle with Armageddon are familiar to many whose knowledge of the Bible and Christian tradition is otherwise negligible.

Yet however influential this book has been, its meaning can hardly be said to be transparent. For many, John's Apocalypse is less a book of *revelation* than a book of *concealment*. This introduction sets out to tackle two fundamental issues. First, and without being too prescriptive, it hopes to offer some clues as to how a contemporary interpreter might approach this book. Much has been written on this book by New Testament scholars in recent years (some might say too much!), which has shed fresh light on some of its obscurities. In the chapters which follow, I have attempted to distil what I have found most helpful and insightful. Nevertheless, there is a danger that the insights of interpreters from past centuries can be overlooked in the recent scholarly preoccupation with the historical setting of John and the churches to whom his book was first read. Therefore, my book is as much a dialogue with some of them and their interpretative methods.

The second question is in some ways more interesting, and impinges upon the interpretation of the whole. What precisely did John see on the island of Patmos? Was he given access to the heavenly realm, as he claims? Did he see what his visions describe, and if so in what sense? Many different answers have been and continue to be given to this question. For some, John is a kind of first-century clairvoyant, gazing into a crystal ball to view events of the distant future. For others, he looks out longingly across the Aegean Sea, conscious of those seven Christian churches he has left behind on the mainland. Others still consider Revelation's distinctive contribution to the New Testament to be its ability to see clearly the truth about humanity, and the world which it inhabits. The metaphor of 'seeing', indeed, covers a wide spectrum of meaning. In this book, I will attempt to explore some of these different kinds of 'seeing', not prejudging whether or not they are all mutually exclusive. If I take more seriously than some the possibility that John describes actual visionary experience in his literary work, I do so in the knowledge that others in the wider fields of apocalyptic and mysticism are also less willing than their predecessors to close the door on such a prospect. Moreover, I do so in the conviction that, through whatever he saw, John of Patmos gained new insight into the ways of the world, and that something of this insight remains a possibility for those prepared to sit patiently with the book he has bequeathed us.

1

Beginning to Read

I do not reject the things which I do not comprehend, but rather I
marvel that I have not understood them.

(Dionysius of Alexandria, d. *c.* 265)

As Many Secrets as Words

The reader of the Apocalypse of John faces a veritable minefield of
interpretative difficulties. How does one begin to read and interpret a text
such as this, with its claims to prophetic utterance and visionary insight
(e.g. Rev. 22.7)? What is the critical reader to make of a book which purports
to offer a vision of heaven itself, and claims an authority which demands the
assent of those who hear its message? What kind of literary genre does this
work represent, with its strange, often fantastic and always highly fluid
imagery, and what are the ground rules for interpreting such a text? Does it
refer, in a veiled way, to historical events and personages, and if so, how does
one go about uncovering their identity? Are these veiled events to do with
the end of the present world order, rather like the prophecies of Nostradamus?
Or does this book describe, at least in part, events which from the present
reader's perspective have already taken place, whether in the history of the
world from its beginnings, in the lifetime of its author and original
addressees, or in the history of the Church subsequent to the first coming of
Christ? These are all ways in which this book either has been or continues
to be read.

Or is any attempt to decode the visions an inappropriate way to read
this apocalypse? Is it concerned in a more allegorical way with the ongoing
battle within the world, and the human soul, between good and evil? Or
does it simply recount the visionary experience of John the seer, with little
or no conscious reflection upon that experience, and therefore few explicit
allusions to the events of history? How did this unusual work find its way
into the New Testament Canon, and does it really deserve its place there?
Why is it so rarely read by Christians in the mainstream churches, and why
has it achieved such popularity among sectarian and religious fringe
groups?

Some of the questions traditionally asked about the Apocalypse are, of
course, involved in the attempt to read and understand any ancient biblical
book. When and where was this book written? Are there any clues in the text

as to the circumstances of its composition, and the concerns of its author and first addressees? But perhaps more than any other biblical writing, the not dissimilar book of Daniel included, the multi-faceted and multi-layered book of Revelation continues to confound and to elude those who would understand it, a fact to which the colourful history of its use and interpretation over two millennia stands as bold testimony (Wainwright, 1993; van der Meer, 1978). As one early commentator put it: 'The Apocalypse of John has as many secrets as words' (Jerome, *Ep.* 53.9). The rest of this chapter will explore some of the distinctive difficulties faced by the interpreter of this book.

Reading with All the Senses

The Apocalypse of John possesses a unique and puzzling quality which singles it out among New Testament writings. One may pick up one of the ancient letters written by Paul of Tarsus, and, for all the obscurities involved in listening to one side of a conversation between the apostle and a largely unknown community from a very different age and culture to ours, some degree of understanding is possible. The letter remains an intelligible mode of communication for the contemporary reader, and Christians continue to turn to the Pauline Epistles for insight and guidance. The interested reader may turn to one of the canonical Gospels, and, however complex the process and however many the layers underlying its composition, its relatively straightforward narrative form enables some access to the evangelist's distinctive portrait of Jesus Christ. But when one turns to the book of Revelation, one is immediately plunged into new and unfamiliar territory. One encounters a universe populated by myriad angelic beings, by fantastic and often terrifying beasts (even the Lamb, despite its generally tame depiction in Christian art, has seven horns and seven eyes!). One enters a world in which the veil covering the unseen, heavenly realm is temporarily removed from before the reader's eyes, to enable a privileged vision of that sacred space where even angels fear to tread. One is confronted with a text dominated by unnerving mythological language which evades straightforward translation into conceptual discourse. This kind of book (known to scholars as an *apocalypse*, a designation which derives from the opening word, and subsequent title, of this very book) was relatively well known among and, one may presume, intelligible to literate Jews in the late Second Temple period, but it remains largely obscure to the uninitiated modern reader.

Moreover, the demands which this book makes upon its audience should alert us to the fact that the process of reading such a text is far from straightforward. To begin with, one needs to recognize the profound differences in the reading process between the ancient world and our own, differences apparent in the very first verses of this book:

Blessed is the one who reads out and those who hear the words of the prophecy and keep the things written in it, for the time is near.

(Rev. 1.3, author's translation)

It is important to note the sequence here: 'read' (or 'read out'), 'hear'. The automatic and immediate response of the contemporary Western reader, when requested to read a book, is to sit down in a comfortable chair or at a desk, and read silently to oneself. But the distinction which this verse makes between 'the one who reads' (singular) and 'those who hear' (plural) should remind us of just how alien such a concept would have been to the earliest Christians and their contemporaries (Gamble, 1995). Even private reading involved the audible enunciation of the words on the page, probably necessitated by the fact that books were generally written in a continuous script (*scriptio continua*), which did not differentiate between individual words. Books for public consumption commonly received a public reading (*recitatio*), in which the role of the reader was clearly distinguished from that of the audience, for whom the work was intended. Public reading was the customary practice in the Jewish synagogue for the reading of sacred texts, a practice apparently continued by the earliest Christians, not simply for the scriptures, but for other authoritative communications, such as letters from founding apostles (e.g. 1 Thess. 5.27; Col. 4.16).

The Apocalypse, by its own admission (1.3), was likewise written to be read aloud, by the reader, who would doubtless have prepared carefully for the task. The use of *scriptio continua*, mentioned above, meant that ancient texts, particularly those written in Greek, lacked not only divisions between individual words and other structural markers such as paragraphs, but even punctuation. Though the earliest copies of the Apocalypse, like those of other biblical writings, have not survived, the opening passage of the document (probably a scroll, βιβλίον) originally sent by John would have looked to the human eye (allowing for modifications in the Greek script) something like Figure 1. Though the ancient eye would have been more practised than the contemporary one in reading such manuscripts, it was nevertheless a skilful art which would have required careful preparation. Moreover, it is likely that even by this stage, the reader would have chanted rather than simply read the passage in question, as became established practice by the fourth century.

The corollary of this is that the Apocalypse, like other New Testament texts, was written to be heard by the congregations to whom it was sent (originally, given Rev. 2—3, to seven Christian communities in proconsular Asia, and only subsequently circulated more widely). This book places particular emphasis on the sense of hearing (e.g. 1.10; 5.11; 6.1; 8.13; 16.1), and hearing a text can have very different effects to reading a text. Just as the ancient reader would have been trained to read *lectio continua*, so too one may presume that the ancient audience would have had a much greater capacity to follow the plot of even a relatively lengthy text than the twenty-first-century reader, more accustomed to the short sharp bursts of television and internet. Attention to structure, order, repetition and location would have enabled the hearer to retain some sense of the whole, even when the text was read not in one sitting but in a number of instalments. The reading of the book would have enabled the sensitive auditor, like the audience of a play or a participant in a liturgical celebration, to enter into the drama of the story and the symbolic world created by the text.

Figure 1. The opening section of the Apocalypse

ΑΠΟΚΑΛΥΨΙΣΙΗΣΟΥΧΡΙΣΤΟ
ΥΗΝΕΔΩΚΕΝΑΥΤΩΟΘΕΟΣΔΕΙ
ΞΑΙΤΟΙΣΔΟΥΛΟΙΣΑΥΤΟΥΑΔΕ
ΙΓΕΝΕΣΘΑΙΕΝΤΑΧΕΙΚΑΙΕΣΗ
ΜΑΝΕΝΑΠΟΣΤΕΙΛΑΣΔΙΑΤΟΥ
ΑΓΓΕΛΟΥΑΥΤΟΥΤΩΔΟΥΛΩΑ
ΥΤΟΥΙΩΑΝΝΗΟΣΕΜΑΡΤΥΡΗ
ΣΕΝΤΟΝΛΟΓΟΝΤΟΥΘΕΟΥΚΑ
ΙΤΗΝΜΑΡΤΥΡΙΑΝΙΗΣΟΥΧΡΙΣ
ΤΟΥΟΣΑΕΙΔΕΝΜΑΚΑΡΙΟΣΟΑ
ΝΑΓΙΝΩΣΚΩΝΚΑΙΟΙΑΚΟΥΟΝ
ΤΕΣΤΟΥΣΛΟΓΟΥΣΤΗΣΠΡΟΦΗ
ΤΕΙΑΣΚΑΙΤΗΡΟΥΝΤΕΣΤΑΕΝΑ
ΥΤΗΓΕΓΡΑΜΜΕΝΑΟΓΑΡΚΑΙΡ
ΟΣΕΓΓΥΣΙΩΑΝΝΗΣΤΑΙΣΕΠΤ

AREVELATIONOFJESUSCHRI
STWHICHGODGAVEHIMTOS
HOWTOHISSERVANTSTHOS
ETHINGSWHICHMUSTHAPPE
NSOONANDHESENTHISANG
ELTOMAKETHEMKNOWNTO
HISSERVANTJOHNWHOBOR
EWITNESSTOTHEWORDOFG
ODANDTHETESTIMONYOFJE
SUSTOALLTHATHESAWBLE
SSEDISTHEONEWHOREADS
OUTANDTHOSEWHOHEART
HEWORDSOFTHEPROPHECY
ANDKEEPTHETHINGSWRITT
ENINITFORTHETIMEISNEARJ
OHNTOTHESEVENCHURCHE

Hearing the Apocalypse could have other surprising effects, as David Barr has suggested in an illuminating article on this subject (Barr, 1986). In oral performance, for example, the reader functioned dramatically as the 'voice' of John, making the absent prophet 'present' in a manner akin to the performance of the Pauline letters: in the repeated 'I, John' (1.9; 22.8), the distance separating the seven churches of Asia and the seer's island exile was temporarily removed. Having established this relationship between the reader and the prophetic author, the oral performance of the Apocalypse was then in a position to create another, even more dramatic and to modern sensibilities shocking, as the reader, now clothed with the prophetic mantle, became the mouthpiece of Jesus Christ himself. The words are all the more powerful, and irresistible, in the hearing than on the written page: 'I am the first and the last' (1.17); 'See, I am coming like a thief!' (16.15); 'See, I am coming soon; my reward is with me, to repay according to everyone's work' (22.12).[1] As for the oral performance of the seven letters, one can only imagine the impact, in an assembly of the Christians of Laodicea, of the following words, chanted or declaimed *in persona Christi* by the reader of the text: 'I know your works; you are neither cold nor hot … I am about to spit you out of my mouth' (3.15–16).

Oral enactment can also highlight the variety of sounds which can often remain unnoticed in a purely mental reading of the text typical of modern private reading. The Apocalypse is an extremely noisy book. Visions of heaven, and of activity in the heavenly temple, are frequently accompanied by thunderclaps and loud noises (e.g. 4.5; 8.5; 11.19; 16.18). The voice of the Son of Man is like the sound of many waters (1.15). The sound of the heavenly song, apparently on the lips of the 144,000 on Mount Zion, is so loud that it can be likened not only to many waters, but also to 'loud thunder' and 'harpists playing on their harps' (14.2). Music, indeed, permeates this book, whether by indirect allusion or through direct citation of hymns and canticles. The four living creatures and twenty-four elders sing before the throne night and day (4.8–11), and break into a 'new song' when the Lamb takes the scroll from the One on the throne at 5.6–10. Those who are victorious over the beast sing the song of Moses and of the Lamb (15.3–4). Though it is not clear whether singing or simply speaking (or better, shouting) is at issue at this particular point, the aural image created by a recitation of Revelation 5.11–14 would be impressive indeed, as the congregation is told, in gradual stages, what John hears: the sound of the angelic host, thousand upon thousand, indeed ten thousand times ten thousand, proclaiming that the Lamb is worthy, taken up by an even greater chorus, comprising 'every creature' in heaven, earth, sea and underworld, offering praise and honour to the One on the throne and to the Lamb in an eternal act of worship.

Nevertheless, the interpreter of the book of Revelation should not simply attend to the effects of hearing: the context in which a text is heard, and read, also has a profound effect on how it is received. The initial vision of the risen Christ (Rev. 1.12–20), standing in the midst of seven golden lampstands, and the recurring liturgical language, imagery and hymnody throughout the remainder of the Apocalypse (as in the examples just offered from Rev. 4 and 5) suggest that this particular book was meant to be read, and heard, in the context of worship. Indeed, some would be even more specific, positing a eucharistic setting for the reading of this book, and pointing to strong parallels between Revelation and the eucharistic passage in *Didache* 9—10 (Barr, 252–5; Garrow, 1997). Yet a survey of the lectionaries – both ancient and modern – of most Christian churches will reveal how rarely the worshipping community has been exposed to this highly liturgical text during its public worship, in particular during its eucharistic worship. Most contemporary Roman Catholics, for example, will only hear small excerpts from the book read liturgically twice a year, at Mass on the solemnities of All Saints (Rev. 7.2–4, 9–14) and the Assumption of Our Lady (Rev. 11.19; 12.1–6, 10); in Year C (of a three-year cycle) further readings are set for the Sundays in Eastertide, but even this is a tiny exposure when compared with the size of the whole book, perpetuating the widespread ignorance of this book among Catholic Christians.[2] Only those who are daily Mass-goers will benefit from the more extensive (though still filleted) lectionary provision for weekdays in the last few weeks of the liturgical year. Similarly, the new Church of England *Common Worship Lectionary*, for use at the main Sunday service (whether eucharistic or not), prescribes the Apocalypse for Eastertide of Year C, a further three Sundays in Year B (Epiphany 2, 3 and 4), and a smattering of festivals and other occasions (such as St George, St Michael and All Angels and the Blessed Virgin Mary).[3] Here too, substantial sections of the book (the letters to the seven churches, the sequences of seals, trumpets and bowls, the vision of the beasts, Babylon and the last judgement) will never be heard at a principal Sunday liturgical celebration.

In other words, the most appropriate context for hearing the Apocalypse read, the appropriate context for entering into it and understanding its message – the context of eucharistic worship – is unlikely to be the context in which reading/hearing actually takes place, if this book is read at all. To read it silently to ourselves, in our favourite armchair or in our study, while at least ensuring that the Apocalypse does not remain a totally closed book, may actually be the wrong imaginative context within which to approach this text. Ironically, although public liturgical *reading* of the Apocalypse never occurs within the Orthodox tradition, the celebration of the Divine Liturgy, both in its language so evocative of the Apocalypse, and in its dramatic movement between the earthly and heavenly realms on either side of the iconostasis, has vividly retained something of that original imaginative context, that sense of the lifting of the veil between heaven and earth.

Yet reading and hearing do not complete the interpretative process. Whatever context in which we read this book, or hear it read, it is clear that its message demands a response. The verse quoted above actually demands a threefold sequence: read, hear, *keep*. To hear the words of this prophecy read is not enough, unless it issues in a change, a renewed commitment, on the part of the hearers. In other words, the demand made upon the hearer of the Apocalypse is not so much to *comprehend* the message as to be *apprehended* by the message. The aim of the seer is to convince his audience of the truth of his revelation, to lead them to view the world as this book views it, with the corresponding demands that makes upon them. This is a fundamental hermeneutical key for the interpretation of the book, particularly crucial given the frequency with which its interpreters, in every age, have used it as a stick with which to beat their enemies, finding in the figures of the Dragon, the Beasts and Babylon the Great those with whom they disagree (ranging from the Renaissance papacy to Martin Luther, from Saddam Hussein to Margaret Thatcher). Any reading of the Apocalypse which challenges only one's opponents, without impinging on oneself also, is likely to be suspect, for it fails to bring the reader under the spotlight of its prophetic message.

As one continues to read the book, or rather to hear it read, the complexities involved in appreciating its message increase even further, as it becomes clear that its contents are as much about *seeing* as they are about reading and hearing. In the introductory section, we are told how John, the author of this book, was on the island of Patmos 'because of the word of God and the testimony of Jesus' (1.9), when he 'saw' one like a Son of Man, the risen Lord, who entrusted him with seven messages for seven churches. After this, the same John describes how, in mystical ascent, he 'sees' the divine throne-room, the One seated on the throne, and the Lamb (Rev. 4—5), while the ensuing chapters describe vision after vision which John 'saw'. This book, unlike any other New Testament book, is a book dominated by *visions*, by what is seen: the Greek verb for seeing (εἶδον in its various forms) occurs about sixty times in this book, as opposed to approximately fifty occurrences of the verb for hearing.

Indeed, in a very profound sense, an hour or two spent in the National Gallery in London, or the Sistine Chapel in Rome, or before the iconostasis in the Cave of the Apocalypse on Patmos, may well offer greater insight into the message of this book than many days spent poring over hefty biblical commentaries and monographs. That is not to deny the crucial role of the professional biblical scholar in illuminating many of the obscurities of this difficult book, only to set the exegetical task within a wider framework. For artists, like poets and prophets, have not lost that capacity to see, to behold that which is so often hidden from our eyes, that capacity for profound insight which is the focus of an apocalypse.[4] Indeed, for many centuries of the Church's life, it has been primarily through art and iconography that the Apocalypse has made its impact upon the majority of Christians. The apocalyptic Lamb and his martyr-band still dominate the ancient basilicas of Rome and Ravenna. The great medieval cathedrals have retained their ability to evoke the glory and splendour of the heavenly Jerusalem. The Apocalypse woodcuts of Dürer and Cranach, no less than the text which they were designed to accompany, remain testimony to the power of these striking visions to speak afresh to Christians in an age of change and reform. The image of Our Lady of Guadalupe in Mexico, clothed with the sun, standing on the moon and cloaked in the stars of heaven, continues to inspire Latin American Christians to hold firm to their vision of a better and more just world. It should come as no surprise, given the visual richness of this book, that it has often been through the work of artists and sculptors that John's challenging vision has been kept alive over the past two millennia.

And yet, paradoxically, even the *vision* of John in this apocalypse is far from straightforward. Even artists have struggled to portray the complexity of the vision of the Son of Man from chapter 1, without making it overloaded, or unreal, or static (it is a highly dynamic vision). It is not an easy task to visualize the paradox of washing robes white in red blood (Rev. 7), or recreate the seductive charm of the Harlot-City, Babylon (Rev. 17). The fluid, polyvalent nature of Revelation's imagery, the kaleidoscopic way in which visionary aspects merge into one another, as in the case of human dreams, makes even pictorial description a difficult task. A Christian of first-century proconsular Asia, hearing John's vision of the Woman clothed with the Sun read in the Christian liturgical assembly, is likely to have experienced a multiplicity of imaginative images flashing before the mind's eye, images drawn from both the Jewish biblical tradition and, we must surely presume, the surrounding Graeco-Roman culture. This vision may well have recalled the figure of Eve, the mother of us all, who according to a particular exegesis of Genesis 3.15 would crush the head of the serpent; or Israel, the mother of God's people, who had suffered much in salvation history for fidelity to God's covenant, and yet now stands gloriously crowned with the twelve stars of heaven (cf. Gen. 37.9–11), borne to safety on the wings of an eagle (Exod. 19.4). The woman also bears traits of Jerusalem, the pregnant mother, who cries out for her children to be delivered (Isa. 26.16–18), and Mary of Nazareth, that faithful Israelite who gave birth to the Messiah. Local Asian Christians may also have seen echoes of Diana-Artemis, the great mother-goddess of the Ephesians, or Leto, pregnant with Apollo, escaping from the dragon Python, or Isis the queen of heaven and mother of Horus, pursued by the red dragon Set. The location of this 'great sign' in heaven may well have called to mind the constellation Virgo, a recognition of the powerful influence of astrological concerns throughout the ancient world. What impact this kaleidoscope of images had, what new shapes were formed and what meanings were discerned in the mind of the hearer, one can only hazard a guess. To visualize even this one image of a woman has exercised the minds and imaginations of artists and poets ever since.

Indeed, the symbolic world which the book of Revelation describes blurs even the fairly solid distinction between hearing and seeing. In his inaugural vision on the Lord's Day on the island of Patmos, John first hears a voice telling him to write what he sees. What follows shakes the reader like a bolt from the blue, as John recounts how he turned 'to *see* whose voice it was that spoke to me' (Rev. 1.12, my emphasis). How is it possible to see a voice? How are even the Michelangelos, or the Dürers or the William Blakes of this world to paint the heavenly voice? The Apocalypse, far from reinforcing our normal perceptions of the way the world is, pushes our senses to their limits. All our faculties, our hearing, our seeing, even our smelling (for the aroma of heavenly incense is never far away from the pages of this book, e.g. 5.8; 8.3–4; 18.13) are stretched almost to breaking point, impelling us onwards to ever newer horizons and spheres of vision and understanding. To embark on a reading of the Apocalypse is to embark on a risky journey which will not leave us unchanged but may well turn our world and our apprehension of reality on its head. Yet it requires the flexing of our imaginative muscles, no less than our intellectual ones.

The Literary Puzzles

Uncertainty about the appropriate senses through which to approach this book is not the only reason why Christians have tended to shy away from Revelation over the centuries, or continue to do so today. There are also what one might call the *literary* difficulties: structure, chronological pattern and genre, each of which will now be considered in turn.

To comprehend any text, it is felt necessary to be able to detect some kind of order to it, to identify some structural clues within it to aid comprehension. That has been true almost from the beginning, yet the conclusions of interpreters regarding structure have rarely coincided: the sixth-century Greek commentary of Andreas of Caesarea, so influential upon Apocalypse interpretation in Eastern Christianity, detected twenty-four sections in the book, each of which could be subdivided by three. On the other hand, Andreas' contemporary, the Latin commentator Primasius of Hadrumetum, divided the Apocalypse into a mere twenty sections. The paradox of Revelation, at least to many readers, is that it seems to combine clarity of structure in certain chapters with apparent muddle and confusion in others.

Most contemporary commentators, for example, accept that the number seven is an important structural key, seven being a number designating perfection or completeness in the ancient world. After an extended superscription (1.1–3) and introduction by the author (1.4–8), an account of John's inaugural vision prefaces seven 'letters' or 'prophetic messages' to seven churches in the Roman province of Asia. These seven letters give way to further series of sevens: the opening of seven seals by the Lamb, enabling the heavenly scroll containing God's purposes to be unravelled; the blowing of seven trumpets, inaugurated by the opening of the seventh scroll, which herald visions of cosmic disaster; the pouring out of seven bowls of divine wrath, provoking events reminiscent of the plagues of Egypt. There are also seven distinctively Johannine beatitudes punctuating the text (1.3; 14.13; 16.15; 19.9; 20.6; 22.7; 22.14). Evidently, the repetition of the number seven, and cycles of sevens, is structurally significant.[5] But much more ambiguous, and controversial, is how to interpret the events between the seven trumpets and the seven bowls, or the final eschatological events after the pouring out of the seventh bowl. Here the structural clarity of the series of sevens is rather less evident, though some commentators have found implicit septets within the text. Nor is it always clear how and why the seventh element is separated from the sixth: in the case of the trumpets, by nearly two chapters (10.1—11.14), incorporating no less than three visions (the angel with the little scroll and the commissioning of John; the measuring of the temple; the two witnesses). A tentative attempt at navigation through these treacherous textual waters is offered in Chapter 3 of this book.

The question of what one might call 'chronological pattern' or 'chronological sequence' is also a difficult one in relation to the apocalyptic visions of this book. Is it possible to trace a neat chronology of events throughout the book, from beginning to end? Given the rather fluid nature of its visions, and the location of many of them beyond our earthly temporal plane, it is often difficult to discern in any one vision whether one is being presented with events of the past, the present or the future, or a combination of all three. Are the visions of the Lamb that was slain, for example, visions of the present reality in heaven, where Christ, both priest and victim, pleads before the throne of grace, or of Christ's future victory, when the last enemy will ultimately be destroyed (cf. 1 Cor. 15.26), or of his historical death on Calvary, or even of that which has been the case 'from the foundation of the world' (Rev. 13.8)? It is not surprising to find that, from the earliest years, commentators have had difficulties in determining precisely how the text works on a chronological level.

Victorinus of Pettau (died c. 304), in what is the earliest surviving Latin commentary on the book, developed his famous theory of *recapitulation* which explained the recurring cycles of sevenfold seals, trumpets and bowls as describing essentially the same events, rather than plotting a straightforward chronological chart of the events of the End, such as the widespread millenarian interpretation suggests. In more recent years, particularly in the late nineteenth and early twentieth centuries, there have been a host of source-critical solutions which attempt to attribute various parts of the book to different stages of composition or to the use by the author of earlier sources, or even to different authors. R. H. Charles is well known for the particular difficulties he found with the chronology of eschatological events in Revelation 20—22, forcing him to propose a radical theory of displacement at this point (Charles, 1920, II, 144–54). Given the structural clues that can be detected in certain parts of Revelation (as in the role of the number seven mentioned above), one might be forgiven for wondering whether such source-critical and other literary solutions represent more an impatience with sitting with the text than an accurate description of the historical process of its composition. Nevertheless, most would concur that the structure of the book as a whole is not at all straightforward.

A further literary difficulty is determining the precise genre of this text. To understand any text, whether poem, historiographical work, romantic novel or birth announcement in the newspaper, one needs to pay some attention to its literary genre, if one is to lessen the risk of seriously misunderstanding its message. This task is difficult enough in the case of the Gospels, or the Acts of the Apostles. It is even more complex in the case of the book of Revelation, which represents not one but a combination of three different genres, at least one of which is largely unfamiliar to the modern Western mentality (Bauckham, 1993, 1–17).

The literary framework of the book of Revelation, 1.4–8 and 22.16–21, is an epistolary one, connecting this book, for all its dissimilarities, to the letters of Paul, or the circular epistle known as 1 Peter, sent to a number of different Christian communities in 'Pontus, Galatia, Cappadocia, Asia, and Bithynia' (1 Pet. 1.1). Following the pattern of other early Christian letters, a reference to the author and addressees of this book is followed by the form of greeting made famous by Paul: 'Grace to you and peace ... ' (Rev. 1.4). Like the opening of 1 Peter, and of Galatians, which is addressed to various churches in the region of Galatia (Gal. 1.2), Revelation 1.4 similarly describes itself as a letter sent to 'the seven churches that are in Asia', and Revelation 2—3 purport to contain seven specific messages to these churches from the risen Christ. These epistolary characteristics mean that, far from being a generalized exposition or account of visions, this book was originally intended for specific, and named, Christian groups.

Yet, even before this epistolary framework, this book has already designated itself as a prophetic work: it contains words of prophecy (1.3); they are prophetic words which are not to be sealed up (22.10), for the time is near; blessings are promised on both reader and hearers of this prophetic message, and curses on those who tamper with it (1.3; 22.18–19). Does this mean that we are meant to read it on a par with the canonical prophetic books of the Hebrew scriptures, such as Isaiah, Jeremiah and Ezekiel? This book is certainly heavily influenced by the prophetic words and imagery of these and other Israelite prophets, and indeed John at one point will receive a commissioning closely resembling that of Ezekiel (Rev. 10; cf. Ezek. 2—3).

Yet it is also unashamedly a work of Christian prophecy, and therefore stands on a par with those examples of oracular prophecy found elsewhere in the early Christian movement, particularly in a liturgical context (e.g. Acts 13.1–3; 1 Cor. 14; Matt. 7.15–20; *Didache* 11—13). The letters to the seven churches claim to be messages spoken directly in the name of the Lord Jesus, while other prophetic oracles, spoken in the name of the risen Christ (e.g. Rev. 16.15), or of the prophetic Spirit (e.g. 14.13b), punctuate the visions of this book at strategic points. A fundamental difference in the case of Revelation is that John, unlike other community or wandering Christian prophets, is not present during the delivery of his prophetic message, due to his island 'exile'. His 'prophetic letter', again like the letters of Paul (e.g. 1 Cor. 5.3–4), would compensate for his absence when read out during the liturgical assemblies of the seven churches.[6]

Understanding Apocalyptic

Yet it is not sufficient to see this book as a 'prophetic letter'. Despite some misgivings, the majority of scholars are united in seeing the book of Revelation, for all its epistolary and prophetic characteristics, as belonging to the body of early Jewish and Christian texts known as *apocalypses* (indeed, it gives its name to this genre: Rev. 1.1). But it is precisely this aspect of its literary genre which makes this book so difficult for the modern reader. The contemporary (mis)use of words such as 'apocalyptic' and 'apocalypse', both in popular usage and, to a lesser extent, even by theologians and biblical scholars, may have dulled our senses to the distinguishing features of this strange but influential literature (Rowland, 1982).

In scholarly circles, it has become increasingly clear that a word such as 'apocalyptic' has been used in such a diversity of ways as to elude clear definition. Some would now argue that the word should no longer be used in scholarly discourse, to avoid the confusion which hitherto existed, others that it should be used only as an adjective, such as in the phrase 'apocalyptic literature' or 'apocalyptic movement'. However confusing the recent debate about terminology has been, it has resulted in some clarification in the use of terms, such that the word 'apocalypse' is now generally used to describe the distinctive literary genre, or texts which utilize this genre, 'apocalypticism' refers to the social movements or ideology which produced such texts, and 'apocalyptic eschatology' (or 'transcendent eschatology') to that distinctive variety of ideas concerning the End, found not simply in literary apocalypses but in other kinds of texts as well.

The popular misuse of the term is even more pervasive. The title of the cult film *Apocalypse Now*, set against the horror of the Vietnam War, is symptomatic of the problem, for it conjures up images of violent destruction and bloodshed on a nightmarish scale. In general usage, the language of apocalypse, and related words (some of them, like Armageddon, drawn from the book of Revelation), conjure up images of the violent collapse of civilization, cosmic disasters, even nuclear warfare.

Yet recent scholarly study of apocalyptic and the apocalypses has also wanted to play down this popular emphasis upon the 'End of the world'. The word 'apocalypse', after all, is derived from the Greek word ἀποκάλυψις, which literally means 'uncovering' or 'unveiling'. Apocalyptic is concerned, not primarily with *eschatology*, teaching about the last things (other types of biblical literature are also concerned with things pertaining to the last days), but with the *disclosure of divine secrets* by direct revelation. Thus this Judaeo-Christian literature is a particular manifestation of a wider interest in the ancient world in higher wisdom through revelation. An apocalypse provides the narrative framework within which such a revelation can be described, often using fantastic imagery, vivid colours and symbolic numbers, and normally attributed pseudonymously to an authoritative figure of Israel's past, such as Daniel, Enoch, Ezra or Abraham. Within the narrative, the apocalyptic 'unveiling' can take place in a variety of ways: by means of a heavenly journey, or a dream-vision, or the mediation of an angelic being.

Although it is true that the two canonical apocalypses, Daniel and Revelation, have a particular interest in the events leading to the end, due not least to the circumstances within which they were written (Daniel, for example, was almost certainly written as a response to the Maccabean crisis prompted by the provocative policies within Palestine of the Seleucid Antiochus IV Epiphanes during the second century BCE), other apocalypses, such as the earliest sections of 1 Enoch, have little or no interest in eschatology but are much more interested in other secrets, such as cosmology and the origins of evil. As *Mishnah Hagigah* 2.1 (a rabbinic ruling actually written to discourage the kinds of speculations in which the apocalypticists engaged!) puts it, such writings are concerned with the revelation of four types of mysteries: things pertaining to the realm above, the realm beneath, what was before time, and what will be hereafter. To define apocalyptic predominantly in terms of the hereafter, in terms of eschatology, is to do a disservice to its many other aspects.

The Apocalypse of John, then, should not be viewed as a book primarily concerned with the end of this world as we know it (even though it does have profound eschatological concerns), but as a revelatory work which 'unveils' or 'uncovers' a variety of heavenly mysteries, not least among them the truth about the world which John and his addressees inhabit. The apocalyptic distinction between Above and Below, between heaven and earth, should not be understood as advocating a thoroughgoing dualism. Rather, the heavenly visions of apocalypses are perhaps best understood as providing a kind of 'running commentary' on action on earth, offering assurance of a particular outcome in the realm below. Heaven is the realm where God is not only God, but acknowledged as such, where things are seen, in other words, in their true reality. Earth, on the other hand, is the realm where God's authority is yet to be recognized; viewed from an earthly or this-worldly perspective, reality appears askew. The striking claim of an apocalypse, therefore, is to remove the veil which separates the heavenly realm from our limited, earthly perspective, enabling the seer, and those privileged with access to the seer's revelation, to view things, however temporarily, from the divine perspective.

Direct revelation of the things of God, such as an apocalypse claimed to offer, would have provided a powerful (and to many, more satisfying) alternative to the existing ways within Judaism of discerning the will of God. The ancients were not immune to the kinds of question which have troubled human souls to the present day: how does one discern the divine will? why does the way of the wicked prosper? what sense can be made of the suffering of the innocent? These profound human questions would have become all the more pressing in Judaism as a more transcendent view of God began to predominate during the exilic and post-exilic periods. Given the belief among at least some Jewish circles that the age of prophecy had now ceased (e.g. 1 Macc. 4.46; *Tosefta Sotah* 13.3), answers to such questions were largely dependent upon the precarious business of scriptural exegesis, the traditional scribal activity, or the inductive wisdom of sages such as Jesus ben-Sira or the author of the book of Proverbs. The apocalypses' claim to offer direct disclosure of the things of God, authenticated by their attribution to authority figures of the past, would have appeared much more reliable than these more indirect procedures.

But can one go further, and posit a particular social context which would have been especially conducive to the writing of apocalypses? It is sometimes claimed that apocalypses are essentially crisis literature, arising out of a situation of crisis, such as persecution. In other words, the social function of an apocalypse is to comfort the suffering or threatened righteous by the revelation of heavenly secrets, often to do with future salvation, which serve to place their present suffering in a wider context. Given such an understanding, the book of Revelation can be understood as yet another book of consolation for those currently being persecuted or facing impending persecution (according to the traditional Christian explanation, persecution under the Emperor Domitian).

A background of crisis for the people of God is almost certainly the case with some of the apocalypses. Both Daniel and the so-called Animal Apocalypse of *1 Enoch* 85—90 are generally believed to have been provoked by the crisis in Palestine in the second century BCE, during the reign of the Seleucid Antiochus IV. But such is not necessarily the case, and, as will be seen in Chapter 4 below, it is not the only or even the most appropriate explanation of the book of Revelation. To begin with, as John J. Collins has noted, the Jewish apocalypses written as a response to the traumatic events of 70 CE (the fall of Jerusalem and the destruction of the Second Temple), namely *4 Ezra* and *2 Baruch*, were not written in the midst of those events, but perhaps two or three decades afterwards (Collins, 1992, 155f.). Indeed, despite Josephus' claim that some of the rebels during the Jewish War claimed divine inspiration (*War* 2.258–60), there do not seem to be any literary apocalypses surviving from Palestine during that turbulent period. But, in fact, it is not only *4 Ezra* and *2 Baruch* which do not fit the mould of 'crisis-literature': in what sense, for example, can the *Apocalypse of Abraham* (dated between the late-first and mid-second century CE) be viewed as a response to a crisis? Apart from its rather humorous attack on pagan idolatry in the first seven chapters, this is essentially an account of Abraham's journey through the heavens, accompanied by the angel Iaoel, in which various secrets are revealed of 'what is above' and 'what is below'. There is just one brief allusion to the events of 70 in *Apoc. Abr.* 27, but this does not seem to be in the forefront of the mind of the seer. If crisis is not an indispensable feature of these apocalypses, then it need not necessarily provide the catalyst for the composition of the Apocalypse of John either.

Before we move on, we must address one forceful, if not widespread, objection to the apocalyptic nature of the book of Revelation. The apparent mixture of literary types which has been noted for this book has led some commentators to deny that it should be described as an apocalypse at all. Roloff, for example (Roloff, 1993, 6), stresses its unusual epistolary features, but goes further still, pointing to what he sees as differences between the so-called 'Apocalypse of John' and other apocalypses, as evidence that its classification as a literary apocalypse is misguided. He notes, for example, its relative lack of the typical combination of obscure vision and clear interpretation, and the fact that it does not claim to be a long-hidden book from the distant past. Others object that the 'prophetic' claims of Revelation count against its identification as an apocalypse.

To answer the first objection, Revelation is not alone in its combination of various kinds of material in the same book. The undeniably apocalyptic *1 Enoch*, for example, presents a combination of legend, apocalypse proper, and admonition. The biblical apocalypse attributed to Daniel is not simply a series of visions, but contains stories about the hero and his Jewish contemporaries in the Babylonian court. Moreover, though John of Patmos speaks of his work as 'prophecy' (Rev. 1.3; cf. 22.7, 10), he still maintains the characteristic literary elements of an apocalypse: mediation by an angel, or series of angels, and the centrality of visions, rather than a prophetic speaking directly 'in the name of the Lord' (Collins, 1992, 212). Further, the objection that Revelation is a prophetic work rather than an apocalypse represents a failure to recognize the distinctive characteristics of Christian prophecy, such as the belief in the re-emergence of the spirit of prophecy in early Christian circles, so that Christian claims to direct divine revelation can be expected to have a prophetic edge. Moreover, the Christian conviction that the eschatological events have in some sense begun in the life, death and resurrection of Jesus Christ should go some way towards accounting for the lack of pseudonymity in John's Apocalypse. Similarly, other primitive Christian apocalypses (such as the *Apocalypse of Peter* and the *Apocalypse of Paul*) do not claim to be books sealed by one of the ancients at some point in the distant past. In short, Revelation represents a distinctly Christian version of the well-established Jewish genre of apocalypse, tinged with prophetic elements, and sent as a circular letter to the seven churches of Asia.

Puzzles of Authorship

Anyone who has ventured, however tentatively, into the realms of critical biblical study will be aware that the question of apostolic authorship of a host of New Testament writings is a much disputed one. This is no less true for the book of Revelation, which has traditionally been ascribed to John the son of Zebedee, one of the twelve (or 'twelve apostles'), long identified with the unnamed 'disciple whom Jesus loved' of the Fourth Gospel (e.g. John 13.23; 20.2; 21.7). The earliest explicit mention of the Apocalypse of John, found in Justin's *Dialogue with Trypho* 81.4, reveals that, as early as the second century, it was attributed to 'John, one of Christ's apostles (*unus ex apostolis Christi*)', and this claim to apostolic authorship remained widely held into the modern period, and continues to be held by a small number of scholars even today. The strength of this tradition of the apostolic authorship of the Apocalypse, from such an early period, and the related belief that Revelation and John's Gospel sprang from the same pen, is certainly impressive.

  However, even in the early period it did not remain unchallenged: at the beginning of the third century, for example, Gaius, a Roman presbyter, attributed to the gnostic leader Cerinthus 'revelations written, as he would have us believe, by a great apostle'; his description of the contents of these revelations makes clear that he is speaking of the Apocalypse of John (Eusebius, *H.E.* 3.28).[7] But there would seem to be dogmatic grounds for such an attribution, and for the earlier attribution to Cerinthus of all the Johannine writings, the Apocalypse included, by the second-century group known as the Alogoi. At least part of the reason for their rejection of apostolic authorship was their unease with the widespread chiliastic interpretation of the book (a literal interpretation of the 'thousand'-year reign of Christ in Rev. 20). Thus it has little to contribute to any contemporary assessment of the apostolic authorship of the book.

  More compelling may be the questioning, later in the third century, of the book's apostolic authorship on literary grounds. Dionysius of Alexandria, while continuing to regard the Apocalypse as authoritative if obscure (and therefore rejecting the position of Gaius and the Alogoi), concluded that its author could not be identified with the author of the Fourth Gospel and

Johannine Epistles, whom he took to be John the apostle (Eusebius, *H.E.* 7.25). This led him to resort to the tradition that there were two tombs of John at Ephesus in order to account for two different New Testament writers bearing this name. What kind of evidence led him to this conclusion? While one cannot rule out a vestige of the earlier suspicion of Revelation for dogmatic reasons, Dionysius' main arguments are literary. For one, the evangelist and epistle-writer never names himself, whereas the author of Revelation calls himself John on several occasions; moreover, Dionysius noted sharp differences between the two in both theological expression and Greek style and grammar, pointing out the latter's use of 'barbarous idioms'. It is these kinds of literary arguments which have tended to feature in more recent objections to the Johannine authorship of Revelation.

First, it is certainly the case that many of the theological phrases so characteristic of the Johannine Gospel and Epistles are lacking in the Apocalypse: the noun ἀλήθεια ('truth') and adjective ἀληθής ('true'; yet Revelation does use the related Johannine adjective ἀληθινός, 9 times in the Gospel; 10 in Rev.), ζωή ('life'), αἰώνιος ('eternal'), σκοτία ('darkness'), πιστεύειν ('to believe'; though both 'faith', πίστις, and 'faithful', πιστός, are found). Other Johannine phrases, such as 'world' (κόσμος), are found but used in a very different sense. As many examples can be found of terms characteristic of Revelation which are lacking in the Gospel and Epistles. Statistical analysis of these differences has led some scholars to go so far as to deny the book any place within the Johannine stream of early Christianity (Schüssler Fiorenza, 1985, 85–113). Theological differences are also pointed out, not least the contrast between the so-called 'realized eschatology' of the Fourth Gospel and the 'future eschatology' of the Apocalypse. Moreover, some commentators find it difficult to attribute the Greek of Revelation to the same author as the Fourth Gospel: the Greek of the Apocalypse is often regarded as rather eccentric, probably pointing to an author who was more at home in a Semitic language such as Aramaic or Hebrew, while the Greek of the Fourth Gospel, though simple and utilizing a limited vocabulary, is grammatically correct.

Yet it may be premature to cut all links between the Apocalypse and the undisputed Johannine writings. As at least one prominent Johannine scholar has shown (Brown, 1997, 804), for all the differences there are some striking similarities in theological motifs. For example, both Revelation and the Fourth Gospel speak of Christ as source of living water (John 7.37–39; Rev. 22.1), as Word of God (John 1.1, 14; Rev. 19.13) as bridegroom (John 3.29; cf. 2.1–11; Rev. 19.7, 9; cf. 21.2, 9), and as one who 'shepherds' (John 10; Rev. 2.27; 7.17). Both envisage the replacement of the Jerusalem Temple (though in somewhat different ways: John 2.19–21; 4.21; Rev. 21.22); both envisage hostility towards Christians from Jewish groups (John *passim*; Rev. 2.9; 3.9), even if each presupposes a different stage in the relationship between the church and the synagogue. Particularly significant is the dependence of both upon the Theodotion version of Zechariah 12.10, rather than the Septuagint or Hebrew Masoretic text tradition (John 19.37; Rev. 1.17).

While some of these agreements may appear superficial (though both describe Christ as Lamb, they utilize different words, ἀμνός in the case of the Fourth Gospel, ἀρνίον in the Apocalypse), others run much deeper, pointing to a quite profound sharing of theological vision, as an exploration of the common use of the language of 'witness' or 'testimony' within both texts reveals. Though it may be true that 'bearing testimony' has a more overtly christological focus in the Fourth Gospel (e.g. John 5) than in Revelation, underlying both there is a strong sense that the Christian vocation, like that of Jesus Christ, is to bear witness to the truth, whether that be about Christ, the Father, the world or the beast (e.g. John 3.32–33; 18.37; Rev. 1.2; 11.7). Similarly, the effects of the death and exaltation of Christ, and of the steadfast witness of believers, can be spoken of in terms of 'conquering' or 'being victorious' (νικάω; 1 in the Fourth Gospel; 6 in 1 John; 17 in Rev.). This is a motif which ties in well with a mythological tradition utilized by both, describing the downfall of the 'ruler of this world' or the satanic dragon (John 12.31; Rev. 12.9). Likewise, the frequent use of verbs denoting ascent to and descent from the heavenly realm (ἀναβαίνω and καταβαίνω) are characteristic of both Revelation and the Fourth Gospel. Nor is the difference in eschatological outlook quite so pronounced as is often claimed, particularly if one allows for development in theological perspective with the passing of time. While the subject matter of the Apocalypse means that it has a particular focus upon the future consummation of God's salvific purposes, it nevertheless emphasizes the 'already' of the Lamb's victory, a feature especially pronounced in the succession of heavenly canticles, which describe a salvation as 'realized' as anything in the Fourth Gospel (e.g. Rev. 5.9–10; 11.15–18).[8] So too, the 'coming' of the risen Christ is not simply connected to his future coming in glory: already in the seven letters of Revelation 2—3 he comes in judgement and salvation to those who follow him (cf. John 14.18–19). There do, in other words, seem to be good reasons for continuing to claim some connection between the book of Revelation and the other writings attributed to John 'the son of Zebedee'.

Yet, while the similarities point to this book originating in the same circle as the Fourth Gospel and Johannine Epistles (or at least in an early Christian circle which had close contact with the Johannine stream), the differences would seem to confirm the conclusions of Dionysius of Alexandria that Revelation is not the work of the same author as the other Johannine writings. But does this mean that apostolic authorship of the Apocalypse is thereby ruled out? The answer to this is not a straightforward yes, given recent developments in Johannine scholarship (Brown, 1979; Ashton, 1991). There is a tendency now among commentators on John's Gospel to distinguish between the 'Beloved Disciple', who stands at the source of the Johannine tradition (e.g. John 19.35; 21.24) and the person (evangelist) or persons who put this distinctive tradition into its present literary form in the Gospel. Many, indeed, will go even further, to question the identification of this mysterious Beloved Disciple (who is never named in the Gospel) with John the apostle. This recognition that the Gospel was not necessarily written by the disciple who inspired it, still less by one of the apostles of Christ, means that the rejection of common authorship of the Gospel and Apocalypse does not thereby automatically rule out the apostolic authorship of the latter book, as it did for Dionysius. Indeed, one solution sometimes posited is that the Apocalypse represents an early stage in the Johannine tradition, which would allow this rather stormy book to be the work of 'the disciple whom Jesus loved', even the work of John, son of Zebedee, otherwise known as 'son of thunder' (Mark 3.17). It remains a fact that the first attribution of Revelation to John the apostle (by Justin) is earlier than the claim (by Irenaeus) that this John also wrote the Gospel.

But is this a plausible solution? Two sets of evidence need to come into play here: external evidence about the life of John son of Zebedee, and internal evidence from the Apocalypse itself which offers clues as to the kind of person who wrote it. The external evidence is rather sketchy. John, son of Zebedee and brother of James, was called to be a disciple of Jesus of Nazareth from the family fishing business probably based in Capernaum on the north shore of the Sea of Galilee (Mark 1.19–20 and parallels): though his first language would most likely have been Aramaic, he would probably have known a certain amount of Greek, for business purposes. The two Zebedee brothers were known in at least one early stream of tradition as Βοανηργές or 'sons of thunder' (Mark 3.17 and par.), and a story about them in Luke exhibits traits in their character which might provide a possible explanation for their nickname (Luke 9.51–56; cf. Mark 9.38).[9] The synoptic evangelists often present John, together with his brother James and Simon Peter, as a kind of 'core group' within the wider circle of the twelve, called apart to witness the raising of Jairus' daughter (Mark 5.37//Luke 8.51), to experience the Transfiguration (Mark 9.2–8 and par.), or to pray with him in Gethsemane (Mark 14.33//Matt. 26.37), though it is unclear whether this reflects the period of Jesus' earthly life or John's subsequent prominence within the Christian community, 'read back' into the ministry. Certainly other New Testament sources suggest that he subsequently came to prominence, alongside Peter (e.g. Acts 3.1–11; 4.13–22; 8.14) and eventually another James, the 'brother of the Lord' (Gal. 2.9), in the mother church of Jerusalem.[10] Contradictory traditions about John's subsequent movements take us beyond the pages of the New Testament. One such tradition, that he was martyred alongside his brother James, is relatively late, contradicts the first-century tradition of James's death enshrined in Acts 12, which knows nothing of John's demise at this point, and could well have been read out of Mark 10.38–40.[11] The other, rather more likely, is that he lived to a ripe old age (which could admittedly have been read out of John 21.23), and eventually settled in the city of Ephesus in Asia. The Ephesus connection was well established by the end of the second century, when it is cited by Irenaeus (*Adv. Haer.* 3.1.1). Indeed, Irenaeus may have received it via Polycarp of Smyrna, who claimed to have known John personally.

Our second task is to consider how far this traditional portrait of John son of Zebedee tallies with the internal evidence from the Apocalypse itself about its author, at least in so far as the latter can be reconstructed by the reader from partial glimpses provided by the text. First, and most obviously (unless the work is pseudonymous),[12] he is a Christian bearing the name John, further designated as a 'servant' of Jesus Christ (or possibly of God, 1.1). Though he does not describe himself explicitly as a prophet, his book is to be understood as containing prophetic words (1.3; 22.7), and he recounts at one stage his prophetic commissioning (10.8–11). In true Christian prophetic mould, he claims to speak the words of the risen Christ to the addressees of his book, Christians living in seven cities of Roman proconsular Asia (2.1—3.22). He is apparently well known to them, such that he can introduce himself simply as 'John'. He can also claim a certain authority over at least some of them, which suggests that he was active in these cities, including Ephesus, before his sojourn on Patmos. That there are some who would dispute his prophetic authority is suggested by what is said about 'false apostles', the Nicolaitans, the followers of the 'teaching of Balaam', and the devotees of 'Jezebel' (2.2, 6, 14–15, 20). As well as claiming the gift of prophecy, he is a visionary, in the mould of apocalyptic seers of the late Second Temple period. The ambiguous phrase 'all that he saw' (1.2) is probably an allusion to these visions, though it could just imply that he is an eye-witness to the testimony which Jesus bore during his life on earth. His Jewish background is implied by a number of other factors. Allusions to the scriptures of Israel permeate virtually every verse of this book, suggesting an author schooled in these texts from an early age. The hostile references to 'those who say that they are Jews and are not, but are a synagogue of Satan' (2.9; 3.9) bear the marks of one whose self-designation is Jewish, and seeks to deny claims of Jewishness to rival groups. Further, the Semitic features of his rather eccentric Greek point to someone who originates from a part of the world where Jews habitually spoke, or read, Aramaic or Hebrew: Palestine is the obvious candidate. Finally, he may have experienced some hostility from non-Christian quarters during the exercise of his ministry, given that he describes himself as 'your brother and sharer with you *in the tribulation and the kingdom and steadfastness in Jesus*' (1:9, my translation).

Some may be impressed by the similarities between the traditional portrait of John, son of Zebedee and the picture reconstructed from the text of Revelation of the kind of person likely to have written it. Both present a Jewish-Christian leader, originating in Palestine but subsequently finding his way to the Roman province of Asia, including the great city of Ephesus. Both present a figure whose authoritative status is likely to have been acknowledged by a number of different Christian communities, though perhaps not without some dissenters (Gal. 2.9 points to tensions, at an earlier period, between Paul and John no less than between Paul and Cephas). Many, indeed, have thought 'son of thunder' a not inappropriate designation for the author of the Apocalypse, with its dramatic visions of divine judgement as well as divine salvation. All this, while falling short of conclusive evidence, does mean that the thesis that this book was written by John son of Zebedee, rather than another, otherwise unknown figure connected in some way to what is called the 'Johannine tradition', deserves serious consideration.

Yet there are also differences between the two portraits, which others have found to be compelling objections to the apostolic authorship of the Apocalypse. First, the prophetic character of the author of Revelation seems to fit uncomfortably alongside the apostolic status of John son of Zebedee. One would surely expect the latter to designate himself as an 'apostle' (or, if the same figure as the rather shadowy one behind the Fourth Gospel, 'the disciple whom Jesus loved' or 'the Elder').[13] This is not as decisive as it might at first appear, however: Paul, after all, can allude on occasion to his prophetic gifts (1 Cor. 14.19), and indeed also to his visionary experiences (2 Cor. 12), yet he is equally adamant about his apostolic credentials (e.g. 1 Cor. 9.1; 15.8–10). Similarly, Paul, no less than our John, can describe himself on occasion as a 'slave of Jesus Christ' (Rom. 1.1; Gal. 1.10; Phil. 1.1), and a similar designation is used in texts attributed to other apostolic figures (cf. Jas. 1.1; 2 Pet. 1.1; Jude 1). Biblical scholars are sometimes in danger of making too rigid distinctions, such as those between 'prophet', 'apostle' and 'apocalypticist', which the ancients would not necessarily have regarded as mutually exclusive. More compelling may be the fact that, in describing the vision of the New Jerusalem, our author can speak of it as built on twelve foundations, bearing the names of the 'twelve apostles of the Lamb' (21.14). This phrase and the similar one found at Ephesians 2.20 seem to presuppose that the twelve apostles (John included) belong to an earlier, foundation period upon which Christians can now look back. Some have found this a crucial objection; readers of the book will need to decide for themselves, however, whether it is quite as insurmountable as is often claimed.

Moral Revulsion

The biblical designation of the sons of Zebedee as 'sons of thunder' points us, finally, towards an aspect of the Apocalypse of John which perhaps causes the greatest difficulty to the contemporary reader: what one might call the 'moral' objections to the book. Although its cataclysmic visions have provided the Western cultural tradition with some of its most potent symbolism, influencing artistic masterpieces as wide-ranging as Michelangelo's *Last Judgement,* Dante's *Divine Comedy,* William Blake's *Death on a Pale Horse* and Ingmar Bergman's classic film *The Seventh Seal,* they have also provoked profound moral soul-searching. What is the reader to make of a book which, at least in places, appears dominated by images of death and destruction, some of which at least would seem to be divinely ordained? Visions of war (e.g. 19.11ff.), the cry to avenge blood (6.9–11), at least two lists of horrendous plagues, reminiscent of the plagues of Egypt, afflicting humanity (8.6—9.21; 16.1–21), the treading of the winepress of God's wrath, with blood flowing from it as high as a horse's bridle (14.19–20), the lake of fire and sulphur into which God's enemies are to be thrown (20.10), all conspire to create a theological dilemma even for the believer. There is something about the violent imagery of the book, its visions of chaos and destruction, which can cause even its staunchest supporters to blanch. While not all would wish to go as far as Carl Gustav Jung, who described Revelation as 'a veritable orgy of hatred, wrath, vindictiveness, and blind destructive fury that revels in fantastic images of terror' (Jung, 1984, 125), many Christians come to the reluctant conclusion that it is somehow 'sub-Christian' and unworthy of the gospel of Christ.

First of all, a word of warning is called for. It is possible that our sense of moral revulsion may reveal as much about ourselves as it does about the theology of this book. For what disturbs and horrifies one generation of readers may be very different to that which disturbs and horrifies another generation, as a survey of the history of Revelation's interpretation reveals. What readers in the fourth century, such as Eusebius, found difficult about this book was not its language of chaos, violence and divine vengeance, but rather what appeared to be its literalist, this-worldly understanding of the Millennium or thousand-year reign of Christ. To ignore what to our culture (though not necessarily to another) is problematic or even morally reprehensible in Scripture may mean that we are never forced to face that which we would rather not face, even to engage in difficult theological wrestling. Yet what appears to be the case, in many a contemporary liturgical lectionary, is an ecclesial decision to encourage this very avoidance: in the two recent eucharistic lectionaries discussed above, only a tiny percentage of the Apocalypse is set for public reading, while even in the lectionary accompanying the widely used Anglican Office *Celebrating Common Prayer,* which can pride itself in a fairly extensive coverage of Revelation for Morning Prayer in the Easter Season, the sequences of seals, trumpets, and bowls, the vision of the two beasts and the judgement of Babylon are notable for their absence. One might legitimately ask whether this 'policy of avoidance', which includes avoidance of our own 'darker side', is the best or most fruitful one to employ.

Indeed, even in our own day, particularly but not exclusively beyond the northern hemisphere, it is precisely these visions of cosmic collapse and transformation, judgement and vindication, to which many Christians turn for inspiration in their own struggle to follow the Lamb. A renewed exploration of the biblical concept of 'justice', and a sense of affront at the world's manifest injustices, within the context of a rediscovery of the nature of apocalyptic imagery, has led such readers to value the prophetic challenge of this book and relocate it much closer to the heart of the biblical canon (this recent trend, which in fact represents a very ancient way of reading Revelation, will be explored in more detail later in this book). Alongside such 'engaged' readings representing the cries of the victims of injustice, liberal Western 'moral objections' to the book can appear hopelessly naive, the preserve of the privileged few.

This is not completely fair, however. There are passages in the book in which the reader seems to be encouraged to rejoice in the destruction of his or her enemies (e.g. 18.20; 19.3), and where even God appears to approve the violent destruction of his creation, humanity included (e.g. 8.6—9.21). Few readers can fail to be disturbed by the cry of the angel inviting the birds of heaven to God's great feast, to 'eat the flesh of kings, the flesh of captains, the flesh of the mighty, the flesh of horses and their riders – flesh of all, both free and slave, both small and great' (19.18). The precise meaning of such passages, and their theological implications, can only really be explored in the context of the Apocalypse as a whole (and will recur again throughout the course of this book). At this point, however, it would seem appropriate to mention briefly some of the other ways in which commentators have attempted to grapple with such difficult texts.

First, it is possible that careful attention to the overall picture will reveal how some of the more violent imagery, drawn from Old Testament antecedents or from the stock-in-trade of Jewish apocalyptic writings, has undergone a 'rebirth of images', such that it comes to mean something very different from what at first appears to be the case. An often-cited comment of George Caird on the vision of the Lamb in Revelation 5 makes this point well:

It is almost as if John were saying to us at one point after another: 'Wherever the Old Testament says "Lion", read "Lamb".' Wherever the Old Testament speaks of the victory of the Messiah or the overthrow of the enemies of God, we are to remember that the gospel recognizes no other way of achieving these ends than the way of the Cross.

(Caird, 1984, 75)

That violent images are often used in quite surprising ways in the Apocalypse cannot easily be denied: the discussion of the vision of the Word of God riding out to battle (19.11-16) in Chapter 3 below may provide another good example of this process, whereby violent Divine Warrior traditions drawn from Israel's scriptures have been dramatically transformed so as to speak powerfully about the victory of the cross of Christ. Whether this can account for the whole picture, however (such as 14.10, or even 19.17–21), and whether, more pertinently, this is sufficient to exonerate John of the charges of malice and vindictiveness, remains a hotly disputed question.

A second way of making sense, theologically, of the violent, destructive imagery of the Apocalypse is to see it in terms of the Judaeo-Christian alternative to a thoroughgoing dualism, preservation from any idea that the battle between light and darkness is a battle between two rival gods, two finely balanced powers. Dualism is a particular danger for the apocalyptic mindset, which tends to draw a sharp contrast between the heavenly and earthly realms, between good and fallen angels, between the present evil age and the age to come. The Judaeo-Christian alternative is to allow God to be God, to admit that God is ultimately in control of his creation, even if that includes those problematic aspects of that creation, evil, disease and natural disaster. This line of interpretation makes much of the repeated use of the Greek ἐδόθη (literally 'it was given', i.e. denoting permission) in visions describing the execution of violent or destructive acts by a variety of figures: the four horsemen (Rev. 6), the four angels at the corners of the earth (7.2), the angel of the Abyss (9.1), the monstrous locusts who arise from the Abyss (9.3–5), the beast from the sea (13.5), the beast from the earth (13.15), the fourth bowl angel (16.8). At least some of these characters are demonic, on the side of Satan. The divine 'permission' given to them is testimony to the final victory of God: although allowed to function temporarily, they are ultimately unable to frustrate the divine plan.

Finally, it is possible that at least part of what we find in Revelation's language of judgement and destruction is a description, albeit in mythological language, of the self-destructive nature of evil. Again, the vision of the four horsemen, bringing in their wake evils in which human beings, and human societies, can find themselves implicated (war, bloodshed, famine, inflated food prices), may be a case in point. Similarly, the vision of the oppressive and arrogant city Babylon the Great (in her present incarnation the city and empire of Rome, Rev. 17), relates how she is to be destroyed by the very beast upon which she sits and on which she relied for her prosperity, as well as by the kings who have made political and commercial alliances with her (17.16). Yet even this beast is destined for perdition (17.11). On this view of Revelation's visions of judgement, it is not that God sets out to destroy, but that what is evil, oppressive and unjust ultimately brings its own destruction upon itself.

Whichever attitude one takes to these more 'problematic' aspects of the Revelation to John, they represent yet another symptom of the complex nature of this biblical book. It will, I hope, have become clear throughout this chapter just how different is the mindset of John of Patmos, and the first hearers of his apocalyptic book, from our own. The nature of this mindset, and the ancient appropriation of his message, will be the subject of the next few chapters.

NOTES

1. Unless otherwise noted, biblical quotations are from the New Revised Standard Version.
2. 2nd Sunday of Easter: Rev. 1.9–13, 17–19; 3rd Sunday: Rev. 5.11–14; 4th Sunday: Rev. 7.9, 14–17; 5th Sunday: Rev. 21.1–5; 6th Sunday: Rev. 21.10–14, 22–23; 7th Sunday: Rev. 22.12–14, 16–17, 20. Those who attend the Mass of the Chrism during Holy Week will be exposed to a further four verses (Rev. 1.5–8). This reading is also set for the Solemnity of Christ the King in Year B (three-year cycle). The Apocalypse does receive relatively full coverage in the Office of Readings for the Easter Season, yet this is in a non-eucharistic context.
3. Rev. 7.9–17 is set for All Saints' Day in Year A, Rev. 21.1–6 in Year B.
4. The word 'apocalypse' literally means 'unveiling' or 'uncovering': an apocalypse is to do with unveiling the divine reality normally hidden from our limited sight.
5. There are also seven spirits before the throne (1.4); the Son of Man holds the seven stars in his right hand (1.16), as he stands in the midst of seven lampstands; seven lamps burn before the heavenly throne (4.5); the lamb has seven horns and seven eyes (5.6); the cry of the mighty angel with the little scroll is answered by seven peals of thunder (10.3); the dragon, in a divine parody, has seven heads (12.3), as does his vicegerent, the beast from the sea (13.1; 17.7–10).
6. Early Christian prophecy could also be literary, as well as oracular: e.g. *Shepherd of Hermas*.
7. Cited from A. Roberts and J. Donaldson, *Ante-Nicene Fathers* vol. 5 (Peabody, MA: Hendrickson, 1995), p. 601.
8. Similarly, the Fourth Gospel retains elements of a future eschatology despite its primary focus on the 'now' of salvation: e.g. John 5.28–29; 6.40b, 54.
9. They also appear together in a synoptic story asking for privileged seats in the Kingdom (Mark 10.35–40//Matt. 20.20–23): that the request comes from their mother in the Matthean version, and the story is omitted entirely in Luke, may be due to redactional changes reflecting increasing reverence within the Church for the original twelve.
10. Interestingly, the Beloved Disciple of the Fourth Gospel, like the John of the Synoptics and Acts, generally appears in close proximity to Peter (e.g. John 13.23; 20.2; 21.7, 20–22).
11. Writers from the fifth century onwards attribute this tradition to an otherwise unknown passage of Papias. It is also found in some martyrologies, certain

Syrian traditions, and the Manichean Psalms (3rd century?), which state that the two sons of Zebedee were compelled to drink the 'cup of martyrdom' (clearly using the language of Mark 10).

12. This is unlikely, for a writer wanting to claim the authority of a prominent figure of the early Church would surely have been more specific: John 'apostle of Jesus Christ', or 'the Elder'.

13. In fact, the dominant view within Johannine scholarship is that the Beloved Disciple (the authority behind the tradition enshrined in the Johannine writings) and the Elder (the author of the Johannine Epistles) are different figures.

REFERENCES

Ashton, J. (1991), *Understanding the Fourth Gospel.* Clarendon Press, Oxford.

Barr, D. L. (1986), 'The Apocalypse of John as Oral Enactment', *Interpretation.* July 1986, pp. 243–56.

Bauckham, R. (1993), *The Theology of the Book of Revelation.* Cambridge University Press, Cambridge.

Brown, R. E. (1979), *The Community of the Beloved Disciple.* Geoffrey Chapman, London.

Brown, R. E. (1997), *An Introduction to the New Testament.* Anchor Bible Reference Library; Doubleday, New York, pp. 773–813.

Caird, G. B. (1984), *The Revelation of St John the Divine,* 2nd edn. Black's New Testament Commentaries; A. & C. Black, London.

Charles, R. H. (1920), *A Critical and Exegetical Commentary on the Revelation of St John.* International Critical Commentary; T. & T. Clark, Edinburgh.

Collins, J. J. (1992), *The Apocalyptic Imagination.* Crossroad, New York.

Gamble, H. Y. (1995), *Books and Readers in the Early Church.* Yale University Press, New Haven and London.

Garrow, A. J. P. (1997), *Revelation.* New Testament Readings; Routledge, London and New York.

Jung, C. G. (1984), *Answer to Job.* ET Routledge & Kegan Paul, London.

Meer, F. van der (1978), *Apocalypse: Visions from the Book of Revelation in Western Art.* Thames & Hudson, London.

Roloff, J. (1993), *The Revelation of John. A Continental Commentary.* ET Fortress Press, Minneapolis.

Rowland, C. (1982), *The Open Heaven.* SPCK, London.

Schüssler Fiorenza, E. (1985), *The Book of Revelation: Justice and Judgement.* Fortress Press, Philadelphia.

Wainwright, A. W. (1993), *Mysterious Apocalypse.* Abingdon Press, Nashville.

2

What Did John See?

I, John, … was on the island called Patmos because of the word of God
and the testimony of Jesus. I was in the spirit on the Lord's day, and
I heard behind me a loud voice like a trumpet saying, 'Write in a book
what you see and send it to the seven churches, to Ephesus, to Smyrna,
to Pergamum, to Thyatira, to Sardis, to Philadelphia, and to Laodicea.'
(Rev. 1.9–11)

Vision and Audition

There are two famous traditions within Christian artistic representation of
John of Patmos, which reflect rather different understandings of the nature
of his revelation. One, found particularly in the West – and represented by
Diego Velázquez's *Saint John the Evangelist on the Island of Patmos*, now in
the National Gallery in London – presents a youthful John, traditionally the
youngest of the apostles of Christ, sitting with an open book and a pen in
hand, gazing intently into the sky. Far above him, the sky has been torn
apart, and a heavenly vision, no larger than a man's hand, can just be made
out (often, as in the case of Velázquez, the vision is that of the woman clothed
with the sun and the great red dragon, from Rev. 12). The second tradition,
common in the iconography of the Apocalypse in the East, presents an aged
John, John the Elder, generally seated in the cave in which, according to local
Patmian tradition, his revelation was received. Here too he is found gazing
into heaven, ready to write, or rather to dictate. In some icons depicting this
scene, however, a further element is introduced: a tiny angel whispers in
John's left ear, the vehicle of the divine Apocalypse, and the complementary
Johannine Gospel, which John is about to record for posterity through the
pen of his disciple and scribe, Prochoros. This latter tradition highlights
what John hears, the message whose authoritative status is authenticated by
the mode of its transmission, heavenly voice or angelic interpreter; the
former stresses what John sees, his visionary apprehension of divine revelation,
which is transmitted to subsequent generations by means of the vivid
pictorial descriptions in this text. Audition and vision: both are crucial
aspects of an apocalypse. What John heard is described vividly enough in his
book: claps of thunder, trumpet blasts, mighty angelic choirs, the sound of
many waters. But it is what John saw that has perhaps made the greatest
impact in the history of the interpretation of Revelation.

The Western artistic tradition, typified by Velázquez, highlights the question which is so often overlooked or downplayed in scholarly discussion of the book of Revelation: what precisely did John see? Metaphors of 'seeing', 'vision', can encompass a whole spectrum of meaning, from physical sight to mental apprehension, from visionary ecstasy to spiritual insight. The common phrase 'I see what you mean', Martin Luther King's famous 'I have a dream' speech with its vision of a world free of racial inequality, or the claim of Bernadette Soubirous to have seen 'a little girl' at the rock of Massabielle, all employ the language of sight; yet in each case, the nature of the 'seeing' is very different. In the light of this diversity of meaning, is it possible to reach any conclusions as to the nature of John's vision? In particular, given the introductory claim of the author at 1.9–11, is his book in fact based on any kind of visionary experience? This chapter will attempt to explore some of the ways in which John can be spoken of as a seer, a visionary.

A Complex Visionary Book

One should, of course, be wary of any sentimental naivety about the visionary status of the book of Revelation, which views it either as a straightforward description of what John saw (following the tradition found in Velázquez), or the faithful record of what was dictated to him by a heavenly emissary (following the iconographical tradition of the East). Such an understanding, first of all, fails to take seriously the Jewish apocalyptic tradition within which this work stands, which, as we have already seen, uses the literary genre of apocalypse as a vehicle for its religious message. Whatever visionary, and indeed auditory, experience underlies the Apocalypse of John, it has now been translated into something written, contained within a literary text, with its own distinctive rules and grammar. Many commentators find evidence that, at least in its present form, it is a carefully crafted literary masterpiece. Different types of material and literary genre stand side by side in this book: canticle and prophetic oracle; myth and historical allusion; letter, prophecy and apocalypse.

Moreover, for the most part, vision and interpretation have been closely interwoven. In a few rare cases it is relatively simple to isolate later interpretation of earlier material, such as the vision of the seven-headed beast on which Babylon sits (Rev. 17.9–11), where at least two different explanations are provided of the significance of the seven heads. However, this clear division between vision and interpretation is the exception rather than the rule in this book, in marked contrast to apocalypses such as Daniel or *4 Ezra*, where there is often a straightforward differentiation in the text between descriptions of what is seen and commentary upon these visions (e.g. Dan. 7; *4 Ezra* 11—12). Moreover, some though by no means all would claim that there are indications within the book of Revelation, just as there are in the Fourth Gospel with which it is traditionally paired, that its final form is the result of a rather complex literary process in which perhaps several writers have played a role. All of this complicates the quest for underlying visionary experience at the very least, and has led some commentators to view the Apocalypse of John as a careful literary fiction rather than as an account of an actual revelation.

Any attempt to address the question of what John saw is also complicated by the question of how the book of Revelation relates to earlier biblical and extra-canonical traditions. Clearly John of Patmos is steeped in the traditions and imagery of Israel, and these have profoundly influenced the way in which the apocalyptic visions of this book are described. Although Revelation contains hardly any direct quotations from the Old Testament, it is true to say that virtually every verse of this book breathes the air of the biblical tradition, and biblical stories and traditions are reshaped, often in quite surprising ways (e.g. compare Dan. 7 and Rev. 13). Does this not suggest that the author of this book is better viewed as an interpreter of Scripture, or of the more fluid Jewish religious tradition, than as the recipient of visions? This is certainly how he has often been regarded.

Finally, many commentators have noted parallels with, and possible dependence upon, the Jesus tradition, including the so-called 'Little Apocalypse' (Mark 13 and parallels). The interjection during the bowls sequence at Revelation 16.15 ('See, I am coming like a thief!' cf. 3.3) represents a surprising parallel to words found on the lips of Jesus at Matthew 24.43–44 and Luke 12.39–40, and known already to Paul when he wrote to the Thessalonians in what is perhaps the earliest surviving Christian document (1 Thess. 5.2). The seal visions of Revelation 6, and the activity of Satan and the two beasts (Rev. 12; 13; 20), echo the language and imagery of the lengthy eschatological discourse of Jesus in Mark 13 and its synoptic parallels. Both the Synoptics and Revelation, for example, warn of those who 'deceive'; war, famine and earthquakes mark the 'beginning of the birth-pangs' at Mark 13.7–8 and par., and are also among the features of the first stage of judgement in Revelation 6; Mark 13.22 (cf. Matt. 24.24) warns of the coming of false messiahs and false prophets (ψευδόχριστοι καὶ ψευδοπροφῆται), echoing the activity of Revelation's beast from the earth, which parodies the Lamb, the true messiah (Rev. 13.11), and is later identified as the 'false prophet' (ψευδοπροφήτης, Rev. 16.13; 19.20; 20.10); the darkening of sun and moon and the falling of stars from heaven are signs of the imminent end found alike at Mark 13.24–25 and parallels, and at the opening of the sixth seal at Revelation 6.12–13.

To reconstruct the history of the origins and development of the gospel sayings tradition is notoriously difficult, especially so in the case of the eschatological teaching of Mark 13; to establish the precise relationship between this 'Jesus tradition' and the parallel traditions in Revelation is even less straightforward. Scholars remain divided as to whether the parallels are due to direct literary dependence of one upon the other, or to shared use of common traditions, whether written or oral. In favour of the former may be the opening verse of Revelation, which describes the book, somewhat surprisingly, not as the 'Apocalypse of John', but the 'Apocalypse of Jesus Christ, which God gave him to show to his servants what must happen soon' (Rev. 1.1, my translation). In favour of the latter is the stereotypical nature of apocalyptic imagery, particularly that which is concerned with the End, which means that similar motifs can be found in a wide range of texts which do not necessarily have a literary relationship to one another. Attempts to settle this issue are not helped by the range of scholarly opinion as to the origins of Jesus sayings, not least whether some of them derive from early Christian prophetic oracles, in which the prophet claims to speak 'in the name of the Lord Jesus', rather than from the lips of the historical Jesus of Nazareth. It may not be coincidental that one clear echo of a synoptic saying of Jesus is alluded to in the letter to the angel of the church in Sardis (3.3), i.e. in the context of a prophetic oracle spoken by the exalted Son of Man through the mouthpiece of his prophetic servant John. But if John is in some way dependent upon the Jesus tradition for the contents of his visions (such as some antecedent to the synoptic 'Little Apocalypse'), does this not undermine his claim to direct revelation on Patmos? Or should we not be surprised that the teaching of Jesus, so fundamental to the self-identity of the early Church, has left its mark on the way in which this early Christian leader has recounted his actual visionary experiences?

John as Apocalyptic Visionary

Yet the project of this chapter is not yet doomed to failure. While acknowledging the complex process which was involved in the formation of the literary apocalypse we know as the book of Revelation, and its indebtedness to Israel's literary past and early Christian tradition, there nevertheless remain good grounds for taking seriously the claim that actual visionary experience on the part of the author underlies this text. There has in recent years been a greater willingness among scholars to take seriously the claims of heavenly ascent and other direct access to the divine made by the authors of Jewish apocalypses and related visionary texts, and there are no a priori reasons for ruling out John's Apocalypse from consideration in this regard (Lindblom, 1963; Gruenwald, 1980; Rowland, 1982, Ch. 9). On the one hand, Revelation and other apocalypses have elements in common with texts from other periods which describe, by common consent, actual visionary experience, such as writings and traditions about the so-called *Merkavah* mystics (Jewish mystics who claimed visions of the Throne-Chariot or *Merkavah* of Ezekiel 1, as described, for example, in the Jewish mystical *Hekhalot* or 'palace' texts of a later period), and the writings of Christian mystics such as Bridget of Sweden and Teresa of Avila. On the other hand, the apocalypses manage to combine fairly stereotypical literary features with the rather more chaotic, fluid imagery and dream-like quality that one might expect of records of actual, as opposed to purported visions. The manner of the experience may differ from text to text, ranging from dream-vision to ecstatic trance, from angelic encounter to descriptions of actual journeys to the heavenly realm ('whether in the body or out of the body', 2 Cor. 12.2), but the claim to 'direct and intimate consciousness of the Divine Presence' remains a constant feature of them all (Scholem, 1946, 4).

To begin with the latter point, the rather tentative descriptions, and fluid nature, of some of the visions provide a reasonable starting point for the hypothesis that John underwent actual visionary experiences prior to writing his literary work. The repeated use of similes, indeed the necessity of piling one such simile upon another, appears to reflect the seer's struggle to express the inexpressible in recounting what he has seen and heard. This is particularly the case with his inaugural vision of the 'one like a son of man' in Revelation 1, and the account of his ascent to the heavenly throne-room in Revelation 5, though it is not lacking in certain other visions throughout the book. The head and hair of the one like a son of man are white 'as white wool, white as snow' (Rev. 1.14), his feet are 'like burnished bronze', as if refined in a furnace, the voice 'like the sound of many waters' (1.15). This struggle to articulate the elements of his vision remains significant, even when one acknowledges the influence of the language of Daniel 7 and 10 on John's account.[1] The vision of the heavenly throne-room creates even more difficulties, as the seer strives to find words from his cultural tradition to describe what he sees on the throne: 'And the one seated there looks like jasper and carnelian'; the brightness surrounding the throne is 'a rainbow that looks like an emerald' (4.3); the space before the throne can only be described as 'something like a sea of glass, like crystal' (4.6). Other visions exhibit a fluid, dream-like quality: hideous creatures like locusts defy description as they exhibit in turn the features of scorpions, horses, human beings, lions and winged creatures (9.1–11); horses wear lions' heads and serpents' tails (9.13–19); a city is transformed into a young woman, dressed as a bride (21.1–4). Similar fluid descriptions, and the repeated use of similes and metaphors, can be found in a wide variety of other visionary texts, not least those Jewish texts (such as Daniel) which seem to have provided John with much of his religious vocabulary.

That John of Patmos is to be regarded primarily as a visionary rather than a writer or biblical exegete finds confirmation when one pays attention to a variety of features shared by his apocalypse and other visionary texts. First of all, Revelation seems to presuppose particular dispositions on the part of John for visionary experience. There are allusions in a number of apocalypses to the various preparations to be undertaken by the seers prior to their purported visionary experience, including prayer, fasting and other such practices, echoing those found in the later *Hekhalot* texts and the earlier Israelite prophetic material. In *4 Ezra* (a Jewish apocalypse roughly contemporaneous with Revelation), the seer, in the guise of the scribe Ezra, is told to fast for seven days, mourning and weeping over the fate of Israel, in preparation for subsequent encounters with his angelic interpreter (*4 Ezra* 5.13; cf. 6.35). Likewise, a period of fasting forms the prelude to Baruch being carried over the city of Jerusalem (*2 Bar.* 5.7; cf. 20.5, 11; 21.1; 47.2; Dan. 10.2–3). In the *Apocalypse of Abraham*, we are told that the seer, accompanying the angel Iaoel, refrains from bread and water for forty days and nights (*Apoc. Abr.* 12.1). Other preparations include a strange diet which might account for a particular disposition for receiving visions (Ezra is told by the angel Uriel to eat only of the flowers he finds growing in the field, prior to his vision of the mourning mother who is transformed into the established city of Zion: *4 Ezra* 9.24–25), and a period of intense prayer (*4 Ezra* 9.25; cf. Dan. 9.3).[2] At least two of these elements, prayer and eating divinely provided food, seem to be reflected in Revelation. John is seized by the spirit and receives his inaugural vision 'on the Lord's day' (Rev. 1.10), implying a context of prayer and waiting on God. A key turning point in the narrative is initiated by John being bidden, like Ezekiel before him (Rev. 10.9; cf. Ezek. 2.8—3.3), to eat a scroll delivered to him by an interpreting angel.

Similar preparations (though by now rather more complex) were used by those who were in some sense the spiritual heirs to the apocalypticists, the Jewish mystics behind the *Hekhalot* writings. These underwent a rigorous programme of fasting, ritual immersions and incantations as well as the careful preparation of seals to ensure successful progress through the various heavenly palaces, free of attack from hostile angels, in order to attain the vision of the *Merkavah*. Set alongside the practices of these visionaries, the preparations of the apocalypticists appear positively restrained (those attributed to John of Patmos particularly so). Nevertheless, that fact that at least some of the apocalypses record practices similar to those that are known to have been used elsewhere in preparation for actual visionary experiences must force us to consider the real possibility that similar experiences underlie these texts also.

One aspect of visionary preparation that is particularly interesting for our purposes is the place of speculation about and meditation upon Scripture as a prelude to visionary experience. In chapter 9 of the book of Daniel, for example, it is while meditating on Jeremiah's prophecy about the 'seventy years' of Jerusalem's desolation (Jer. 25.11–12) that the seer receives his vision of the angel Gabriel. But as Christopher Rowland has shown, it was meditation upon Ezekiel's vision of the *Merkavah* or Throne-Chariot (Ezek. 1) which had particular pride of place in the preparations of the apocalypticists for mystical encounter with the divine. Ezekiel's vision has clearly influenced visionary descriptions in apocalyptic texts spanning a wide chronological period, including what is generally thought to be one of the earliest surviving Jewish apocalypses, *The Book of the Watchers*, which forms chapters 1—36 of *1 Enoch* (probably composed in the third century BCE). *1 Enoch* 14 describes Enoch's mystical ascent to the heavenly Temple, where he beholds a high throne, and one seated upon it whose appearance echoes that of the Ancient of Days of Daniel 7. Such a tradition of a heavenly ascent to the *Merkavah* is found again and again, not only in later strata of the Enoch literature (*1 Enoch* 60; 71; *2 Enoch* 20—21), but also in the *Testament of Levi* 5, the *Apocalypse of Abraham* 18, and, not least, Revelation 4 (Rowland, 1982, 214–47). The *Merkavah* is no less of interest in the so-called *Songs of the Sabbath Sacrifice* from Qumran. It has long been recognized that the throne-chariot vision of Ezekiel had had a crucial preparatory role for the later *Merkavah* mystics in their attempts to see what Ezekiel himself saw. As was the case for these mystical successors, Ezekiel's vision seems also to have provided the raw material for the visions of God described by the writers of at least some of the apocalypses, and the interpretative lens through which they made sense of these visions.

That we are not speaking simply of literary borrowing here is shown by Rowland's analysis of two important visions of the *Merkavah* in the apocalypses, Enoch's ascent to the heavenly throne-room in *1 Enoch* 14 and that of John in Revelation 4. In neither of these is there a slavish repetition of the details of Ezekiel's vision (or of the temple vision of Isa. 6, which has also greatly influenced both), such as one might expect if they were merely a case of literary dependence. John's vision, for example, lacks the ordered, sequential discussion of the details of Ezekiel 1 typical of an exegetical exposition, and exhibits little verbal dependence upon the original text. Indeed, as Rowland notes, even the differences between Revelation 4 and *1 Enoch* 14 are 'remarkable' for two texts rooted in the same Old Testament visionary passages (1982, 219–26). We are left with the distinct probability that there underlies the vision of the heavenly throne-room in Revelation 4—5 an actual visionary experience in which John himself saw what Ezekiel had seen, namely the heavenly *Merkavah*, albeit with a distinctly Christian edge in the appearance of the Lamb. Ezekiel's vision has certainly given John much of the language with which he can articulate what he saw (so, for example, he follows Ezek. 1.28 in describing the brightness around the throne in terms of a rainbow, Rev. 4.3). His visionary account, however, does not bear the traces of straightforward literary borrowing from that source.

This complex relationship between Ezekiel 1 and Revelation 4—5 ought not to surprise us. Articulating religious experience in categories and imagery provided by one's religious and cultural heritage is a consistent feature of accounts of visions, trances and other similar phenomena, whether mystical ecstasy, Marian apparitions or 'near death experiences', and one should not be surprised to find it also in accounts of apocalyptic visions, particularly when a religious text containing such imagery has been important in preparing the ground for those visions. Indeed, many commentators on mystical experiences would want to claim that the mystic's religious and cultural tradition will actually have laid the foundations for such experiences, setting down established patterns to which the actual visionary encounter will conform (Ashton, 2000, 114f.). In this case, then, Ezekiel's vision of the *Merkavah* can be expected to provide the raw materials for John's own visionary experience on Patmos. One can only speculate as to how far, and to what extent, John's meditation upon other Old Testament texts besides Ezekiel 1 contributed to what he himself saw, though Daniel 7 and 10 are also likely candidates.

A second characteristic shared by Revelation and other apocalypses and visionary literature is the emphasis placed upon the disturbing, emotionally draining, and often frightening effect of heavenly visions and angelic encounters on the seer. *1 Enoch* 14.13 describes the extremities of temperature experienced by the seer on entering the first house in heaven: 'hot as fire and cold as snow';[3] he finds himself overcome with fear and trembling. The vision of the Head of Days in the *Similitudes* has a similar effect on Enoch: 'And I fell upon my face, and my whole body melted, and my spirit was transformed' (*1 Enoch* 71.11). In *4 Ezra*, the ground on which the seer is standing rocks to and fro at the sound of the heavenly voice (*4 Ezra* 6.29); similarly, Ezra is filled with fear at the glorious vision of Zion, and falls like a corpse at the feet of the angel Uriel who is sent to offer an interpretation of what Ezra has just seen (*4 Ezra* 10.25, 30).

Similar responses to heavenly visions are attributed to John of Patmos. On beholding the vision of the one like a son of man, he falls at his feet 'as though dead' (Rev. 1.17), and feels the hand of the exalted Christ upon him, an experience only too vividly portrayed in the famous icon by Thomas Vathas (*c.* 1596), now in the Cave of the Apocalypse on Patmos, in which the seer is portrayed lying corpse-like before the awesome vision. Although there are two other places in Revelation where John is said to fall down before another, which might suggest an artificial literary feature, it is only here that the terrifying impact of the vision on the seer is stressed; the other two passages (19.10; 22.8–9), which closely parallel each other in structure and vocabulary, look much more like literary constructs (John falls before the feet of an angel to worship; he is rebuked and told to worship God alone). This present passage, on the contrary, does not function as a critique of angel-worship, but rather describes the expected response to an encounter with the Holy. Nor does the close parallel at Daniel 10.10–12, part of a vision which almost certainly provides the inspiration for John's account here, rule out John's describing an actual experience at this point.

A third and related aspect which Revelation shares with other visionary texts is the claim that John is no passive observer of what is described, but an active participant in his visions. *1 Enoch* 71 describes how Enoch is 'carried off' in spirit, and guided by hand by the archangel Michael. In *Apocalypse of Abraham* 10, an angel takes Abraham by the right hand and lifts him to his feet, in order that he might carry out the sacrifice which God has demanded. So too, at the beginning of the apocalypse proper (Rev. 4), John ascends 'in the Spirit' (ἐν πνεύματι) or perhaps 'in a prophetic trance' to the heavenly throne-room (cf. *Ascension of Isaiah* 6.10ff.); later in the book, he is twice taken 'in spirit' by an angel, journeying to see Babylon the Great and the New Jerusalem (17.3; 21.10). When he hears that no one has been found worthy to open the scroll in the hand of the One on the throne, he weeps (Rev. 5.4). He eats the little scroll given him by the mighty angel (10.10), and the result is similar though not identical to the effect of a scroll on the prophet Ezekiel (cf. Ezek. 3.3). He plays an active role in the vision of the Temple, being given a measuring rod with which to measure its dimensions (11.1). He 'is amazed' or 'wonders' when he first catches a glimpse of the vision of Babylon in her seductive luxury, and has to be warned of her dangers by the accompanying angel (17.6b). The seer is portrayed again and again as one who has not simply been privileged to behold the unseen world, but has actually entered into it.

Finally, one cannot rule out the influence of liturgical and cultic experience upon the articulation of visionary experience on the part of the apocalypticists, particularly John, whose writing is saturated with liturgical actions and hymnody, and allusions to the heavenly temple. Just as Isaiah's inaugural vision apparently took place while he was in the Jerusalem Temple (Isa. 6), so too his description of what he saw may well reflect the layout of the First Temple in the eighth century BCE. Similarly, the various parts of the temple itself (the Holy Place and the Holy of Holies), or the various courts of the wider Second Temple structure, no less than biblical accounts relating to the sanctuary (whether actual or ideal), may well have provided the interpretative key for what a number of visionaries saw, and might suggest that at least some of the visions of heaven described in the apocalypses were seen while they were at prayer in a temple setting: this would account, for example, for the twofold division of the heavenly realm according to *1 Enoch* 14 (cf. also Acts 22.17–21). This is all the more likely if the Second Temple were regarded, at least by some Jews, as a microcosm of the cosmos, the gateway between heaven and earth, with the High Priest playing a particular role in mediating between the two.

Clearly John claims that his vision was received not in or around Jerusalem but on Patmos; nevertheless, it occurred while he was 'in the spirit on the Lord's Day', which implies a liturgical context, albeit a distinctly Jewish-Christian one. Yet the Jerusalem Temple and its cult would appear to have impacted on his description of a number of visions in his book, and this is unsurprising for a visionary of probable Palestinian origin. Indeed, the early Christian tradition attributed by Eusebius to Polycrates of Ephesus

(*H.E.* 3.31.3), that John the Beloved Disciple was a priest wearing the 'mitre', is understandable given the strong priestly imagery dominating the visions of the John who wrote the Apocalypse. His inaugural vision utilizes Temple liturgical symbolism (specifically the menorah-like seven lampstands) to celebrate the presence of the risen Lord in the midst of his people (1.12). A succession of further visions, punctuating the narrative at strategic points, likewise presuppose aspects of the Temple liturgy: angelic activity at the altar of incense (8.3–5); the opening of the heavenly sanctuary to enable a glimpse of the ark of the covenant (11.19); the emergence of seven priestly angels from the tent of witness to receive the bowls of the last plagues (15.5–8). Commentators have long considered that the measuring of the Temple of God at Revelation 11.1–2 has at least some connection with events related to Jerusalem during the Jewish War of the late 60s. But equally there are allusions to the festivals which regulated the cycle of temple worship: the vision of the 144,000 bearing palm branches (7.9) almost certainly alludes to the festival of Tabernacles; Passover allusions can be detected in the presentation of the slain Lamb (5.6), and in possible Exodus motifs at 15.2–4. At least one commentator, indeed, has wanted to claim that all the major festivals of the Jewish liturgical year are built into the structure of this highly liturgical book (Farrer, 1949).

Despite the obvious literary character of this work, then, there are good grounds for taking seriously John's claim that underlying his literary work there are actual visionary experiences, even if it is now well-nigh impossible to separate out the precise content and nature of those visions from their present interpreted literary form. In a number of significant ways, John has been seen to stand firmly in the tradition of apocalyptic and other visionaries, with their claims to direct access to the heavenly realm through dreams, visions or heavenly journeys. John too, whether through trance or some other 'out-of-the-body' experience, had visions of the heavenly realm which enabled him to view the world in a new light, and may even have been given a glimpse, like Ezekiel before him, of the heavenly *Merkavah*.

Revelation of Divine Secrets

The process of identifying actual visionary experience within the book of Revelation may be a precarious one, given its literary form; but there is another visionary aspect, another aspect of *seeing*, which is a widely recognized feature of the apocalypse genre. As we have already seen, one feature of the rather complex scholarly debate about the nature of 'apocalyptic' has been the recognition that apocalypses are to do with the revelation of divine secrets, of mysteries generally hidden from human eyes. The Greek word from which our term 'apocalypse' comes literally means 'unveiling' or 'uncovering'. In an apocalypse, the veil separating the heavenly world from the earthly is, as it were, lifted, and the seer is able to see and understand the things of heaven, which enable a profounder understanding of this earthly realm also. The nature and content of these heavenly mysteries will vary from apocalypse to apocalypse. Some of the earliest apocalypses such as the *Book of the Watchers* and the *Astronomical Book* (*1 Enoch* 1—36; 72—82) are more interested in cosmological concerns than in the emerging eschatological crisis which dominates Daniel and the *Animal Apocalypse* of *1 Enoch* 85—90 as well as the Apocalypse of John. But these texts share the belief that things ordinarily hidden from human beings can be and indeed have been revealed to privileged visionaries, allowing them to see the world they inhabit in a very different light. In the words of Daniel, 'there is a God in heaven who reveals mysteries' (Dan. 2.28). Whatever John did or did not see in the heavenly realm, the visionary book that he wrote certainly claims to unveil profound truths about the world in which he lived, offering insight ordinarily inaccessible to mortals.

This indeed is one of the most challenging, and disturbing, aspects of the book of Revelation: it forces the reader (and the hearers) to look at the world and their place in it in a radically new way. This revelation takes place in two main ways in John's Apocalypse: through the direct prophetic addresses spoken in the name of the risen Christ (the 'seven letters' of Rev. 2—3), and through the 'apocalypse' proper of Revelation 4—22. In the letters to the seven churches, the actual (as opposed to apparent) state of Christians in these communities is revealed in what is, in certain cases, quite a shocking way. The angel of the Ephesian church (probably the heavenly personification and protector of this city and its Christians) has abandoned the love it had at first (2.4). The members of the church in Laodicea, perhaps too reliant upon the economic prosperity of their city, with its banks, wool industry and medical school specializing in ophthalmic treatment, are not rich, as they suppose, but 'wretched, pitiable, poor, blind, and naked' (3.17), in need of the true gold, garments and eye-salve which only Christ can provide (3.18). The church in Smyrna, in contrast, is rich though it thinks itself poor (2.9). Perhaps most shockingly of all, some Christians in Pergamum and Thyatira learn that what they believed was an appropriate mode of following Christ is, in the all-seeing eyes of this same Christ, tantamount to apostasy, no better than the false prophecy of Balaam, who in one biblical tradition stands accused of leading the Israelites astray towards idolatry (Num. 31.16; cf. 25.1–9), or the equally idolatrous practices of the pagan queen Jezebel (e.g. 1 Kings 16.31). The letter to Thyatira renames an unknown prophetess in that church as 'Jezebel'; the letter to Pergamum tells some of its members that they are followers of the teaching of 'Balaam'. Their crime is that they eat 'meat sacrificed to idols' and 'practice immorality' or 'fornication' (2.14, 20). The second phrase is probably to be taken metaphorically, as in the Old Testament, where it habitually refers to Israel's turning away from her Lord to serve foreign gods (the New Jerusalem Bible may be close to the mark in its translation 'commit the adultery of eating food which has been sacrificed to idols'). To the modern reader, the eating of idol meat may seem a quaint irrelevance; to urban Jews and Christians in the ancient world, however, the issue would have been symptomatic of a whole attitude towards society (Theissen, 1982, 121–43). Most of the meat on sale in the markets of ancient Graeco-Roman cities would first have been offered in sacrifice in pagan temples; as was also the custom in the Jewish Temple in Jerusalem, the priests were entitled to their share of the offering, and what was left over was sold on the open market. Meat was, however, expensive, and well beyond the everyday reach of the lower strata of society. Surviving evidence suggests that grain provided the staple diet under both Greece and Rome. It was only when it was distributed during civic religious celebrations, or perhaps by an individual benefactor intent upon municipal office, that the poorer urban dwellers would be in a position to eat meat; thus, to the poorer members of the early Christian urban communities it would always have had religious connotations (some, indeed, seem to have followed diaspora Jewish practice in avoiding meat altogether, because of its idolatrous associations).

For the richer members of society, however, meat would have featured more regularly in their diet, not simply in clearly religious contexts, and so wealthier Christians would not so readily have made the connection between meat and idolatry. They would have been in a better position to buy meat at the market, for example. They would have received, and been expected to offer in return, invitations to dine with their pagan neighbours. Involvement in the civic life of their respective cities would have meant greater exposure to contexts in which sacred meat was expected to be eaten. Those with business interests would have been under pressure to maintain their membership of local trade guilds or other voluntary associations, with their regular meals in honour of the patron-god (the city of Thyatira, home to the idol meat-eating 'Jezebel', was particularly remembered for its large number of trade guilds). Finally, those with a certain social status, including Christians, could on occasion even be invited to dine in a temple, as is exemplified by one famous invitation surviving from the ancient world: 'Charemon invites you to a meal at the table of the Lord Serapis in the Serapeum tomorrow, the fifteenth, beginning at 9 o'clock' (Theissen, 1982, 128).

The issue was, therefore, a particularly pressing one for Christians in the first-century Graeco-Roman world. It was a bone of fierce contention within the church in Corinth, as is testified by Paul's careful, and rather complex, dealing with the issue at 1 Corinthians 8—10, where the 'weak' are almost certainly the poorer members of the Corinthian church, who suffer scruples regarding the eating of such food, and the 'strong' are the wealthy and those who are socially upwardly mobile. For the poor, meat would almost always exhibit its sacrificial character; the rich may well have been more 'enlightened', recognizing that 'no idol in the world really exists' (cf. 1 Cor. 8.4). Acknowledging the social implications for the church of this controversial issue, Paul seems to steer a mediating path between 'weak' and 'strong', permitting the eating of such meat in certain (though not all) contexts, yet insisting upon the priority of not offending another's conscience. He is no doubt aware of the potentially disastrous implications for the Christian assembly in Corinth if its prominent members, those like Erastus, the 'city treasurer', or Gaius, who provided a meeting place for the church (Rom. 16.23), were forced to withdraw from city life. Later strands of the Pauline tradition, possibly building upon the kind of stance which Paul took in Corinth, would see the evangelistic possibilities of an attitude of openness to the world (e.g. 1 Tim. 2.1–4; 3.7; Titus 2.1–5).

Paul's is not the only position on this volatile issue in the New Testament, however. A demand that Gentile converts to the Jesus movement should abstain from that which had been sacrificed to idols had already been made by the Jewish-Christian leaders, according to Luke in an authoritative letter to the Christians in Syrian Antioch (Acts 15.20, 29). Interestingly, Paul makes no mention of this letter in his dealings with the Corinthians. John's visionary book, on the other hand, not only alludes to this apostolic letter (compare Acts 15.28–29 with Rev. 2.14, 20, 24), but goes much further in its condemnation. The divine revelation received in this book claims that such accommodation to their society has dangerous, even demonic consequences. For Christians to eat meat sacrificed to idols, contrary to the attitude taken by Pauline Christians in Asia no less than Corinth, is tantamount to idolatry, or, to use the metaphor prominent in the Hebrew scriptures for Israel's occasional meanderings into the worship of other gods, 'playing the harlot'. The reason for this will become clear in the apocalyptic visions in the second part of his book.

Two visions are particularly helpful for locating the apocalyptic discourse of Revelation on the plane of first-century imperial history, and highlighting the shocking, even subversive nature of the 'unveiling' which John's apocalypse presents, in the light of his own visionary experience of the celestial realm. The first is the famous vision of the woman clothed with the sun and the great red dragon in Revelation 12, the second, the shockingly seductive vision of the harlot Babylon in Revelation 17. Both visions are given particular poignancy when set against certain prevailing myths which played a crucial role in supporting and maintaining the great empire of Rome.

Classical authors at the turn of the Christian era and beyond extolled the virtue of the *Pax Augusta*, the achievements of the great Augustus in establishing peace throughout the borders of Rome's empire, or, as it later came to be called, the *Pax Romana*. Already in the late first century BCE, Virgil had spoken of the glory of Augustus and his restoration of a golden age to Latium in his *Aeneid* (6.791–5). In the city of Rome itself, the senate set up an altar celebrating Augustus' victory, the so-called *Ara Pacis Augustae*. This was not a universally held view of Augustus' reign (Tacitus for one testifies to an alternative assessment after Augustus' death, which saw his peace as peace 'with bloodshed', *Annals* 1.10.4), but it was a very widespread view. As late as the mid-second century, the Greek orator Aelius Aristides could write:

> People no longer believe in wars, indeed doubt whether they ever happen; stories about them are usually regarded as myths. But if wars should flare up somewhere on the frontiers, as is natural given such an immeasurably great empire, ... these wars disappear again, just like myths, as do the stories about them. So great is the peace that you now have, though waging war is a tradition among you.
>
> (Wengst, 1987, 17)

That this view was shared by at least the upper classes in the provinces, not least in western Asia Minor, the location of the seven churches to whom John writes, seems to be confirmed by inscriptions found in the area. One such inscription, from Priene near Ephesus, and dated to 9 BCE, describes Augustus as the one 'who has brought war to an end and ordained peace'. Another, from the city of Halicarnassus further to the south, not only acclaims Augustus as 'saviour of the whole human race', but goes on to provide the reason for such a title:

> Land and sea have peace, the cities flourish under a good legal system, in harmony and with an abundance of food, there is an abundance of all things, people are filled with happy hopes for the future and with delight at the present.
>
> (Wengst, 1987, 9)

One of the ways in which Rome was 'made present' to those living in the provinces such as Asia, apart from the emperor cult which became popular among Asians during the early empire, was the cult of the goddess Roma. Emerging out of the Greek tendency to attribute patron-gods to city-states, the cult of Roma had a temple in Smyrna as early as 195 BCE, and her influence increased alongside that of Rome in the East. Pergamum began constructing a temple to Roma and Augustus in 27 BCE, while Ephesus had its own temple to Roma and Julius Caesar. Paying homage to Roma represented one of the ways in which provincials could assert their loyalty to their overlord; her cult was only officially accepted in the city of Rome itself in 118 CE (Court, 1979, 148–53). Her image has survived in a variety of sculptures from this period, where she is often portrayed in military garb, or seated receiving the spoils of war. She is also portrayed seated on a number of coins minted in Pontus and Bithynia in the first century BCE. On the obverse of an oft-mentioned sestertius minted in Asia during the reign of Vespasian (71 CE), she reclines in military garb on the seven hills of Rome.

Despite the occasional suggestion that she is unfaithful Jerusalem, Revelation's vision of the woman Babylon is almost certainly to be equated in some sense with Rome. She is described as the great city who has authority over the kings of the earth (17.18). Although a number of Old Testament antecedents have obviously coalesced in this potent vision, it is likely that something of the contemporary presentation of Roma has also left its mark upon what John now describes. Like Roma, John's 'Babylon' is the personification of a great city. Though the military characteristics of Roma's depiction are largely lacking in Revelation 17, they may be represented in the colour of Babylon's dress (scarlet and purple). She sits on 'seven hills', as does Roma on the sestertius of Vespasian. Given the parallels between the two, the shocking nature of John's apocalyptic unveiling now comes to the fore. The great city and empire of Rome, paraded as a noble and victorious woman in the imperial iconography of Graeco-Roman cities, and worshipped in their temples as the divine Roma, is unmasked as nothing less than a Roman prostitute, clothed in obscene luxury, and drunk on the blood not only of the saints and the martyrs of Jesus (Rev. 17.6) but of 'all who have been slaughtered on earth' (18.24), that is, not least, of all the silent victims of the *Pax Romana*.

A second example of how John's divine apocalypse subverts those myths which lie at the very heart of the *imperium Romanum* can be found several chapters earlier, in the strange vision of the woman and the dragon in Revelation 12. Yet again, ancient myths, Old Testament figures and traditions, and contemporary historical allusions have merged to create a multivalent vision with an almost indefinite number of resonances. But leaving aside for the moment echoes of ancient chaos myths associated with Leviathan and his Ugaritic counterpart Litan, the Genesis story of Eve and the serpent in Eden, and traditions about the birth and exaltation of Christ, John's vision can also be understood as a subversive challenge to another widespread myth which came to play an influential role in the exaltation of the emperor, namely, that associated with Apollo.

A variety of similar stories circulated in the Mediterranean and Ancient Near East (generally known by the umbrella term of 'combat myths'), which told of a cosmic struggle between two divine figures, one of whom was generally a dragon or some other monster (Yarbro Collins, 1976). One of the more famous versions of this combat myth, known in the Greek and Roman world, was associated with the god Apollo: Apollo's mother, Leto, pregnant by Zeus, is carried on the north wind to the island of Delos to escape the great dragon Python, sent to destroy Leto's child by Zeus' irate consort, Hera. On Delos (significantly, not many miles from John's island exile of Patmos), both Apollo and his sister Artemis are safely born. Ultimately, the Python is slain by Apollo, the very divine child he sought to destroy. Though this is in essence a Greek myth, it came to hold particular force for Romans during the early empire, given that several emperors explicitly identified themselves with Apollo. Apollo was Augustus' own favoured patron; indeed, in 28 BCE he built a temple in his honour on the Palatine hill in Rome. But particularly potent was the self-identification with Apollo of the Emperor Nero, the first imperial persecutor of Christians. Evidence from elsewhere in the Apocalypse suggests that Nero was not far from the mind of the seer as he attempted to make sense of his apocalyptic visions: the vast majority of commentators accept that the reference at 17.8 to the beast that 'was and is not and is to come' (cf. 13.3; 17.11) is an allusion to the *Nero redivivus* myth which circulated in the last decades of the first century, after Nero's death in 68. Suetonius tells us in his assessment that Nero was popularly regarded as equal to Apollo in music and to the Sun in driving a chariot (*Nero* 53). Tacitus goes further, presenting Nero as justifying his own predilection for singing to the lyre as a practice sacred to Apollo (*Annals* 14.14.1f.). Moreover, coins minted in the latter years of Nero's reign exploit these parallels by portraying the emperor as Apollo the lyre-player (Kreitzer, 1996, 208, Figure 5).

Given the popular identification of the emperor (particularly Nero) with Apollo, John's vision of the woman and the dragon has particularly potent force. For it yet again subverts a fundamental Roman myth: the divine child born of the woman, far from being Apollo, or the Roman emperor who rules in his stead, is revealed instead as Jesus Christ, the Lamb that was slain by the very empire which makes such exalted claims for itself. But even more offensive is the revelation that Rome, and its emperors, lie on the wrong side of the mythical divide, identified with the beast from the sea, the earthly instrument of the fiery dragon, known variously as Leviathan, or Satan, or the Python.

The recognition that apocalypses offer, or claim to offer, privileged insight into a divine perspective on the world, through the revelation of divine mysteries, has particular potential for the book of Revelation. John's apocalyptic vision of the divine One seated on his heavenly throne-chariot, a throne now shared with the slain Lamb, enabled him to see the 'rulers of this world', and particularly the contemporary empire of Rome, in their true colours. The alternative vision which he describes in his book may well have proved shocking even to some members of the Christian communities in the cities of Asia, constantly bombarded as they would have been with images of Rome's power and dominance, and the rhetoric of the beneficent *Pax Romana*. But to shock, to challenge, and to overturn received visions of the way the world is, no less than to comfort and exhort those in need of God's reassuring word, remain fundamental purposes of Judaeo-Christian apocalypses.

Seeing New Patterns in Scripture

Nevertheless, John's visionary accounts have clearly not been influenced simply by prevalent pagan myths. Both visions alluded to above are saturated with the imagery of the Hebrew scriptures and subsequent retellings of the biblical story. Indeed, it would not be untruthful to make the same claim for virtually every verse of this lengthy book, despite the lack of explicit biblical quotation. John's text breathes the air of the Israelite biblical tradition; the scriptures of his people are pulsating through his veins, such that, almost unconsciously at times, he can evoke well-known biblical passages. Especially notable are the preponderance of allusions in the Apocalypse to the prophetic books, notably Isaiah and Ezekiel, the Psalms, and the apocalyptic Daniel, as Steve Moyise has shown in a series of graphs which compare Revelation with other New Testament works, namely Matthew, Romans and Hebrews, in which quotations from and allusions to the Pentateuch seem to dominate (Moyise, 1995, 15–16). The influence of Daniel is particularly dominant, proportionate to its size, though perhaps to be expected given that both texts stand in the same apocalyptic tradition. But equally striking is the way in which these biblical allusions have been woven together in often unexpected ways, forming new patterns in the manner of a kaleidoscope. As we have already seen, the vision of the woman clothed with the sun weaves together biblical passages about Eve whose offspring crushes the serpent's head (Gen. 3.15), Israel crowned with the stars of her twelve tribes (Gen. 37.9–11) and borne on eagle's wings (Exod. 19.4), and pregnant Jerusalem, waiting to be delivered from her suffering and from the sea-monster Leviathan (Isa. 26.17–18; 27.1). The appearance of the rider on the white horse at 19.11–16 brings together the Divine Warrior tradition found in Isaiah 63 and Wisdom 18.15–16 with the messianic passage of Isaiah 11. It is as if John's visionary experience has enabled him, whether consciously as a biblical exegete, or rather more unconsciously, to see new patterns in ancient scriptures.

This profound influence from the sacred writings of Israel should not surprise us: visionaries in every age are crucially dependent upon their cultural heritage for making sense of their religious experience. At an even more fundamental level, that same heritage will have been crucial in laying the very foundations for that experience. Steve Moyise reminds us of the frequency of prophetic utterances in Pentecostal churches being delivered not only in biblical language but also in the phraseology of the King James Bible (Moyise, 1995, 40). Ruth Harris's recent book on the visions of Bernadette at Lourdes reveals the extent to which Bernadette's own vision stands in a long tradition of appearances of the Virgin in that region of the Pyrenees (Harris, 1999). The visionary texts of the apocalypticists, similarly, are steeped in the language and imagery of the biblical record. Indeed, the extent of dependence upon biblical tradition may vary even within the same text. A writer may in certain places have engaged in some quite careful reflection upon and reinterpretation of particular scriptural passages, while other references and allusions would appear to be more fluid, drawn less consciously from the deep wells of the biblical tradition. Yet even this is not necessarily incompatible with claims to visionary experience, in a literary work which is partly the result of subsequent reflection upon prior religious experience.

One relatively clear example of where John is dependent upon the Old Testament is in his vision of the two beasts in Revelation 13, the first of which picks up on the Danielic vision of the four beasts in Daniel 7. This chapter was significant not only for other apocalypticists, but also for early Christians, though the focus tended to be upon the two figures of the Ancient of Days and the 'one like a son of man'. John is not uninterested in these figures (e.g. Rev. 1.7, 14), but his main interest in chapter 13 is upon the early part of that chapter. Yet how far is the borrowing the result of careful exegesis of Scripture, and how much due to the role played by Daniel's apocalypse in the formation of John's own mindset?

One can make a good case for some kind of literary dependence of Revelation 13 upon Daniel 7. Both describe beastly visions, in which the chief characters (in Daniel, four beasts, in Revelation, one) come up out of the sea. John's beast encompasses the characteristics of all Daniel's four: leopard-like, feet like a bear's, a lion's mouth, and possessing ten horns. One of the horns of Daniel's fourth beast (almost certainly a reference to Antiochus IV Epiphanes) makes war with the saints (Dan. 7.8 LXX; see also 7.21), as will the beast from the sea which John sees (Rev. 13.7). Just as Daniel's fourth beast will oppress the saints of the Most High for 'a time, two times, and half a time', i.e. three and a half years (Dan. 7.25), so too the beast from the sea is permitted to exercise its authority for the equivalent length of time, forty-two months (Rev. 13.5). Indeed, these similarities reveal linguistic agreements between the two visions: the shared use of the verb ἀναβαίνειν, 'to come up'; the shared expression 'to make war on the saints', the same description used of the speech of Daniel's little horn and John's beast from the sea (στόμα λαλοῦν μεγάλα, lit. 'a mouth speaking great things', Dan. 7.8; Rev. 13.5).

There are firm indications, then, that the Apocalypse of John offers a fresh reading of at least certain sections of Daniel (even though his use of Ezekiel would appear to be even more significant structurally). But whether this is best envisaged as the systematic interpretation of a biblical scholar, is rather less clear. For first, although Daniel 7 is the dominant source for Revelation 13, echoes of other scriptural passages have been detected. A survey of commentaries on this vision will find the following among those identified: Job 40—41 (Leviathan and Behemoth, in John's description of two beasts, one from the sea and one from the earth); Exodus 15.11 (in the parody 'Who is like the beast?'); Exodus 32.32 (the 'book of life'); Isaiah 53.7 (the slain lamb); Jeremiah 15.2 and 43.11 (the 'interruption' of vv. 9–10). This is not straightforwardly a reapplication of Daniel's vision.

In the second place, John's account of the first beast does not systematically follow the Danielic account of the four beasts, as one might expect in the work of a biblical exegete (such is the case, for example, in the Qumran *pesharim* which work their way through a biblical text phrase by phrase). We have already noted this fact in the rather loose relationship between John and his biblical antecedents found in the 'son of man' and throne visions of Revelation 1 and 4. In Revelation 13, likewise, even the order of the beasts is different: Daniel has (1) lion, (2) bear, (3) leopard, (4) ten horns; John has (1) ten horns, (2) leopard, (3) bear, (4) lion. Whereas Daniel then goes on to describe the appearance of the 'one like a son of man' before the Ancient of Days, this does not happen in Revelation, which has already echoed this vision in two places, and will do so again at a later stage. Moreover, whereas Daniel (like some other apocalypses such as *4 Ezra*) follows up these visions with a fairly precise interpretation of the four beasts and their fate, John eschews this in favour of a mere exhortation to endurance and the account of the second beast, leaving his readers to reckon for themselves the identification of these two figures (aided only by the rather cryptic allusion to the beast's number, 666). In short, John's use of his biblical predecessor here seems rather more fluid than is sometimes suggested.

There is a danger of turning the visionary John into a rather bookish don, cutting and pasting diverse biblical passages, or at least into a first-century equivalent of a medieval monk, scouring a variety of manuscripts on the desk in front of him, checking and double-checking textual variants, in order to achieve his finished product. One might want to ask, not least, what access John would have had to scrolls containing biblical texts while on Patmos. The answer to this question depends only in part on the nature of his sojourn there (an issue which will be discussed in Chapter 4), and in part on the presence of a Jewish or Christian community on this tiny island.

Yet surely a mediating position is possible, given the documented role of scriptural study in the Jewish mystical tradition. Apocalyptic visionaries, and their successors, seem to have had their preferred biblical books and key passages which provided a focus for their preparatory meditations. Daniel, it will be remembered, is found meditating upon a prophecy of Jeremiah prior to his dramatic vision of the archangel Gabriel (Dan. 9.2). Ezekiel's throne vision has been shown to have been immensely influential for a variety of apocalyptic texts. The seer in *4 Ezra* is explicitly told by the *angelus interpres* that his vision of the Eagle from the sea is 'the fourth kingdom which appeared in a vision to your brother Daniel' (*4 Ezra* 12.11), now reapplied to encompass the apparently victorious empire of Rome. It would not be out of place, therefore, for Daniel's vision to have been a prominent meditative text for John of Patmos also, alongside Ezekiel's vision of the heavenly *Merkavah*. This would account, then, for the explicit and dramatic reworking of Daniel 7 into a visionary onslaught on the empire of Rome, while allowing for rather more unconscious biblical allusions to weave their way from other texts into the overall picture, a natural process for one so steeped in the biblical tradition.

Concluding Thoughts

There is a tendency amongst many biblical scholars to over-categorize, such that visionary experience, prophetic insight and biblical exegesis are generally treated as mutually exclusive possibilities. The tendency has manifested itself in a particular way in scholarly discussions of John of Patmos and the book which bears his name. It is often presupposed, for example, that if John had meditated on Israel's scriptures in preparation for writing his book, then that rules out his having had actual visions; that if he saw himself as a prophet, speaking the word of God to his own generation, then he could not also have stood in the tradition of the apocalypticists. What is needed instead is a rather less inflexible paradigm, which refuses to regard these options as mutually exclusive. I hope this chapter has gone some small way towards intimating how the balance might be redressed. Prophets need not ignore the written traditions of their forebears; apocalyptic seers can utter oracles in the name of the Lord; exegetes can dream dreams and have visions. It is now time to turn in rather more detail to that one great vision of the earliest Christian era which has been our subject hitherto, and which seems to bring together the crucial tasks of prophet, exegete and visionary. Such will be the focus of the next chapter.

NOTES

1. Indeed, the repeated use of similes in Daniel's two visions may be symptomatic of the same dilemma for apocalyptic visionaries generally, as they attempted to compose their literary apocalypses.
2. It is unclear whether the drink that Ezra is given by the angel at *4 Ezra* 14.38–39 refers to an actual substance drunk, or is a metaphorical description of the divine inspiration which the seer receives in order to accomplish his task of dictating the books.
3. *1 Enoch* 14.13. Translation by M. A. Knibb in H. F. D. Sparks (ed.), *The Apocryphal Old Testament* (Clarendon Press, Oxford, 1984).

REFERENCES

Ashton, J. (2000), *The Religion of Paul the Apostle.* Yale University Press, New Haven and London.

Court, J. (1979), *Myth and History in the Book of Revelation.* SPCK, London.

Farrer, A. (1949), *A Rebirth of Images.* Dacre Press, Westminster.

Gruenwald, I. (1980), *Apocalyptic and Merkavah Mysticism.* E. J. Brill, Leiden.

Harris, R. (1999), *Lourdes.* Penguin, Harmondsworth.

Kreitzer, L. J. (1996), *Striking New Images.* Sheffield Academic Press, Sheffield.

Lindblom, J. (1963), *Prophecy in Ancient Israel.* Basil Blackwell, Oxford.

Moyise, S. (1995), *The Old Testament in the Book of Revelation.* Sheffield Academic Press, Sheffield.

Rowland, C. (1982), *The Open Heaven.* SPCK, London.

Scholem, G. G. (1946), *Major Trends in Jewish Mysticism.* Schocken Books, New York.

Theissen, G. (1982), *The Social Setting of Pauline Christianity.* T. & T. Clark, Edinburgh.

Wengst, K. (1987), *Pax Romana and the Peace of Jesus Christ.* SCM Press, London.

Yarbro Collins, A. (1976), *The Combat Myth in the Book of Revelation.* Scholars Press, Missoula, MT.

3

Viewing the Whole Tapestry

[The Apocalypse] is the one great poem which the first Christian age produced, it is a single and living unity from end to end, and it contains a whole world of spiritual imagery to be entered into and possessed.

(Austin Farrer, 1949, 6)

The Angers Apocalypse

A chance discovery in the garden of the bishop's palace of Angers, France, in the summer of 1843, preserved for the world one of its most magnificent artistic treasures. The fourteenth-century Apocalypse tapestry of the Dukes of Anjou (of which the dirty piece of 'carpet' found in the episcopal greenhouse proved to be part) had been one of the most impressive works of its kind, in its completed form some 420 feet long, comprising seven sections, each containing fourteen scenes from the Apocalypse of John. This set of tapestries had hung in the cathedral of St-Maurice on festival days from the fifteenth until the eighteenth century, when it was relegated to the storerooms, and eventually to the dump, victim to the demise of the Gothic style. Now restored as close to its former glory as possible, and housed in a special gallery in Angers Castle, it presents to the visitor the whole panoply of John's mysterious visions, in vivid scenes silhouetted against dark backgrounds of red and blue.

The metaphor of a tapestry is an appropriate one for the task of interpretation, of reading this book with insight. For it is often the case, whatever approach is taken to the Apocalypse, that more attention is paid to the interpretation of specific passages than to the work as a whole: there is a tendency to focus on a vision here, a canticle there, such that the wood is rarely seen for the trees. Whether a commentator wishes to use Revelation to plot the sequence of eschatological events, or to learn about the nature and timing of the Millennium in particular, or to 'decode' specific characters or images, or to locate the book and its original addressees in their historical setting, or to dig for supposed sources beneath the surface of the text, certain passages become central to the detriment of others, and thus to the whole. The creator of a tapestry, on the other hand, is attempting to produce a unified vision, an overall effect, through the skilful interweaving of the various threads, sensitive to pattern, to colour and to texture. Recent literary approaches to the Bible have made commentators increasingly aware of the importance of similar features within what we might call textual tapestries; used with care, they may help us better to understand this book as a whole, and not simply in its constitutive parts.

The rest of this chapter is intended as an aid to viewing the Apocalypse as a whole, rather like a complete tapestry. What follows, therefore, should not be taken as set in stone, definitive, but simply as a guide to an initial read-through of this elusive and apparently impenetrable book, pointing out both clear and possible structural clues, attempting to offer explanations where these might be helpful, highlighting passages where interpretations are controversial and disputed, and suggesting how individual parts might be related to the whole. Readers will need to make up their own minds about how useful such hints are, accepting some and revising or rejecting others in the light of their own subsequent re-readings of the book.

Of course, even to attempt something as elementary and provisional as this is a precarious task. As David Barr has written, not without some frustration, of the seemingly endless scholarly attempts to uncover the structure of the book: 'There are, unfortunately, nearly as many outlines of the Apocalypse as there are commentators on it' (Barr, 1984, 43). This should warn us against too readily accepting any one schema as definitive. Nevertheless, as has been mentioned in Chapter 1, there are certain structural clues (such as the various series of seven) upon which the majority of commentators agree, and these can provide a solid starting point for our initial reading. Those who wish to take things further will want to refer to one or more of the plethora of commentaries on the book of Revelation.

1.1–8 Prologue

Beginnings and endings are always important for understanding a text. The first eight verses of Revelation form a prologue which provides crucial keys to the genre of this book. Verses 1–3 are a kind of superscription or title to the whole book, which identifies its revelatory character: it is an 'apocalypse' or 'revelation of Jesus Christ' (not, despite the title subsequently attached to this book, 'revelation of John'), i.e., a book which claims to offer insight into the unseen world, direct access to heavenly mysteries. The genitive here is ambiguous, perhaps deliberately so: is this a 'revelation about Jesus Christ', or a 'revelation from Jesus Christ' to his servant John? Both are possible, but the following phrase ('which God gave him') suggests a preference for the latter. Whatever is the case, a chain of transmission for this divine revelation is being set up: God – Jesus Christ – his angel – his servant John. The heavenly secrets to be revealed over the following twenty-two chapters of this apocalypse have reached John by means of intermediaries, of whom one is Jesus, and the other his messenger or angel.

Moreover, we may have here our first clue to the structure of this book, for the giving of the revelation by God to Jesus Christ sounds very much like the event described in Revelation 5, when, in the heavenly throne-room, the One seated on the throne gives the sealed scroll to the Lamb, while the sending of Christ's angel to John may well allude to the episode in Revelation 10, in which a mighty angel descends from heaven holding a little scroll, which the seer is then commanded to take and eat (Rev. 10.9). From that point in the narrative, John takes on a new role, no longer being a simple observer but bidden to prophesy actively. Is this opening verse of the book an early warning that these two events will herald important turning points in the structure of this book?

Three further features of the introductory statement are worthy of note. First, the content of this revelation is described as that which 'must soon take place' (or 'quickly', 'without delay'). Despite the fact that readers often plunder this book for details of end-time scenarios in our present or near future, the author seems to claim for the events so described a chronological proximity to his own day, over nineteen centuries ago. Second, this revelation has been 'made known', or, better, 'signified' (Greek ἐσήμανεν) by an angel; John uses a verb from which comes the Greek word for 'sign' (σημεῖον). In other words, this revelation is not conveyed in any straightforward manner, but through signs, which are notoriously elusive and need to be carefully interpreted. This provides an early warning that understanding this text will require slow and patient study, and not least an appreciation of its symbolic nature. Finally, a blessing is promised in verse 3 for both the reader (singular) and the hearers (plural), an early indication that this text was intended to be read out loud to the Christian assemblies to which it was sent. Whether it was to be read in one sitting, or in more manageable instalments, remains to be decided.

After this titular superscription, we come (in vv. 4–8) to the author's greeting proper, which gives the book the character of a letter, akin to the letters attributed to Paul, and has led some commentators to question whether it should be considered an apocalypse at all. The recipients of this apocalyptic letter are described as the seven ἐκκλησίαι which are in Asia (as elsewhere in the New Testament, 'Asia' refers to the Roman province of Asia, comprising the former regions of Mysia, Lydia, Caria, Ionia, and the larger part of Phrygia, in western Asia Minor, e.g. Acts 6.9; 19 *passim*; 21.27; Rom. 16.5; 1 Cor. 16.19). Though ἐκκλησία was a word frequently used in the ancient world to describe a host of political and religious assemblies, the present context makes clear that these are seven Christian assemblies or churches. Whatever wider application the Apocalypse would come to have – and subsequent interpreters have made much of seven being the number of completeness, i.e., this book is addressed to the whole Church – the primary focus of this book is upon these seven early Christian assemblies in proconsular Asia.

The greeting echoes that of letters in the Pauline tradition, which also wish their addressees both 'grace' (Greek χάρις, a theological modification of the typical Hellenistic greeting χαίρειν) and 'peace' (the traditional Jewish greeting *shalom*) But John's greeting wishes grace and peace not, as in the case of Paul, 'from God our Father and the Lord Jesus Christ' (e.g. 1 Cor. 1.3; 2 Cor. 1.2; Phil. 1.2), but using a threefold (we are probably not yet in a position to say Trinitarian) designation distinctive to this particular writer. God is described is 'him who is and who was and who is to come', the latter verb (where one might have expected 'who will be') creating a dynamic phrase which underlines the sense of imminent eschatological salvation of this book. Along with God, there are the 'seven spirits who are before his throne': is this a poetic description for what is called elsewhere in the New Testament the 'Holy Spirit' or 'Spirit of God', playing again on the significance of the number seven as symbolizing completeness or perfection, and perhaps influenced by the description of the sevenfold gifts of the Spirit in Isaiah 11, or the seven 'eyes' of the Lord in Zechariah 5? Or is this an echo of the Jewish belief that there were seven principal angels standing before the divine presence in heaven (e.g. Tobit 12.15; cf. *1 Enoch* 20.2–8; angels are sometimes referred to as 'spirits', cf. Heb. 1.14), so that 'grace and peace' are transmitted to the Christian recipients by angelic mediators? The reader will want to pay attention to further descriptions of the Spirit/seven spirits, and of the role of angels, as the book proceeds, in order to answer this question (what is the connection, for example, between 1.4 and 8.2?). Finally, grace and peace come also, as for Paul, from Jesus Christ, whom John designates as 'the faithful witness' (Greek μάρτυς, from which comes our English word 'martyr'), 'the firstborn of the dead, and the ruler of the kings of the earth'. Many commentators have seen this designation as significant. In so describing Jesus, is John wanting to strengthen the resolve of his hearers in their own Christian witness, even in the face of potential or actual hostility or persecution, assuring them that, however slight and ineffectual it might appear, it has the capacity to withstand even the might of the 'kings of the earth'? This strengthening of resolve would then be heightened by the way in which the addressees themselves are described: as a 'kingdom' (or possibly 'empire', in direct opposition to the empire of Rome), and as 'priests serving his God and Father', those who have direct access to the divine presence. Finally, expectation is raised of the imminence of Christ's coming 'with the clouds' (v. 7), and confirmed by the direct intervention of the heavenly voice: 'I am the Alpha and the Omega, says the Lord God, who is and who was and who is to come, the Almighty' (v. 8).

1.9—3.22 *Seven Letters/Messages*

After this careful literary introduction, the first main section (clearly delineated, as we shall see) now begins: a series of seven 'letters' or 'prophetic messages' to the seven churches of Asia, prefaced by an autobiographical statement from John and an account of a vision of the risen Christ which provides these messages with their authority. Letters or messages are unusual in an apocalypse (though not unknown, e.g. *2 Baruch* 77—87); but their presence here is less surprising when we remember that they are addressed to angels, not humans. More importantly, they are crucially important for understanding this book as a whole. For they root the apparently other-worldly visions of chapters 4—22, and thus the divine revelation they purport to offer, firmly in the socio-political realities of life in first-century Roman Asia. Themes introduced in this vision, and in these seven messages, will be taken up, reused and developed in the ensuing visions, weaving the various chapters of this book into a coherent whole.

John begins by telling us that the vision and messages to be described in the next few chapters were seen and heard by him while he was on the small, rocky island of Patmos, in the Aegean, not many miles off the coast of western Asia Minor. What precisely he means by saying that he was there 'because of the word of God and the testimony of Jesus' will be discussed further in the next chapter. What is important here is his claim to visionary experience: John shares with many of different times and cultures the belief that, given the right circumstances, direct access is possible to the normally unseen realities of a higher realm.

The vision which he goes on to describe (1.12–20) seems to have a twofold function within this section, and within the book as a whole. It functions as a kind of commissioning vision for John the seer, rather like the stories of the commissioning of the prophets Isaiah, Jeremiah and Ezekiel (Isa. 6; Jer. 1; Ezek. 1—2), though John is commanded here to write rather than directly to prophesy (that will come later, in chapter 10). But it also provides the immediate context, and the divine legitimization, for the seven messages: these are not letters sent by John so much as direct communications, to the angels of these churches, from the mouth of the Son of Man himself. The description of the vision has echoes of a number of biblical and other apocalyptic texts, such as the vision of the 'glory of the Lord' at Ezekiel 1.26–28, or the Ancient of Days and the celestial being of Daniel 7 and 10 respectively, but retaining the fluidity to be expected of a description of actual visionary encounter.

There are strongly liturgical characteristics in this vision: the one like a Son of Man appears standing in the midst of the seven golden lampstands, reminiscent of the seven-branched lampstand of the Jerusalem Temple (Exod. 25.31–37; cf. 1 Kings 7.49). Indeed, some commentators have suggested that he is portrayed in the garb of a priest, even the High Priest, though that remains disputed. Certainly he is an exalted figure, more associated with the heavenly than the earthly realm. Early Christian writers plundered the existing titles and categories of their religious heritage in order to speak meaningfully of Christ, and, while many of them explored traditions which would stress Jesus' role as a divinely appointed human being, such as messiah or prophet, John's encounter on Patmos leads him to speak of Christ in terms hitherto restricted to figures from the angelic, heavenly realm. Indeed, such is the awesome nature of this encounter with one of the heavenly realm that John falls down at Christ's feet, as if dead, and is only restored to his previous condition by the initiative of the heavenly figure (Rev. 1.17; cf. Dan. 10.9–10). Later in the book there will be occasions when worship, expressly forbidden towards angels, will be directed towards the person of Christ (e.g. 5.8, 13; cf. 19.10; 22.9).

Chapters 2 and 3 present the content of the seven 'letters' or 'messages', each with a similar structure. Each one, first of all, is addressed to the ἄγγελος of the church/assembly in the respective city. It is unlikely that we should translate ἄγγελος as 'messenger', as if the messenger (i.e. the deliverer) of this book to the seven churches was also to be addressed by it. Rather, we should probably translate it as 'angel'. But even this translation remains ambiguous: some have thought that 'angel' is to be taken as a designation of a human authority figure, the bishop or overseer of the specific churches. Yet Revelation seems to know nothing elsewhere of the monepiscopate which was found in some of these Asian churches by the time of Ignatius of Antioch a few decades later (John seems far more interested in the ongoing ministry of the prophet, e.g. 11.10; 22.6, 9). It is more likely, particularly given the apocalyptic nature of the text, that the messages are addressed to angelic beings. Nations were believed to have their own heavenly counterparts or guardians (Michael was understood to be the guardian of Israel), and those mentioned here may well then have been the angelic personifications or guardians of these fledgling Christian communities.

Second, there is the equivalent to the Old Testament 'prophetic messenger formula', the 'Thus says the Lord ... ' of the canonical prophets (translated in the Greek Septuagint as Τάδε λέγει, a phrase picked up here in each of the seven letters). But Revelation is thoroughly christological. It is the Son of Man, rather than 'God' or 'the Lord', who introduces himself in this divine manner, and he does so differently to each community, in terms largely drawn from the inaugural vision, such that by the end of the seventh letter, the whole vision has been recapitulated, and supplemented by further titles of Christ which will be echoed later in the book: 'the holy one, the true one, who has the key of David' (letter to Philadelphia, 3.7; cf. 19.11; 22.16); 'the Amen, the faithful and true witness, the origin of God's creation' (letter to Laodicea, 3.14; cf. 19.11; 21.6). Vision and prophetic utterance are thus inextricably interwoven in this section of our apocalyptic tapestry.

There then follows the main body of each message, in which the One who searches the mind and heart offers a divine diagnosis of each community to its angelic guardian. This section reveals just how intimately the exalted Son of Man, or his prophetic messenger John, knows the state of each of these churches. The important historical and archaeological work of Sir William Ramsay, and the later research of Colin Hemer, have shown the extent to which local allusions, highly pertinent to the city in question, have been woven into each of the messages (Ramsay, 1904; Hemer, 1986).

Figure 2. Possible local allusions in the seven letters (Rev. 2—3)

City	Allusion	Possible Reference
Ephesus	Promise of 'tree of life' in God's paradise	Temple of Artemis contained a tree-shrine, with right of asylum
Smyrna	'Who was dead and came to life'	Smyrna destroyed c. 600 BCE and refounded c. 300
	Exhortation to be faithful to death	City's Greek name is the same as word for 'myrrh', associated with death and burial
	Promise of 'crown of life'	Smyrna's games, at which victor received a 'crown' or 'wreath'
Pergamum	'Throne of Satan'	Possible allusions include: Statue of Jupiter, Altar of Zeus, Temple of Augustus, Asklepion healing-shrine (associated with serpent), or acropolis as a whole, dominating the skyline
Thyatira	'Burnished bronze' of Christ's feet	Thyatira had an important metal industry
Sardis	Christ will come 'like a thief'	Sardis' acropolis was attacked twice at night
Philadelphia	Promise of a 'new name'	Philadelphia took new name of Neocaesarea under Tiberias
Laodicea	Claims to be rich and prosperous; urged to buy white garments and eye ointment	Laodicea had reputation for financial prosperity; famous pharmaceutical industry, and black wool
	Church is 'lukewarm, and neither hot nor cold'	Close to hot springs at Hierapolis, and cold waters of Colossae

More telling for the analysis of the specific Christian assemblies is the mixture of praise and rebuke, noted already, which reveals the very diverse challenges faced by these Christian communities. Some receive encouragement in the face of actual or potential hostility, apparently provoked by rival Jewish synagogues (2.9; 3.9), but this seems to be a relatively minor concern within this sevenfold prophetic letter. Others are praised, or criticized, for the way in which they have responded to alternative presentations of the Christian gospel, whether from the so-called 'apostles' of Ephesus (2.2), the mysterious Nicolaitans at Ephesus and Pergamum (2.6; 2.15), those at Pergamum who 'hold to the teaching of Balaam' (2.14), or the followers of the Christian prophetess rather derogatively named 'Jezebel' in Thyatira (2.20). Only two churches, those at Smyrna and Philadelphia, come out of the divine assessment unscathed, while one of them, Laodicea, has nothing for which to be praised. Those who would see the Apocalypse primarily as a work of consolation for the persecuted need to take seriously the strong element of rebuke within these letters. In each of the seven messages (2.5, 10b, 16, 24–25; 3.3, 11, 19), the main body concludes with a prophetic remedy or challenge, normally introduced by the word 'therefore', and in several cases issuing in a call to repentance. There is nothing fatalistic or predestined about the state of the churches: even the pitiable Laodiceans are given an opportunity to repent (3.19).

The conclusions to each of the seven letters/messages are also similar. There is in each the recurring phrase, reminiscent of a gospel saying of Jesus often connected with his parables (e.g. Mark 4.9, 23), for those with an ear to 'listen to what the Spirit is saying to the churches', which is the penultimate phrase in letters 1–3, and the ultimate one in letters 4–7. This is then followed (in the first three), or preceded (in the last four), by a promise made to those who are victorious. In each case this is expressed in language and images which will reappear later in the book, and especially, though not exclusively, in the final glorious visions of chapters 20—22. The victors in Ephesus, for example, will eat of the tree of life, which is later found, bearing plentiful fruit and leaves for the healing of the nations, in the New Jerusalem (2.7; 22.2); the Smyrnean conquerors will not be harmed by the second death (2.11; 20.14–15); the faithful in Sardis can be assured of finding their names written in the book of life when the dead are gathered for judgement (3.5; 20.12). Thus not only are the seven letters bound into the preceding inaugural vision of the Son of Man, they are also inextricably linked within this apocalyptic tapestry with what is yet to come, especially those visions of eschatological salvation in which this book culminates. Before the implications of divine salvation and judgement are worked out for the world, they are worked out for the Church. The Church is not immune to compromise with the kingdom of this world and the seduction of Satan, yet authentic life in

Christ is life in anticipation of the glorious future in which God will be all in all.

4.1—8.1 Seven Seals

At this point in the narrative there is a noticeable shift of tone and location, as a new sequence of visionary revelation begins. We are granted visions of 'what must take place after this' (4.1), of the state and fate of the world, in which the already significant number seven continues to play an important structural role. These visions will continue, strictly speaking, until the middle of chapter 22. Up to this point, John has functioned as prophetic mediator of the Lord's relatively straightforward words to his Church. Now he is taken up 'in the spirit' (the New Jerusalem Bible may provide a better rendition of John's sense with its paraphrase 'fell into ecstasy') into the heavenly throne-room, and becomes an apocalyptic seer proper, the privileged observer of symbolic visions. As in the previous section, here too an initial vision serves as an introduction to a series of seven, this time the opening of seven seals.

What John describes in the vision of Revelation 4—5 lies firmly in the tradition of Jewish visions of the heavenly *Merkavah*, rooted in the throne-chariot vision of Ezekiel 1, though with a certain fluidity which argues against direct literary dependence upon existing written accounts of similar visions. As in Ezekiel's vision, the throne is jealously guarded by four living creatures, the cherubim, though they have become in Revelation four different creatures rather than each bearing characteristics of lion, ox, human and eagle (Ezek. 1.5–14; they have not yet become the four evangelists of later Christian symbolism). The precise identity of the twenty-four elders seated on thrones encircling the great throne (4.4) is rather more controversial, indeed has been the subject of controversy for centuries. Are they angels, or, more probably, human figures? If human, then are they representatives of the people of God of both old and new dispensations (including the twelve apostles), or the twenty-four divisions of the Aaronite priesthood (1 Chron. 24.4ff.)?

In contrast to Ezekiel, John has little interest in the chariot itself; he moves swiftly on to the figure seated upon the throne. But even here, there is a noticeable reserve in his description of what, or whom, he sees. Ezekiel can speak, albeit elusively, of the figure on the throne as 'something that seemed like a human form' (Ezek. 1.26). John's description is even more reluctant to use human characteristics to signify what he sees, using instead images from the mineral world, 'like jasper and carnelian'. In this, of course, he reflects his own Jewish heritage. Nevertheless, to his first audiences, such reserve would have provided a powerful contrast to the highly anthropomorphic depiction of the gods, and the deified emperors, in the cities in which they lived and worked. The God who revealed himself to John is wholly other than the cult statue of Apollo, which featured on coins minted by the city of Thyatira, or Ephesian Artemis, whose great cult statue was the envy of the ancient world, or the deified Augustus, whose temples graced the skylines of Pergamum and Sardis. The One whom John sees on the throne may not be venerated by the hoards of suppliants in the temples of Ephesus and Pergamum; but in the unseen realm, not only the four living creatures, not only the twenty-four elders, but the myriads of angels, 'ten thousand times ten thousand', render fitting worship to the Almighty, who was, and is, and is to come.

There is an even more fundamental difference between the visions of Ezekiel (and *1 Enoch* 14 and *Apocalypse of Abraham* 18) on the one hand, and that of John on the other: the place of Jesus Christ. John sees in the hand of the One sitting on the throne a scroll, with writing on both sides, sealed with seven seals. We are not told explicitly what this scroll contains, though it has the characteristics of a Roman legal document. Is it Scripture as a whole, the record of God's careful plan for the human race; or specifically his eschatological plan for salvation in the last days? Or does it contain a record of the events about which we shall read in the remaining chapters of this book, such that, when the scroll is opened, these events will begin to unfold? Nor are we told, in chapter 10, what relationship, if any, there is between the 'little scroll' brought to John by a mighty angel and this scroll now in the hand of the One on the throne (though, as we saw, there may be a clue in 1.1). We are told, however, that only one is worthy to open this scroll and see inside it, namely, the Lion of the tribe of Judah (a Jewish messianic title echoing Gen. 49.9). Moreover, the movement of the rest of the book suggests that there is indeed some direct connection between the opening of the scroll and the unfolding visions of judgement and salvation.

The Jewish apocalyptic tradition frequently utilizes animals to symbolize human beings – the *Animal Apocalypse* of *1 Enoch* 85—90 is one of the more famous examples, in which the history of salvation is played out in visionary form utilizing characters from the animal world – so that the initiated may well have understood that the Lion of the tribe of Judah signifies the Messiah. But having heard tell of a lion at this stage, the reader might be understandably surprised that what John *sees* is not a lion but a lamb. The relationship between *hearing* and *seeing* in this apocalypse is an important, and much discussed, issue. In this passage, it is what John sees which provides true insight into what he has heard, identifying the true nature of the Messiah and of the redemption which he has achieved. Nor is the lamb-like appearance of the lion the only paradox of this section of the vision. The Lamb is described in terms reminiscent of a warrior, a powerful apocalyptic lamb or ram, with seven horns and seven eyes (just as, in *1 Enoch* 90, Judas Maccabeus is described in terms of a victorious horned ram; cf. also *Testament of Joseph* 19:8). Yet the real emphasis is placed upon the traits of sacrificial death which this animal bears, signs of apparent weakness ('as if it had been slaughtered') juxtaposed with those of profound strength (the Lamb is 'standing'). The Christian reader will recognize in this vision the story of the victory of the cross, and thus, in the Lamb, the person of Jesus Christ. Because of his death, spoken of in this book in terms of 'witness' or 'testimony', he alone is worthy to break the seals of this mysterious scroll and enable the divine salvific plan to take its course. The hosts of heaven, and indeed all creation, break out into songs of victory, proclaiming the worthiness of the Lamb to receive honours hitherto directed only towards the One seated on the throne: 'Worthy is the Lamb that was slaughtered to receive power and wealth and wisdom and might and honour and glory and blessing' (5.12; cf. 4.11).

But as was the case with the initial vision in chapter 1, this vision too inaugurates a series of seven as the Lamb opens the seven seals of the scroll (6.1—8.1), heralding a series of events which have provided Western culture with some of its most evocative and chilling imagery. The breaking of the first four leads into the visions of the Four Horsemen of the Apocalypse (cf. Zech. 1.7–17). Although these four can be grouped together, in that each horseman is summoned by the thunderlike 'Come!' of one of the four living creatures, they should not be over-separated from the visions heralded by the breaking of the fifth and sixth seals (the souls under the altar, and the dramatic signs in earth and sky). What is more striking, structurally speaking, is the fact that there is a substantial interlude between the sixth and seventh seals, while the servants of God are sealed on their foreheads to protect them (7.1–17; we shall see that this is a recurring feature of this book). The reader may well find this delay frustrating. Yet when one remembers that this work was written to be performed orally, such a delay at the penultimate stage in the sevenfold sequence comes to have an understandable and powerful function. One can imagine the dramatic impact of these repeated delays in the execution of divine judgement, rooted in the very structure of the book (Bauckham, 1993, 12). They locate the reader, and hearers, of the book in the penultimate stage, on the verge of eschatological salvation but still in the throes of the prelude to it. As with other New Testament writers, the author of Revelation grapples creatively with the tension between the 'already' and the 'not yet' resulting from the inauguration, by the death and resurrection of Jesus in the past, of the eschatological times.

There are two further questions prompted by the seven seals sequence. The first concerns the relationship between the scroll and the visions its unsealing provokes. Is the mission of the four horsemen, and the content of the other seal visions, part of the contents of the scroll, or do these visions simply describe the prelude to the outworking of divine judgement, or the state of affairs in the world as it already exists? Richard Bauckham maintains, for example, in a carefully argued article, that the contents of the scroll are not actually revealed until after they have been imparted to John in the 'little scroll' of chapter 10. The seal visions cannot describe the contents of the scroll, because these cannot be read until all the seals have been broken and the scroll fully opened (Bauckham, 1993, 243–66). Others might object that this demands a logic inappropriate to the fluidity of apocalyptic imagery, and that the contents of the scroll begin to be revealed from the moment that the first seal is ruptured.

The second question, though related to the first, is rather more theological, and echoes the moral revulsion which contemporary readers of Revelation often experience. This is particularly pronounced in the light of the activity of the horsemen, described in terms of conquering, war and bloodshed, famine and death. Are these four horsemen sent out to execute the divine will, or do they represent in mythical form the destructive and disordered forces at the heart of human society? Some commentators make much of the similarities between the first rider, on a white horse, and portrayals elsewhere in the book of Christ and those who follow him. The appearance of the Word of God is described at 19.11–16 as the coming out of a rider on a white horse. White is the colour associated with the faithful followers of the Lamb (e.g. 7.9; 19.14): on the significance of colours in this book, see Figure 3. The verb 'to conquer' (Greek νικάω) is associated with the Lamb's victory (e.g. 5.5; 12.11), though it can occasionally be used of the activity of the beast against God's saints (e.g. 11.7; 13.7, omitted in some ancient manuscripts). Thus the four riders are viewed as angels sent by God to carry out his destructive will. Others are more impressed by the repeated use of the verb ἐδόθη (literally 'it was given' 'it was permitted'), which might imply that these mysterious figures represent rebellious spiritual forces currently permitted to function by God, but ultimately contrary to the divine will and destined for destruction:

- The first rider 'was given' a crown (ἐδόθη, 6.2).
- The second rider 'was permitted' (ἐδόθη) to take peace away, and 'was given' a sword (ἐδόθη, 6.4).
- The fourth rider Death, and his companion Hades, 'were given authority' to kill (ἐδόθη, 6.8).

Such a line of interpretation (which sometimes identifies the rider on the white horse as Antichrist) has a good deal to commend it. Certainly much that these horsemen accomplish – conquest, war, famine, and death by the sword – are all evils in which human beings, and human institutions, can play their part. But even if one exonerates God from direct involvement in the destructive activity described in the seals cycle, this difficulty will need to be faced at a later stage, in the ensuing cycles of trumpets and bowls.

Figure 3. The significance of colours

White	**Heaven, Victory**, associated with God (20.11), the Son of Man (1.14; 14.14; 19.11), the twenty-four elders (4.4) and the followers of the Lamb (2.17; 3.4–5, 18; 6.11; 7.9, 13; 19.14); the first horseman at 6.2 may be a parody of Christ, i.e. Antichrist
Red	**Blood, Violence, Slaughter**, associated with the second horseman (6.4), and the Dragon/Satan (12.3)

Also reflected in its derivatives:

Scarlet	**Wealth and Debauchery**, associated with the beast (17.3), the clothing of Babylon (17.4; 18.16), and her luxury imports (18.12)
Purple	**Royalty and Debauchery**, the imperial colour (cf. John 19.2), associated with the clothing of Babylon (17.4), and her luxury imports (18.16)
Black	**Disaster, Famine**, associated with the third horseman (6.5); at the sixth seal the sun becomes black (6.12)
Green ($\chi\lambda\omega\rho\acute{o}\varsigma$)	**Death**, associated with the fourth horseman (often translated 'pale' at 6.8, but used of the colour of grass at 8.7; 9.4)

The interlude of chapter 7 (also described by the technical term 'intercalation') functions, as we have seen, as a delaying tactic in the unfolding narrative, locating the reader within the penultimate stage of the eschatological scenario. John sees the four angels of the winds, standing at the four corners of the earth, who are restrained from carrying out their task until the servants of God have been sealed on their foreheads, like the remnant of faithful Jerusalemites of Ezekiel's day (Ezek. 9.4–6), presumably to protect them from the imminent judgement. John then hears of the number of those to be sealed, one hundred and forty-four thousand, twelve thousand from each of the tribes of Israel. As was the case of the vision of the heavenly throne-room, so too there is an interesting relationship here between what John hears and what he sees, for the ensuing vision (7.9–12) is of a huge multitude of people, 'that no one could count' (v. 9). This is a proleptic vision, providing a glance into the future on the other side of the Great Tribulation, which in the chronology of the narrative still remains in the future. What is the relationship between the 144,000 of which John hears, and the great multitude which he sees? Are the former the faithful Jews, or Jewish

Christians, while the latter are the great company of all the faithful, or only Gentile Christians? Or are they specifically the company of Christian martyrs (given that, according to the rare interpretation provided by one of the elders, these have washed their robes and made them white in the blood of the Lamb, 7.14)? Many commentators will want to distinguish between the two groups. This twofold division is often necessitated by the literalist interpretations of fringe religious groupings, such as Jehovah's Witnesses, which reject the symbolic nature of numbers in the ancient world. Thus 144,000 becomes a restrictive number: *only* 144,000 will participate in the thousand-year reign of Christ (the 'Millennium') described in Revelation 20, understood by the Witnesses as a heavenly kingdom. The 'great multitude' then describes that much larger group of those not privileged to share in the Millennium, who will nevertheless find a place in a renewed paradise on earth.

However, there is a strong possibility that the reader is not intended to differentiate between the two multitudes. According to the conventions of ancient numerology, 144,000, being a multiple of twelve, a number denoting completeness (the number of God, 3, multiplied by the number of the universe, 4), far from being a restrictive number, is rather a number of *inclusion*, ultimate completeness (12 x 12 x 1000 – 144,000). So it is far from established that this specific number must refer to something other than a huge multitude, 'which no one could count'. Moreover, given the precedent already set in Revelation 5, when the true nature of the Lion of Judah of which John hears is revealed in the vision of the Lamb, might it not be that the multitude which John actually sees, 'from every nation, from all tribes and peoples and languages' (7.9), is to be identified with the group he hears as being sealed from the ancient people of God, so that God's servants are shown to be no longer restricted, in the Christian dispensation, to one particular nation? [1]

The delay has been long enough, and so now, at the beginning of chapter 8, the Lamb finally opens the seventh seal. Instead of the expected culmination of divine judgement and salvation, however, the narrative takes two unexpected turns at this point. First, the result of the opening of the seventh seal is not, as one might expect, cataclysmic cosmic disasters, thunder and lightning and the sun turning to blood; instead, we are told that there was 'silence in heaven for about half an hour' (8.1). This is the prolonged, and profound silence of worship. One eye-witness account of the cult of the Second Temple claims that the priests ministered in complete silence (*Epistle of Aristeas* 95), and, although this appears to be contradicted by other sources, it is seen as the appropriate response to the awesome presence of the deity, as also reflected in one of the Qumran *Songs of the Sabbath Sacrifice*, which speaks of the silent blessing of the angelic priests in the heavenly sanctuary (4Q405.11–13). The reference to silence here ensures that the

Figure 4. The significance of numbers

1   primary number, excellence (e.g. 1.17; 2.8; 22.13 'the First and the Last')

½   limited, restricted time (e.g. 8.1 silence in heaven 'for about half an hour')

2   number of witness in Jewish tradition (two witnesses at 11.3; cf. Deut 19.15)

3   number of the divine (1.4f.; parodied by the 'three unclean spirits' of 16.13)

3½   half of seven: imperfection, suffering, time of trial and persecution (three and a half years, also appears as 'a time, times, and half a time'; 'forty-two months'; 1,260 days)

4   number of universe: hence four winds, four seasons, four corners of earth (7.1), and four living creatures (6.1); universal, and therefore all humanity (the four angels, and four living creatures, act on behalf of humanity)

5   natural round number (fingers on hand and toes on foot): demonic locusts permitted to torment humans for 'five months' (9.5, 10)

6   seven minus one: number of Antichrist, penultimacy and therefore number of evil; intensified, it is the number of the beast, 666 (13.18)

7   four plus three (number of God plus number of universe): completeness, the perfect number (seven stars, days of week, etc.); in Revelation there are seven stars, lampstands, churches, spirits of God, seals, trumpets, bowls and beatitudes; beast has seven heads (but its number is 666!)

8   number of Jesus (in Greek, the number of Ἰησοῦς is 888), seven plus one: first day of a new creation (cf. parody by Antichrist at 17.11)

10   number of human completeness: hence dragon and beast have ten horns (12.3; 17.3); there are ten kings (17.12)

12   four times three (number of God multiplied by number of universe): number of completeness (like seven); twelve months, tribes of Israel (hence 12,000 are sealed from each of the twelve tribes, 7.5ff.); woman clothed with the sun is crowned with twelve stars (12.1); holy city has twelve gates and twelve foundation stones, inscribed with names of twelve apostles of Lamb (21.12–14); its dimensions are 12,000 stadia in height, length and breadth

1000 incalculable number: a round number denoting a great multitude (e.g. 5.11; the 'thousand year' reign of 20.2)

Numbers are intensified by multiplication:
e.g. 144,000 – square of 12 (tribes of Israel), multiplied by a thousand (not a limited number, but a countless multitude).

seals section ends, as it began, in a profoundly liturgical ambience. Liturgical 'moments' seem to punctuate the narrative of this book at crucial points, a point already recognized by Alan Garrow in his excellent structural analysis (Garrow, 1997, 14–65). We have already noted the liturgical visions of Revelation 1 and especially Revelation 4—5; there will be another liturgical moment in a couple of verses, to inaugurate the new section. Second, the climax to the sevenfold seal cycle inaugurates a new cycle of seven trumpets, so much so that it is difficult for the interpreter to know precisely where to make the break between the two. I have opted for 8.1 as the end of the previous cycle, which allows neatly for the appearance of the seven trumpet angels in verse 2 (though one could equally conclude the section with 8.2, or 8.5).

8.2—11.18 Seven Trumpets

This new section, structured around a cycle of seven trumpets, is inaugurated, like the last, by liturgical activity in the heavenly temple (8.2–5) during which the trumpets, the traditional heralds of the day of the Lord's judgement (e.g. Zeph. 1.14–16; 1 Cor. 15.52; *4 Ezra* 6.23; *Apoc. Abr.* 31), are given to the seven angels of the Presence. It has other similarities too with the previous section. There is an intercalation, very lengthy in this case, between the blowing of the sixth and seventh trumpets (10.1—11.14), reiterating that element of delay already embedded in the narrative (a lesser sense of delay is introduced after the fourth trumpet). There is also a liturgical conclusion to this section associated with the seventh trumpet (11.15–18). But equally, as we shall see, the contents of the trumpet visions tie this section thematically to the sevenfold bowl sequence which occurs in chapter 16.

The inaugural liturgical action at the heavenly altar of incense, reminiscent of the daily priestly ritual of incense-offering in the Jerusalem Temple (cf. Luke 1.8–23), in part recalls the vision at the opening of the fifth seal, in which the souls of the martyrs beneath the heavenly altar cry out for vindication for the shedding of their blood (6.9; cf. 5.8). For at this point we are told that the angel with the golden censer is given a great quantity of incense to 'add to' or 'offer with' (literally 'give to') the prayers of the saints. Back at the opening of the fifth seal, the souls of those slain 'for the word of God and for the testimony they had given' were told to wait a little longer. These souls probably encompass not simply recent Christian martyrs, such as those killed in Rome under Nero, and Antipas of Pergamum, but all those killed for their witness to God throughout salvation history, as far back as righteous Abel (cf. *Targum Neofiti* on Gen. 4.10; 4 Macc. 18.11; *1 Enoch* 47.2; Matt. 23.35). Now, in the true heavenly Temple, despite the appearance of things upon earth, their prayers are being heard and answered. As this apocalypse now progresses, the language of ascent and descent will be increasingly important. At this point the ascent of the prayers of the saints, mingled with the rising of heavenly incense, provokes the descent to the earth of the golden censer, heralding the descent, the throwing down of the seven trumpet plagues. The martyrs and saints, actual and potential victims of the injustice of the Great Empire, have cried out for justice to be done; here, we see the first stirrings of the divine response to the cries of the human heart, the downward response to the upward prayer of God's people.

As was the case with the seals, the first four of which were associated with four horsemen, so too the first four trumpet-blasts form a particular group, separated from the others by the vision of an eagle, flying overhead (the fourth living creature of 4.7?)[2] to herald the three woes associated with the last three trumpets. There are some echoes in the contents of these visions, and those of the fifth and sixth trumpets, of the plagues of Egypt in Exodus 7—12, directed long ago against the oppressors of God's people. The allusions to the Egyptian plagues will become even more explicit in the bowls sequence in chapter 16, raising the question of the relationship between the trumpet and bowl cycles. Does the latter simply reiterate the former, though with heightened intensity, such that essentially the same events are being described in both (Victorinus of Pettau thought so in what is the earliest surviving Latin commentary on the book)? Or do we have a chronological progression of eschatological events from one cycle to the other (commentators often note that the effects of the trumpet-plagues are limited: only a 'third' is destroyed)? The answer to this question will profoundly affect the way in which the Apocalypse as a whole is understood: those who read it as a guidebook to the end of the world, for example, will naturally prefer the latter explanation.

After the first four trumpet-blasts, the eagle announces three impending woes, linked to the blowing of the final three trumpets (8.13); this has the effect of heightening for the reader the sense that the final victory over evil and injustice is imminent. The blowing of the fifth trumpet (9.1–11) brings with it the first of these woes or disasters (v. 12): terrifying scorpion-like locusts invade the earth from out of the abyss, echoing the plague of locusts in Egypt, but accentuated by the surreal description of these insects. The sixth trumpet-blast provokes something similar: the release of the four angels chained at the river Euphrates, whose cavalry, two hundred million strong, are mounted on grotesque horses with lions' heads and serpents' tails (9.13–19). At this point, the sense of imminent expectancy receives its first blow. Having been told in verse 12 that the fifth trumpet vision represented the first of the three woes, and that two more are still to come, the reader has been prepared for the second woe to follow immediately upon the blowing of the sixth trumpet. But in fact, the appearance of this grotesque army is not yet the second woe; for this we must wait until the middle of chapter 11 (11.14, which apparently refers to the dramatic events which accompany the raising of the two witnesses immediately preceding it).[3] Yet again, narrative suspense is built into the very framework of this book.

The contemporary reader may well experience the same theological dilemma with the contents of the trumpet-plagues as is felt over the opening of the seals, particularly those associated with the four horsemen. Do these describe the outworking of God's will for humanity, with the corollary that natural disaster and the violent destruction of countless human beings are part of the divine plan? Or rather, yet again, is the veil being removed to enable John, and the reader of his apocalypse, to view the world as God sees it, disordered by human sinfulness, injustice and pride, or even by supernatural forces beyond human control (cf. *1 Enoch* 6—10), and bearing the seeds of its own destruction?

The latter interpretation may be hinted at particularly in the fifth and sixth plagues, whose description suggests a demonic rather than divine origin. The plague of locusts is inaugurated by the falling of a star from heaven, an image which could be used in Jewish apocalyptic of the fallen angels (*1 Enoch* 21.6; Luke 10.18 speaks of Satan falling 'like lightning' from heaven), and this particular angel is given the sinister name 'Destroyer' (*Abaddon* in Hebrew, Ἀπολλύων in Greek, 9.11; cf. Job 28.22). But even if this angel with the key of the abyss is more positively understood as an agent of God's will, the place of origin of the locusts remains 'from below'. They arise out of the abyss, the watery deep associated with evil and chaos, out of which the beast will soon arise (11.7). Like the four horsemen of chapter 6, their powers are severely circumscribed. They are not allowed to harm the grass or any plant or tree, nor those bearing the seal of God (v. 4); they are 'permitted' (v. 5) not to kill but only to 'torture' or 'give anguish' to human beings, and that only for the limited period of five months. Similarly, the grotesque nature of the terrifying array of horses which arise at the sixth trumpet, sharing characteristics with the serpent-like Satan (9.19; cf. 12.9) and the fire- and smoke-breathing Leviathan (9.18; cf. Job 41.19–21), points towards their demonic nature.

Moreover, whatever the origin of these visions of chaos and disaster, the narrative makes paradoxically clear their redemptive purpose. Their function is not to gloat over the ruthless destruction of the created order, but to confront humanity with the reality of the world it inhabits, in order to lead it to repentance. That, however, at least at this point in the narrative, fails to achieve its purpose (9.20–21). As Christopher Rowland has perceptively commented, on the culmination to this section:

Humanity longs for release, but does not find it. It is as if humanity is brought face to face with the full horror of the world it has created and is not allowed to escape the consequences of its actions. That leads to darkness, disfigurement, and the unbalancing of the natural world.
(Rowland, 1998, 633)

At this point, the seals cycle has prepared the reader to expect a delay, and that indeed is what now happens, as the mention of the seventh trumpet is briefly preceded by another vision of a mighty angel, bearing in his hand a 'little scroll' (10.1–7). The question of the relation of this small scroll (βιβλαρίδιον) to the scroll given to the Lamb in Revelation 5 (βιβλίον; cf. 10.8) has already been raised above. The angel's descent is accompanied by seven loud thunderclaps, the words of which John is about to write before he is forbidden to do so by a heavenly voice (one is given no indication of what these heavenly words might have been), with the rejoinder that there is to be no more delay in the fulfilment of 'the mystery of God' (10.6–7). Expectation is raised that the seventh angel is about to blow his trumpet, heralding the last great judgement.

It would appear at first that the vision of the angel with the scroll is only a brief interruption to the completion of the trumpet sequence. But in fact it is the beginning of a much larger intercalation, which continues until the end of chapter 11. Despite the expectant reference to the seventh trumpet at 10.7, it is not actually blown until 11.15. What is the reader to make of this lengthy interruption to this trumpet sequence?

First, we should perhaps return to the parallel intercalation in the seals cycle. There the subject matter was the role of the servants of God (the 144,000) in the coming messianic woes, and the accompanying proleptic vision portrayed the glorious victory of the followers of the Lamb (ch. 7). So too here, we have a kind of preparation of the church, and John in particular, for prophetic witness in the trials ahead. John hears the heavenly voice speaking to him again (10.8; a similar phrase has already been used at another crucial point in this book, at 1.12), telling him, like Ezekiel before him (cf. Ezek. 3.1–13), to take the scroll from the mighty angel and eat it. This seems to function as a commissioning story, parallel to the one in chapter 1. There John was commissioned to write what he saw, in the tradition of the apocalypticist. Here he is given the more active role of prophesying 'about many peoples and nations and languages and kings' (10.11), and indeed, in 11.1–2, John is giving the active task of measuring the temple of God (in Ezek. 40, it is an angelic figure who does the measuring). Is this a literary clue that we are on the verge of a turning point in this book (after all, despite the expectation of the imminent climax to judgement, we are still not quite halfway through!), so that we still have to learn of the eschatological fate of the nations, and of the church in their midst, in the succeeding chapters? Those who see a connection between this sweet and sour scroll which John now devours and the scroll previously given to the Lamb would argue that, in the following chapters, the contents of that original scroll are now, finally, to be revealed.

But before the trumpet sequence can be concluded, we are told of the ministry and fate of two prophetic witnesses (11.3–13), who will prophesy for one thousand, two hundred and sixty days in the 'great city', who will be killed by those against whom they speak, but who will ultimately be vindicated by God. The identity of these two witnesses has long been a matter of interest amongst commentators. Because of their ability to hold back the rain and turn water into blood (11.6), and of their subsequent ascent into heaven (11.12), they have sometimes been identified with Elijah (1 Kings 17.1; 2 Kings 2.11) and Moses (Exod. 7.17; Deut. 34.6). They have also been understood as Elijah and Enoch (cf. Gen. 5.24 and the tradition arising from this), or Zerubbabel and Joshua, the 'two olive trees' (11.4; cf. Zech. 4), or Peter and Paul, who bore witness to death before the emperor in the city of Rome.

More likely, however, given the fluidity of the imagery which has enabled all of the above identifications to be made, the reader should understand this passage (along with that which precedes it) as describing the prophetic ministry in general, and specifically that prophetic ministry in which the Church will have to engage in the time of tribulation. John is presented as a particular instance of this prophetic witness, but he is not alone in receiving this commission. Having witnessed in the sequence of seals and trumpets the nightmarish vision of a world marked by chaos and destruction, the reader is now presented with something even more threatening: the word of truth, the prophetic word which cuts more finely than any double-edged sword (Heb. 4.12; cf. Rev. 1.16). To speak the truth in the midst of a hostile world is a dangerous business, as the tragic history of God's prophets and martyrs testifies; but ultimately, in the face of the truth, the lie will be revealed for what it really is. Here the Church is prepared for that prophetic task, with the assurance that it is only temporary. In the symbolic numerology of this book, the two witnesses are sent to prophesy for one thousand, two hundred and sixty days. This is calculated elsewhere in this book as forty-two months (the time of the trampling of the outer court of the temple by the Gentiles, 11.2), or 'a time, and times, and half a time' (the period of the desert exile of the woman clothed with the sun, 12.14), or three and a half years: i.e. half of the perfect period of seven years (cf. Dan. 9.27), or a limited period. What may appear to be the endless trampling of God's people is here revealed to be as nothing within the overarching schema of divine salvation.

At last, with the passing of the second woe (apparently the dramatic effects of the prophetic proclamation and vindication of the two witnesses, 11.11–14), the way is at last open for the blowing of the seventh trumpet (11.15–18). We have already been alerted to the fact, at 10.7, that the sounding of this final trumpet will mark the fulfilment of the mystery of God. Now heavenly voices are heard, victoriously proclaiming that the 'kingdom' (or 'empire') of the world has become 'the kingdom of our Lord and of his Messiah'. The response, marking the conclusion to this lengthy section, is, predictably, a liturgical one: the twenty-four elders prostrate themselves before the throne, and sing a eucharistic hymn giving thanks for the inauguration of the reign of God, with its dual aspect of judgement and vindication. The reader is left with that heightened sense of anticipation which also marked the conclusion to the seal sequence.

11.19—15.4 Seven Visions of the Church in the World

Since the previous three sections (letters, seals and trumpets) have all begun with a liturgical vision, the commentator should be attuned to expecting the same for this new and kaleidoscopic sequence of visions. Hence, though many commentators begin this new section at 12.1, it would seem more appropriate to begin at 11.19, with the opening of the heavenly sanctuary and the revelation of the ark of the covenant, dramatically accompanied by lightning flashes, thunderclaps, an earthquake and violent hail. Nevertheless, at this point that other hitherto constant feature, the clear sevenfold structure, appears to break down, and we must wait for the sequence of seven bowls in the following section for this sevenfold feature to reappear explicitly. There is no objection in principle to John having hidden a septet in the body of the narrative: this is, after all, an intricate narrative which calls for careful and repeated reading. Many commentators, indeed, have detected seven unnumbered visions here, though not always agreeing on the precise divisions (in one scheme, the woman clothed with the sun and the great dragon of chapter 12 are relegated, somewhat implausibly, to separate visions). But is this sevenfold structure quite so clear? Or is the apparently purposeless sequence accounted for by the fact that the contents of the scroll are now being revealed? Commentators continue to puzzle over this section of the book.

However it is to be structured (and an implicit septet can be detected by the present writer), this section certainly contains some of the most vivid and memorable visions in the whole book. The first vision, of the pregnant woman clothed with the sun and the great fiery dragon (Rev. 12, interwoven with a mythical account of the heavenly battle between Michael and Satan), has been particularly influential in the history of Christian theology and iconography, not least due to its frequent mariological interpretation. The dragon is explicitly named as the Devil and Satan, and it is clear that this vision concerns that great cosmic battle between the forces of good and evil typical of the apocalyptic mindset. The identity of the woman is less obvious. Given that she gives birth to the Messiah, she has, particularly since the Middle Ages, been identified with Mary, but she also bears the characteristics of other biblical figures: Eve (Gen. 3.15–16), Hagar (Gen. 16.6–7), the people of Israel, and the city of Jerusalem. Given that two cities will soon be personified as women in this book (Babylon and the New Jerusalem), a more collective interpretation suggests itself: she is perhaps best understood as the heavenly counterpart of the people of God, the community out of which the

Messiah was to be born, and from which he would be 'snatched up' to the Father's right hand (12.5). This does not necessarily rule out the widespread mariological interpretation, but sets it in a broader context (Boxall, 1999).

What is particularly significant is that this vision introduces the interwoven themes of suffering and persecution, which will bind together a number of the visions in this section. The messianic community, and individual members of it, can expect to be persecuted by the dragon, whose loss of power has been denoted by its fall from heaven (12.9), in the lead up to the last days. This is a theme which can be traced into the next few visions, where most commentators find veiled references to socio-political pressures facing the Christian community during the early years of its existence within the Roman empire. Chronologically, this section is quite difficult to locate within the eschatological schema, not least because chapter 12 seems to look back to the past events of the birth and exaltation of Christ (those who would see in the book of Revelation a clear timetable for the events of the End may have some difficulty relating the events described in the previous seal and trumpet visions to what is here described).

The following two beast visions (13.1–10; 13.11–18) seem to bring us forward again to the present time of the seer and his fellow Christians, engaged in the battle against Satan's minions, incarnated in the political realm. The apocalyptic vision of Daniel 7 had already portrayed hostile empires as ferocious beasts (the eagle-like lion, bear, winged leopard and fourth, iron-teethed monster are generally understood to represent the Babylonians, Medes, Persians and Greeks respectively, Dan. 7.17; cf. Dan. 2.36–45). John's horrific beast from the sea, combining all the worst characteristics of Daniel's four, seems in a particular way to personify the blasphemous claims of the current world empire, Rome, 'permitted' (ἐδόθη) to exercise authority for the limited period of 'forty-two months' (13.5). The next vision, of a beast from the earth (13.11–18), continues a similar theme. This satanic parody of the Lamb, with its two lamb's horns and the voice of a dragon, acts as an accomplice to the first beast, encouraging the people of the earth to worship it; that there is a commercial and not simply 'religious' aspect to this is made clear at 13.17. Participation in the economy of this beastly political system is tantamount to bearing the name and number of the beast. Many gallons of ink have been spilt over the centuries in attempts to decipher the number of the beast, 666, and some of these will be discussed elsewhere. Suffice it to note here that six is one less than the perfect number seven, so that whatever else may be implied by 'six hundred and sixty-six' (does 13.18 mean that it is the 'number of a person', or merely a human, as opposed to angelic, number?), it is shot through with a sense of penultimacy, incompleteness.

The fourth vision of this sequence (14.1–5) seems to function as an antidote to the previous three (the woman and the dragon, beast from the sea, beast from the earth), for it offers a reassuring picture of the 144,000, standing alongside the Lamb on Mount Zion, singing a new song which only these redeemed could learn. It is not clear whether we have here a proleptic vision of the future victory of these sealed servants of God (we have come to expect proleptic visions between the sixth and seventh elements of the cycle, so if that is what it is, it appears misplaced here), or a reassuring image of their present preparedness to participate in the final battle, which would then explain the otherwise puzzling reference to their sexual continence (like priests in a state of ritual purity for involvement in the holy war: 14.4; cf. 1QM 7).

That the fourth vision belongs with the first three as a group may be implied by 14.6-13, in which three angels, led by one flying in midheaven (14.6), announce the impending judgement. The first four trumpet visions had been followed by an eagle, flying in midheaven (8.13), proclaiming the three woes, which served to heighten the air of expectancy within the narrative. The proclamation of the 'eternal gospel' by the three angels has a similar effect: they declare the arrival of God's hour of judgement, the fall of Babylon the great (utilizing the 'prophetic perfect', as if this future event has already taken place), and the impending judgement of those who worship the beast or bear its mark. This sense of urgency is completed by a call for the endurance of the saints, and a beatitude on those 'who from now on die in the Lord' (14.12–13).

Two further visions (the fifth and the sixth, if the three-angel episode can be paralleled to the woe-carrying eagle of Rev. 8) raise the stakes even further. In the first, 'one like the Son of Man' (it is unclear whether this is Christ, or an angel) appears on a cloud, with a sharp sickle, and is bidden to cast it down to the earth to reap the harvest (14.14–16). In the second, another angel, also bearing a sickle, is bidden to gather in the grapes of the earth's vine, producing enough blood to reach as high as a horse's bridle (14.17–20). The imagery of harvesting is common as a description of the eschatological judgement (e.g. Mark 4.29; Matt.13.30); the blood of the winepress will make another appearance in chapter 19.

This 'unnumbered' series of seven seems to be concluded by the appearance in heaven of seven angels with seven plagues (15.1), which points forward to yet another cycle of seven, that of the seven bowls of incense (the opening of the seventh seal, it will be remembered, had likewise paved the way for the appearance of the seven trumpet-bearing angels, 8.1). Moreover, as has been the case with the seal and trumpet sequences, this section too climaxes with a 'liturgical moment'. Beside the fiery sea of glass are seen those who have conquered the beast, singing the song of Moses and of the Lamb, proclaiming the just and wonderful deeds of God (15.2–4; cf. Exod. 15). As the trumpet sequence concluded with the singing of a canticle, so too does this sequence.

15.5—19.10 Seven Bowls

The previous section began, according to the liturgically focused structure we have noted, with the opening of the heavenly temple and the revealing of the ark of the covenant. This new bowls sequence begins with the opening of the tent of witness in the heavenly sanctuary, and the giving of the seven golden bowls to the seven bowl angels, appropriately attired for their task (15.5–8). There may well be an intimate connection between the golden bowls of incense at 5.8, identified then as the prayers of the saints rising to God's throne, and these golden bowls, full of the fury of God. The souls of the martyrs under the altar (6.9–11) need no longer cry out, 'How long?' The number of their fellow servants has apparently been completed (cf. 6.11), and the time for their vindication has now come.

A voice tells these seven angels to pour out their bowls upon the earth (16.1; the downward movement of the contents of the bowls picks up again on the upward movement of the prayers of the saints, mingled with the smoke of the incense). There follows a series of plagues, initiated by the pouring out of the seven bowls in succession: some of these overlap with the contents of the trumpet visions, and they echo even more strongly the plagues of Egypt (see Figure 5). Whereas the effects of the seven trumpets were only limited (only a third were destroyed in each case), here the effects are more universal: all those who worship the beast are covered with sores; all sea creatures are killed by the turning of the sea to blood. In the midst of these plagues, the angel of the waters breaks out into a canticle in praise of God's justice, to which the heavenly altar takes up the refrain. Canticles often seem to function in this book as a kind of hymnic commentary on the surrounding action, and the emphasis here upon God's righteousness (God is 'just' in his verdict; his judgements are 'true and just', 16.5–7) may go some way towards contextualizing these horrific events. The major concern seems to be to show how it is that injustice is being confronted, and the deaths of God's faithful vindicated.

As the final three bowls are poured out, it becomes clear that it is the dominance of the beast which is the particular focus of these plagues. The fifth bowl is emptied upon the throne of the beast (16.10), and the 'kingdom' or 'empire' of the beast is darkened (cf. John 1.5). This would, as we saw in relation to chapter 13, have had particularly powerful resonances for the first hearers of John's Apocalypse, those living under the dominance of that empire in seven cities of proconsular Asia. Though meant to lead people to repentance, it has the opposite effect, as those affected bite their tongues in their pain and curse the God of heaven (as the author of the Fourth Gospel recognized, the real judgement upon this world is that, though the light has come, people prefer the darkness to the light: John 3.19). The sixth bowl heralds the drying up of the great river, the Euphrates (the sixth trumpet also initiated activity at the Euphrates, 9.14), as part of the preparations for the

Figure 5. Parallels between trumpets, bowls and Egyptian plagues

Plagues of Egypt (Exod. 7—12)	Trumpets (Rev. 8.7—11.15)	Bowls (Rev. 16.2–21)
1. **rivers turned to blood, fish died** (7.14–24)	1. **hail** and fire mixed with blood on earth; a third of earth and trees, and all grass burnt up (8.7)	1. **sores** afflict those who worship beast or bear its mark (16.2)
2. plague of **frogs** (8.1–15)	2. mountain mixed with fire thrown into sea; third of sea **turned to blood**; third of **sea creatures killed**; third of ships destroyed (8.8–9)	2. sea **turned to blood**; all living **sea creatures killed** (16.3)
3. plague of gnats (8.16–19)		
4. swarm of flies (8.20–32)	3. burning star falls from sky on rivers and springs of water; third of waters turn bitter; many people die (8.10–11)	3. **rivers and springs of water turned to blood**; angel of the water declares God's avenging of blood of saints and prophets (16.4–7)
5. pestilence on livestock (9.1–7)		
6. **sores** afflict humans and animals (9.8–12)	4. third of sun, moon and stars struck, and third of their light **darkened** (8.12)	4. sun permitted to scorch human beings; they curse God and do not repent (16.8–9)
7. **thunder and hail** (9.13–35)	5. **locusts** arise out of abyss; torment human beings for five months (9.1–11)	5. kingdom of beast **darkened**; human beings bite their tongues; they curse God and do not repent (16.10–11)
8. plague of **locusts** (10.1–20)		
9. **darkness over land** (10.21–29)	6. four angels chained at Euphrates released; lion- and serpent-like horses kill a third of human race (9.13–21)	6. waters of Euphrates dried up, and way made for kings of the East; three foul **spirits like frogs** come from 'demonic trinity'; kings of world gather for battle at Armaggedon (16.12–16)
10. death of firstborn; (11.1—12.32); Israelites protected by **blood of lamb**		
	7. Announcement of God's Kingdom (11.15)	7. declaration of end; lightning, **thunder** and mighty earthquake; cities collapse; Babylon remembered; **plague of hail**, for which human beings curse God (16.17–21)

great battle, and culminates in the gathering of the kings of the earth at Armageddon (16.16; almost certainly derived from the Hebrew *Har Megiddo*, the 'mountain of Megiddo').[4] That the powers opposed to God are instrumental in initiating this battle, which bears the seeds of their own destruction, is made clear at this point. Three frog-like demonic spirits arise from the mouths of the dragon, the beast and the false prophet (these form a kind of 'demonic trinity', who parody the One on the throne, the Spirit/ seven spirits and the Lamb, and lead many astray in the process),[5] to summon the kings of the earth for this final war.

There is not, however, the characteristic interlude at this point (unless one counts the verse-long intervention of the heavenly voice, declaring that 'I am coming like a thief' and pronouncing a blessing on those who keep watch, 16.15; cf. 1 Thess. 5.2; Matt. 25.42–44). Rather, as if to move the narrative on, the pouring out of the seventh bowl is immediately described (16.17–21), heralding another liturgical 'moment' (the booming declaration from out of the sanctuary that 'It is done!' accompanied by lightning flashes, thunderclaps and an unprecedented earthquake), and what appears to be the culmination of judgement for the kingdom of this world:

> The great city was split into three parts, and the cities of the nations fell. God remembered great Babylon and gave her the wine-cup of the fury of his wrath. And every island fled away, and no mountains were to be found; and huge hailstones, each weighing about a hundred pounds, dropped from heaven on people, until they cursed God for the plague of the hail, so fearful was that plague.
>
> (Rev. 16.19–21)

Yet although the expected delaying interlude between the sixth and seventh bowls is lacking, so that the sequence moves fairly smoothly on to the announcement of impending judgement upon Babylon and the fall of the world's cities, this conclusion to the bowls cycle is far from being the end of the book. The great battle, prepared for by the sixth bowl, is not finally consummated until chapter 19. Before that can happen, we have first to learn of the identity of this Babylon, whose judgement has just been announced, and who has been obliquely referred to earlier in this book (cf. 14.8).

At this point, however, the clear sevenfold structure of the book is again lost, and commentators struggle in their attempts to explain the relation of what follows to what has gone before. The impressive structural analysis of Adela Yarbro Collins, for example, ties this vision of Babylon the Great following the seventh bowl to the preceding sequence, but treats it as little more than an appendix to the previous section, the so-called 'Babylon Appendix' (Yarbro Collins, 1976, 5–55). Similarly, she regards the similar vision of the New Jerusalem as an appendix to the preceding visions of the

End. Others are more convinced that the bowl sequence has reached its natural climax with the pouring out of the seventh bowl at the end of chapter 16, and that the Babylon vision therefore belongs to the beginning of the next section. Up to this point, the seventh in a sequence has always signalled its conclusion, and pointed towards the inauguration of a new sequence. This is evident, for example, in the textual divisions in the New Jerusalem Bible.

What clues are provided within the text? The author draws a clear literary parallel between the visions of Babylon and the New Jerusalem, which any commentator must take seriously. Both are introduced by the appearance of one of the seven bowl angels, who addresses John in a similar way in each case (17.1; 21.9); similarly, both visions are followed by an episode in which John attempts to worship an angel, and is told that he must worship only God (19.10; 22.8–9). Yet this could support more than one literary analysis. The parallelism could suggest that both visions are meant to conclude different sections of the work, as in Yarbro Collins' analysis (we have seen parallelism used before to link different sections of this book). It is also possible, however, that the parallelism initiates a kind of *inclusio*, according to which the literary parallels between the two visions mark off the beginning and ending of a discrete section, with visions of the End sandwiched between them.

A solution to this dilemma may suggest itself if one remembers that this book was written to be read aloud in the Christian assembly, and that, given its length, it was probably divided into manageable sections (we have suggested, as this analysis has progressed, literary clues as to where these divisions are to be made). To conclude this section after the seventh bowl creates a lection which would be disproportionately small (only 25 verses) in relation to the others (the shortest of which contain 60 verses). To continue until the end of the Babylon vision, however, would create a section only marginally longer than the others, particularly if the brief prologue and epilogue are read along with the main opening and closing sections (see Figure 6).

Figure 6. Possible divisions of the Apocalypse for public reading

1.1—3.22	Prologue and Seven Letters	71 verses
4.1—8.1	Seven Seals	60 verses
8.2—11.18	Seven Trumpets	63 verses
11.19—15.4	Seven Visions	60 verses
15.5—19.10	Seven Bowls and Babylon	77 verses
19.11—22.21	Visions of the End, New Jerusalem and Epilogue	74 verses

Nevertheless, to describe the Babylon vision as an 'appendix' fails to do justice to its careful literary crafting. Rather, it should be seen as the culmination of the bowls sequence, a point made by the central role within it of one of the seven bowl angels. Among the announcements accompanying the seventh bowl (16.19) was one to the effect that Babylon the Great, having been remembered before God, would drink from the cup of God's furious anger. The vision of Babylon (17.1–18), and the subsequent lament over her destruction (18.1–24), now put the flesh upon the bare bones of this announcement.

Since the turning point of the narrative in chapter 10, when John was actively commissioned as a prophet, and the content of the visions turned their attention to the fate of the Christian witnessing community, a major theme has been the activity of Satan in the world, particularly in and through the 'empire' of the beast and the activity of the 'beast from the earth' or 'false prophet'. In this vision of Babylon, whose existence has been hinted at on a number of occasions already, the reader is given a glimpse of the particular focus of this demonic activity. John is taken 'in the spirit' (or 'in ecstasy') to a wilderness, where he is shown a woman seated on a beast. This is almost certainly the same beast which came up from the sea in chapter 13, and bore the characteristics, at least for John's first audience, of the Roman empire (both have seven heads and ten horns). Thus the woman is in some way implicated in that great empire of the beast. Her precise identity has been the subject of fierce debate for centuries, and every generation has seen her features in corresponding figures and institutions of their own time. Though a few commentators have identified her with unfaithful Jerusalem (Jerusalem is called a harlot at Isa. 1.21; cf. Jer. 13.27; Ezek. 16.15ff.), her present incarnation, at least for John's generation, is almost certainly Rome, the city built on seven hills (Rev. 17.9; cf. Virgil, *Georg.* 2.535; Horace, *Carmen Saec.* 7; Tibullus, 2.5.55; Propertius, 3.10.57; Ovid, *Trist.* 1.4.69). This chapter is unusual within the book of Revelation for offering fairly precise interpretations of certain details of the vision (e.g. 17.7–18), and, as shall be seen in the next chapter, features prominently in scholarly attempts to date John's book. Yet even granted the interpretative role of the *angelus interpres*, the identification with Rome does not exhaust her meaning: this vision describes the judgement upon the great city, and the empire of the beast, wherever they may be found.

The vision of the Great Harlot is followed by a series of laments over Babylon from those who have benefited, not least economically, from what she has to offer (18.9–19), bracketed by a series of celestial announcements and the activity of angels (18.1–8, 20–24). The first angel proclaims, in echoes of Isaiah 21.9, the fall of the city seen in the previous vision, and of those nations associated with her. This is taken up by a heavenly voice, perhaps the voice of Christ, which warns 'my people' to 'come out of her' (v. 4), echoing those early warnings in the seven letters against Christian compromise with society. This is followed by a succession of laments over her, from a variety of interest groups: the kings of the earth (18.9–10), merchants (18.11–17), shipmasters and seafarers (18.17b–19). The commercial implications of Babylon's dominance permeate this chapter, and exegetes have often noted how close the cargo lists of vv. 12–13 are to the known imports of imperial Rome (Bauckham, 1993, 338–83): Babylon is under judgement for her arrogance, excessive luxury, and political and economic exploitation. Although a constant factor in the unfolding drama of judgement and salvation in this apocalypse has been the 'prayers of the saints', the climax to this passage reveals, on the lips of another angel, that Babylon is held responsible not simply for the blood of prophets and saints, but of 'all those who have been slaughtered on earth' (18.24).

Few can miss the profound note of pathos in this section, mingled with that very different note of exultation breaking in from the heavenly realm. Indeed, already at 17.6 the seer has admitted that he was 'greatly amazed' at his first sight of Babylon: is chapter 18, with its echoes of Ezekiel's lament over the city of Tyre (Ezek. 27), an indication that John feels some sympathy for the plight of this great city, and those who have invested so much in its continuance? Or is this rather a taunt song, ridiculing the fragility of this apparently impregnable city, and the exploitative use to which Babylon's imports are put? This passage keeps us guessing, particularly when we discover, perhaps on a subsequent rereading, that a number of these imports are found elsewhere in this book, presented in a more positive light (e.g. the precious stones and pearls of the New Jerusalem, 21.19–21; the linen of the bride, 19.8).

But that is not yet the end of this section. We have found up to now that liturgical scenes have provided narrative markers at the end of a sequence, and the same is the case with this rather extended sequence of seven bowls. At 18.21–24, the angel with the great millstone has announced the 'throwing down' of the great city; this solitary angel is now overshadowed by a huge heavenly multitude, singing a canticle of God's victory, his judgement of the great harlot and the vindication of the blood of his servants. The response of the four living creatures and the twenty-four elders, typically, is one of worship and shouts of 'Alleluia', a song taken up by 'what seemed to be the voice of a great multitude, like the sound of many waters and like the sound of mighty thunderpeals' (19.6), which proclaims the imminence of the Lamb's marriage to his bride.

The final scene (19.9–10) of the Babylon vision, and of the wider section of which it is part, will be closely followed at 22.8–9, marking the conclusion to the parallel section containing the vision of the New Jerusalem. Here John is urged by the accompanying angel to write another beatitude, the fourth encountered so far in this book (not surprisingly, there are seven in all: 1.3; 14.13; 16.15; 19.9; 20.6; 22.7, 14), followed by an assurance that these are the true words of God. The scene ends, as will 22.8–9, with John's failed attempt to worship the angel, who rebukes him with the words 'Worship God!' (this raises questions about the status of the Lamb, who has been the object of worship, without the rebuke found here, at 5.8–9). The final phrase continues to puzzle commentators:

it is literally translated, as in the NRSV, 'For the testimony of Jesus is the spirit of prophecy'. 'The testimony of Jesus' (ἡ μαρτυρία 'Ιησοῦ) could be an objective genitive (i.e. testimony to Jesus) or a subjective genitive (i.e. the testimony which Jesus himself bore before the world, which others can continue, cf. 1 Tim. 6.13). Given the use of this phrase elsewhere in this book, the latter seems most likely (e.g. 1.2; 12.17; cf. 6.9). But even this leaves the precise meaning of Revelation 19.10 unsolved, and though most modern translators avoid the issue by opting for a literal rendering of the Greek, commentators resort to a variety of paraphrases in order to convey what this phrase seems to mean in its present context, as a comparison of several commentaries will make clear.

19.11—22.11 Seven Final Visions

A new, and climactic section now unfolds. Up to this point, liturgical activity in the heavenly sanctuary has marked the beginning of a new section. Here, we are confronted with the 'opening' of heaven (paralleling the more overtly liturgical openings at 4.1ff., 11.19 and 15.5; cf. 8.1), inaugurating a new series of visions. Again, the explicit number seven has disappeared from view, and some commentators have resorted to desperate and highly arbitrary rearrangements in order to find some coherence in what appears to them hopelessly illogical and repetitive. Others have made more allowance for the haphazard nature of apocalyptic vision. Indeed, given the parallels with the previous section, in which the vision of Babylon concludes a sequence of seven bowl plagues, it may still be possible to detect seven discrete visions in what follows here, up to the climactic vision of the New Jerusalem. Some have suggested that the repeated phrase 'And I saw' (καὶ εἶδον) functions as a division marker; this is only partly valid, given that καὶ εἶδον is found more than once within what is clearly the same vision, so that not every occurrence of the phrase points to a new scene (a classic example is 20.12, where the dead whom John sees standing before the throne belong to the vision which begins in the previous verse, where John first sees this throne; cf. also 19.17 and 19). Indeed, there are a total of nine occurrences of καὶ εἶδον in this section. Moreover, one passage which almost certainly describes a new scene or stage in the action (20.7–10) lacks this distinctive phrase. A more cautious attention to the use of καὶ εἶδον may lead to the following conclusion, but it is only tentative:

1. Rider on a white horse (19.11–16).
2. Victory over beast and false prophet (19.17–21).
3. Binding of Satan (20.1–3).
4. First resurrection and thousand-year reign (20.4–6).
5. Release of Satan and final victory (20.7–10; lacks καὶ εἶδον).
6. Final judgement (20.11–15).
7. New heavens and new earth (21.1–8).

As was the case in the previous section, then, in which the parallel vision of Babylon was rooted in, and further developed, an element of the seventh-bowl plague, so too the great vision of the New Jerusalem (21.9—22.10) is prepared for by and rooted in the seventh vision in this sequence (21.1–8).

A number of recurring issues and concerns find particular focus in the visions of this section. Not least of these is the moral unease which many readers have felt with the imagery of destruction and bloodshed in this book. The rather terrifying vision of the rider on the white horse, frequently understood as describing the Parousia of the Son of Man (cf. 1.14, 16), provides an illuminating commentary on the nature of the great battle for which the reader has been prepared. Here the full force of the biblical Divine Warrior tradition is brought into play. The rider comes out with robes dripping in blood, like the Lord himself in the vision of Isaiah 63, fresh from his bloody victory over the Edomites; he is described as the Word of God, that stern warrior carrying a sharp sword, who leaps down from heaven from the royal throne (Wisd. 18.15). Yet there are indications that here, as so often in apocalyptic visions, things are not quite what they seem. The robes of this heavenly warrior are dipped in blood even before the final battle commences, calling to mind not the blood of enemies but the blood of the Lamb that was slain (e.g. 5.6; 7.14; 12.11). The weapon with which he will finally engage battle is no military weapon, but the sword of truth which comes out of his mouth, the double-edged sword which is the word of God (19.15; cf. Isa. 11.4; *Pss. Sol.* 17.23–25; *4 Ezra* 13.8–11; Heb. 4.12). Despite all the gruesome apocalyptic imagery of war, slaughter and victory, at no point is military might at issue, nor are Christians bidden to take up arms against their enemies.

This section also brings sharply into focus the chronological question which has underscored, at least implicitly, the interpretation of this book as a whole. From earliest times, when both Justin and Irenaeus saw in this section the promise of a future Millennium or thousand-year reign of Christ on earth, these visions have provoked controversy, and often been given a weight which their size, in relation to the Apocalypse as a whole, cannot really carry. In fact, when compared to visions such as *2 Baruch* 29, John's treatment of the 'Millennium' is markedly restrained. Yet ever since, commentators have wondered how these visions relate chronologically to one another, and to the broader schema of salvation history. Do they all describe events of the ultimate future, still to come for John and indeed for the contemporary reader? Or do some of them look back to that which has already taken place (we have already encountered this possibility in the vision in Rev. 12, which seems to look back to the period of Israel's pregnant waiting, and the birth of the Messiah of the Virgin Mary)? Do certain visions describe the same events in different ways, using a form of recapitulation (Mealy, 1992)? Or is it illegitimate to view them as providing a chronological sequence of events (which might explain the lack of specific numbering here, as also in 11.19—15.4)?

That things are not quite so simple can be seen in the vision of the binding of Satan at 20.1–3, in preparation for the thousand-year reign of Christ. It remains unclear whether Satan is yet to be bound, in some future eschatological scenario, or whether this has already happened. Some might note parallels with the ministry of Jesus as described in the Gospels, where it is clear that the strong man has already been bound with the commencement of that ministry (e.g. Mark 3.26–27). A line of interpretation which can trace its roots back to Augustine of Hippo would take the second view, thus enabling the 'thousand-year reign' to be a symbol of the presence of Christ in his Church, rather than a description of events still in the future. Similarly, there are profound parallels between the two 'battle' scenes, at 19.17–21 and 20.7–10, both of which could in some sense be described as the 'Last Battle'. There are also apparent inconsistencies: judgement is apparently in view with the raising of the martyrs at 20.4, yet in the depiction of the great judgement at 20.11–15, all the dead (including, presumably, the hitherto resurrected martyrs) come before the thrones for the opening of the books. It is far from clear that a neat chronological scheme can, or indeed should, be read out of these visions.

However these visions relate to one another, it is clear that they symbolize the final victory of good over evil, God over Satan, the Lamb and his martyr-band over the beast and its accomplices. The last of the seven describes the new heaven and new earth, and the descent of the New Jerusalem, like a bride prepared for her wedding (some commentators think that we have met this woman before, clothed with the sun, awaiting her final liberation from the wiles of the dragon: Rev. 12.1–6). Typically, a heavenly voice offers commentary on the action: 'See, the home of God is among mortals' (21.3). Fundamental to the Apocalypse up to this point, as to any apocalypse, has been the disjunction between heaven and earth, between the true, heavenly realm, where it is clear that the One on the throne is King, and the earthly, where that royal rule is resisted or denied, with disastrous consequences. As the eschatological events, long delayed by the narrative subtlety of this book, finally reach their climax, that division is now finally overcome. God lives in the midst of humanity; the new heaven and the new earth are as one.

The implications of this last vision are worked out in minute visionary detail in the extended New Jerusalem vision, introduced as its Babylonian parallel by one of the seven bowl angels (21.9). In a kaleidoscope of images and Old Testament allusions (cf. Ezek. 40ff.; Gen. 2), whose complexity artists and poets have struggled to convey, John is taken 'in spirit' or 'in ecstasy' on a guided tour of this celestial city. It is a city marked by order and beauty: foursquare; 12,000 stadia (about fifteen hundred miles!) in length, height and depth; walls 144 cubits thick; founded on twelve precious stones, with twelve gates of pearl; bearing twelve kinds of fruit on its tree of life. This sharply contrasts with the chaos and ugliness of life under the dragon and its beastly cronies. But perhaps most significant is the absence in the New Jerusalem of the one building which so dominated the old: 'I saw no temple in the city, for its temple is the Lord God the Almighty and the Lamb. And the city has no need of sun or moon to shine on it, for the glory of God is its light, and its lamp is the Lamb' (21.22–23). In the new age, the mediatory role of a temple cult will give way to direct access to the divine. It is perhaps not surprising, then, that, in contrast to the conclusion to previous sections, there is here no explicit liturgical action or hymn in the heavenly sanctuary: that has now been superseded.

Instead, the section concludes, as did the last, with an assurance of the truth of these words, a beatitude, and John's frustrated attempt to worship his angelic companion (22.6–9). Finally, the angel forbids him to seal up this book, given that the 'time is near' (ὁ καιρὸς γὰρ ἐγγύς ἐστιν; 22.10), before uttering a concluding warning to evil and righteous alike. This command not to seal the message is in marked contrast to other Jewish apocalypses, attributed to figures of the distant past, which urge the concealment of their visions until the appointed time, or restrict access to the 'wise' among the people (e.g. Dan. 12.9; 4 Ezra 14.46); John's apocalypse, written in his own name and for his own time, has no need for this literary subterfuge.

22.12–21 Epilogue

If attention is paid to order and structure, then one should probably make the break between the conclusion of the angel's words (at v. 11) and the transition to the first person singular in verse 12 (almost certainly the voice of the risen Christ, breaking into the narrative for the last time). The prologue to this book had concluded with the direct words of the Lord God Almighty, declaring himself to be the Alpha and the Omega (1.8), and one should not be surprised if these same words open the epilogue. The words of the exalted Jesus which follow contain two further beatitudes (to complete this particular set of seven), as well as a warning authenticating this book as a work of prophecy (cf. Deut. 4.1–2); they are briefly interrupted by the voices of the Spirit and the Bride. We are now back in 'real time': the climatic vision of the New Jerusalem has again retreated into the glorious future, and once more 'liturgical time' is called for to maintain the vision. The notes of divine presence and eschatological urgency, so reminiscent of the eucharistic liturgy, conclude this highly liturgical book, as the reader, and the hearers, are urged to join the harmonious song of the Spirit and the Bride: 'Amen. Come, Lord Jesus!' (22.20; cf. 1 Cor. 16.22, Maranatha; Didache 10.6).

Concluding Thoughts

This initial read-through of John's Apocalypse has revealed, often in surprising ways, its tapestry-like complexity and integrity. The interweaving of themes, scenes and sections seems to permeate every chapter of this book, from the letters to the seven churches, themselves recapitulating the inaugural vision of the Son of Man, to the climactic vision of the New Jerusalem. The repeated use of the number seven has provided a relatively stable framework within which to test hypotheses about those sections where the structure is much less obvious. Moreover, the oral nature of this book's intended delivery has offered explanations for the otherwise puzzling and irritating tendency towards narrative delay, particularly marked between the sixth and seventh elements of the various sequences. Now, at the end of this first read-through, to step back and view the tapestry as a whole will reveal one more of its secrets. Leaving aside the brief prologue and epilogue, one can see (according to the schema developed in this chapter) not the expected seven sets of seven, but only the penultimate six (1.9—3.22; 4.1—8.1; 8.2—11.18; 11.19—15.4; 15.5—19.10; 19.11—22.11). The element of delay, so recurrent in the individual sections, is now shown to be embedded in the very structure of the book as a whole. The Apocalypse closes, not with the expected culmination of the divine plan, but with that same delay, pointing beyond itself to the imminent and ever-present eschatological future: 'Amen! Come, Lord Jesus!'

NOTES

1. Revelation would not be alone among early Christian writings in ascribing the titles and privileges of Israel to Christian believers, whatever their previous religious and ethnic allegiance: e.g. 1 Pet. 2.9–10.
2. Or possibly a vulture: both birds are denoted by the same Greek word.
3. The precise nature of the third woe is never revealed explicitly.
4. The city of Megiddo is not, strictly speaking, built on a mountain, but it does occupy a strategic location overlooking the valley of Jezreel, the location of many battles (e.g. 2 Chron. 35.22; Zech. 12.11), and thus an appropriate location for the last great battle. Some commentators think that the *har* refers to the nearby Mount Carmel.
5. The 'false prophet' is almost certainly the second beast, from the earth (13.11–17).

REFERENCES

Barr, D. L. (1984), 'The Apocalypse as a Symbolic Transformation of the World: A Literary Analysis', *Interpretation*, January 1984, pp. 39–50.
Bauckham, R. (1993), *The Climax of Prophecy*. T. & T. Clark, Edinburgh.
Boxall, I. (1999), 'Who Is the Woman Clothed with the Sun?' in M. Warner (ed.), *Say Yes to God: Mary and the Revealing of the Word Made Flesh*. Tufton Books, London, pp. 142–58.

Farrer, A. (1949), *A Rebirth of Images.* Dacre Press, Westminster.

Garrow, A. J. P. (1997), *Revelation.* New Testament Readings; Routledge, London and New York.

Hemer, C. M. (1986), *The Letters to the Seven Churches of Asia in their Local Setting.* JSNT Supplement Series 11; Sheffield Academic Press, Sheffield.

Mealy, J. W. (1992), *After the Thousand Years.* JSNT Supplement Series 70; Sheffield Academic Press, Sheffield.

Ramsay, W. M. (1904), *The Letters to the Seven Churches of Asia.* Hodder & Stoughton, London.

Rowland, C. C. (1998), 'The Book of Revelation', in *The New Interpreter's Bible*, vol. XII. Abingdon Press, Nashville, pp. 501–736.

Yarbro Collins, A. (1976), *The Combat Myth in the Book of Revelation.* Scholars Press, Missoula, MT.

4

Looking across the Aegean

Let anyone who has an ear listen to what the Spirit is saying to the churches.

(Rev. 2.7)

John, Patmos and the Seven Churches

According to the opening chapter of Revelation, John was on the island of Patmos when he received his apocalyptic vision (Rev. 1.9), and he subsequently sent it to seven Christian communities located in major cities on the mainland of Asia Minor, in that area of present-day Western Turkey which then formed the Roman province of Asia. These are important clues for the historical-critical approach, that method of interpretation which is particularly interested in the historical process by which a biblical text came to be written. A major concern of the historical critic is to reconstruct the 'world behind the text', and hence the meaning of that text for its author, or to discover how it might have been understood by its first hearers, to set the text in its original historical context, and come to conclusions about its dating and other questions relating to the historical origins of the writing.

This is somewhat complicated in the case of the Apocalypse, given that it claims to mediate a divine revelation received in the form of visions, rather than articulating the conscious message of John. Nevertheless, most scholars accept that this historical rootedness in the first-century Roman world is important for understanding what is going on in the bulk of Revelation, which seems to be concerned not with this world but with the heavenly realm. For its esoteric visions are prefaced by, and intricately connected to, the seven 'letters' or 'messages' to these seven churches which preface them (Rev. 2—3). We have already suggested in the previous chapters that these visions, far from presenting a 'pie in the sky' salvation, offer a profound analysis of the social and political situation of these very earthly churches and the world which they inhabit. As we shall see, however, the details of this historical setting are rather more controversial, and continue to be hotly debated.

To begin with, we are not explicitly told that Revelation was written down in its present form on Patmos, only that John received his visions there, and some have argued (on the basis of early traditions) that the Apocalypse proper was written on John's return from Patmos to Ephesus.

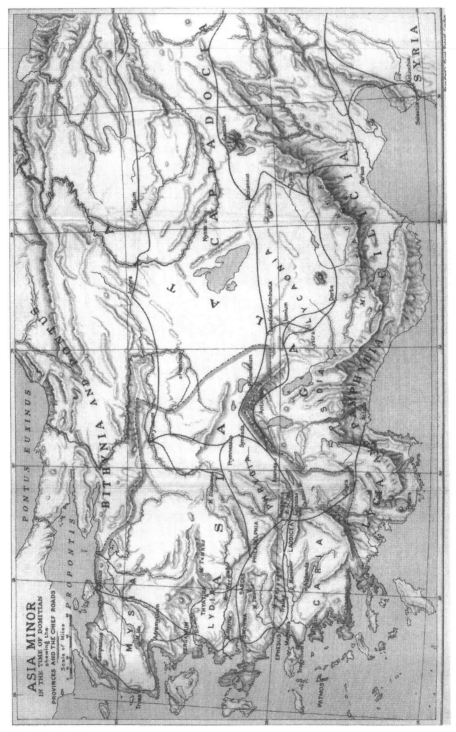

Map of Asia Minor. From H. B. Swete, *The Apocalypse of St John*, Macmillan and Co, London, 1906.

Against this is the fact that, in its present epistolary form, Revelation is sent *to* the seven churches of Asia, Ephesus included (Rev. 1.11). The implication of the text is that it was written from outside proconsular Asia, and the location of Patmos fits the order of the seven churches perfectly: the deliverer of the Apocalypse would have sailed from the island to the port-city of Ephesus, from where a circular course on the main postal routes would have passed through Smyrna, Pergamum, Thyatira, Sardis, Philadelphia and Laodicea, and thence back to Ephesus for the return sailing to Patmos. From these seven centres, copies of the Apocalypse could then have been delivered to other Christian communities in the locale.[1] Such an implication is reflected in the (albeit idealized) Eastern tradition, which portrays John dictating his visions to his disciple Prochoros, one of the seven 'deacons' of Acts 6, in the cave on Patmos.

Second, the precise reason for John's sojourn on Patmos remains somewhat unclear. The most widespread, and very early, explanation is that he was there as an exile, sent by the authorities as a result of his evangelistic activities, an explanation based on a particular interpretation of John's rather more ambiguous statement that he was there 'because of' or 'on account of' (Greek διά) the word of God and the testimony of Jesus (Rev. 1.9). Such a view is reflected in the unambiguous New American Bible translation: 'I ... found myself on the island called Patmos because I proclaimed God's word and gave testimony to Jesus.' There is, however, no explicit evidence that Patmos was used by the Romans as a place of exile, and it is just possible to understand John's words as expressing his purpose in going to the island, a possibility offered by the rather more open King James translation: 'I ... was in the isle that is called Patmos, for the word of God and the testimony of Jesus.' On grammatical grounds, however, the traditional interpretation would appear to be more likely. Elsewhere in his book, the preposition διά is used to describe the cause of an action rather than its purpose. The church in Ephesus has suffered 'on account of my name' (2.3); the twenty-four elders cry out that it was 'because of' the will of the One upon the throne that all things were created (4.11); the souls under the altar were slain 'on account of the word of God, and on account of the testimony which they bore' (6.9, my translations; cf. also 7.15; 12.11, 12; 13.14; 17.7; 18.8, 10, 15; 20.4). This is further supported by John's self-designation at the beginning of his work, which implies that he himself has encountered some hostility for his Christian confession: 'I, John, your brother and sharer with you in the tribulation and the kingdom and endurance in Jesus' (Rev. 1.9, my translation). The evidence is pretty conclusive that it was as a result of God's word and the 'testimony of Jesus', rather than for the purpose of spreading it, that John found himself on Patmos (or at least, that is how John perceives it).

If such is the correct interpretation, it is more likely that John was exiled to Patmos by the local authorities in Asia Minor than that he was sent there at the direct command of the emperor, despite the traditions enshrined in the apocryphal *Acts of John by Pseudo-Prochorus*. Patmos, along with its neighbouring islands of Lipsos (present-day Lipsi) and Leros, belonged in the first century to the mainland city of Miletus, acting as a kind of 'fortress' island (Greek φρούριον) to guard the security of the Milesians (Saffrey, 1975). Far from being a deserted island, it would have been populated by citizens of Miletus; archaeological remains on Patmos today in the 'Castelli' area testify to the long-standing occupation of this part of the island. Moreover, inscriptional evidence points to a temple and priesthood of Artemis (a tradition passed down by the monks of Patmos claims that the Monastery of St John the Theologian is built on the very site of the pagan temple), as well as a temple to Apollo. It is probable, therefore, that John, having preached the gospel in Miletus, provoked the ire of the local authorities, such that they banished him to one of their island fortresses. Although Luke tells us (Acts 20) of a farewell meeting between Paul and the elders of the Ephesian church at Miletus, at some point in the late 50s, he makes no mention of Christians from Miletus itself at this stage. Subsequent preaching activity by John in Miletus could have led to his removal to Patmos, in his words, 'on account of the word of God and the testimony of Jesus'.

Whatever the reasons for John's stay on Patmos, the plight of those seven Christian communities (which, as the seven letters of Rev. 2—3 indicate, he knew so well and over which he claimed a certain prophetic authority) could never have been far from his thoughts, even as, though separated by sea, they were not far geographically from his physical presence. From the Cave of the Apocalypse on Patmos, according to Orthodox tradition the location of John's revelation, the view stretches eastwards down to the port of Skala, across the Aegean to the islands of Arki and Lipsi, and from there to the western coast of Asia Minor some thirty or so miles away. From the north of the island, one can see the mountains of Samos; beyond, in mind if not in sight, lie the great city of Ephesus and her sister churches.

But why precisely was John writing to these seven churches, and transmitting to them, in literary form, the content of his visionary experience? What dangers did he see for them, from his island retreat? The answer to this question used to be considered relatively straightforward: they, like John himself, were the victims of hostility and even persecution, and this book was written to comfort them in their trials and assure them of ultimate victory through the Lamb. Recent scholarship, however, has suggested that the answer is rather less straightforward, and we have already intimated in previous chapters some of the rather different challenges which John foresees. What follows is an attempt to describe the breakdown in the scholarly consensus, and a possible way forward.

Revelation as a Response to Domitian's Persecution of Christians

Perhaps the most widely held scholarly approach to the dating and background of the book of Revelation claims that it was originally written during the reign of the Roman Emperor Domitian, and as a response to the persecution

View of Patmos from the Monastery of St John the Theologian
(by the author)

The acropolis of Pergamum, 'where Satan's throne is', from the Asclepeion
(by the author)

William Blake, *The Four and Twenty Elders Casting Their Crowns before the Divine Throne*

(N05897. © Tate, London, 2001)

Albert Dürer, *The Four Horsemen of the Apocalypse*

(Douce D Subt. 41(3), No. 64.
© Bodleian Library, University of Oxford, Oxford, 2001)

Lucas Cranach, *Babylon Seated on the Beast*

(from Martin Luther's 1522 September Testament. Fol. Theta 346 Sig. Ddiv r.
© Bodleian Library, University of Oxford, Oxford, 2001)

of Christians during his reign. John, in other words, rather like the author of the book of Daniel during the crisis provoked by Antiochus Epiphanes more than two hundred years earlier, writes his Apocalypse to comfort those currently undergoing persecution for their faith. The almost universal position of antiquity, and indeed of the majority of commentators up to the present, follows the second-century bishop of Lyons, Irenaeus, in locating the composition of this text in the latter years of the reign of the Emperor Domitian, that is, the early to mid 90s of the first century. Moreover, at least from the time of Eusebius, the dating of the Apocalypse under Domitian has been connected with a violent persecution by that emperor of the Christian Church, so that the text has often been read as a work of consolation for those facing martyrdom.

Irenaeus is regarded by many as particularly authoritative because of his claim to have known Polycarp, himself an acquaintance of John 'the disciple of the Lord'. In commenting upon the name of the beast in Revelation 13.18, Irenaeus writes:

We will not, however, incur the risk of pronouncing positively as to the name of Antichrist; for if it were necessary that his name should be distinctly revealed in this present time, it would have been announced by him who beheld the apocalyptic vision. For that was seen no very long time since, but almost in our day, towards the end of Domitian's reign.

(*Adv. Haer.* 5.30.3[2])

Irenaeus, it should be noted, does not himself link the Apocalypse with persecutions under Domitian. Nevertheless, from Eusebius onwards, the issues of dating and persecution have become inextricably linked, with the tradition of a large-scale persecution of Christians under Domitian. Eusebius puts it thus, in his *Ecclesiastical History*:

When Domitian had given many proofs of his great cruelty and had put to death without any reasonable trial no small number of men distinguished at Rome by family and career, and had punished without a cause myriads of other notable men by banishment and confiscation of their property, he finally showed himself the successor of Nero's campaign of hostility to God. He was the second to promote persecution against us, though his father, Vespasian, had planned no evil against us.

At this time, the story goes, the Apostle and Evangelist John was still alive, and was condemned to live in the island of Patmos for his witness to the divine word.

(*H.E.* 3.17–18[3])

Eusebius then goes on to cite the above-mentioned passage of Irenaeus about the dating of the Apocalypse, thus linking the writing of this book to the period of Domitian's persecution of Christians, though not even he explicitly states that it was Domitian who banished John to Patmos. In doing so, Eusebius alludes to an existing Christian tradition that Domitian was the first persecutor of the Church after Nero. Tertullian (*Apology* 5), speaks of Domitian as a man equalling Nero in cruelty, and attempting persecution of Christians; though, Tertullian hastily adds, 'as he had something of the human in him, he soon put an end to what he had begun, even restoring again those whom he had banished'.[4] Melito of Sardis, too, as cited by Eusebius, links together Nero and Domitian, claiming that both these emperors, 'persuaded by certain calumniators, have wished to slander our doctrine' (*H.E.* 4.26.9).

Many have found a correlation between this Domitianic scenario and evidence from Revelation itself. Revelation warns its Christian audience, for example, not to worship the beast and its image nor to accept its mark (Rev. 13.4, 12ff.; 14.9, 11; 16.2; 19.20; 20.4), which may well point to conflict over participation in the emperor cult. The seer foresees that a great trial is about to come upon the whole world, which will affect the church also (3.10). Indeed, some Christian blood has apparently already flowed (Antipas in Pergamum: 2.13), Christians in Smyrna may face impending imprisonment (2.10), and the souls of the martyrs cry out for vengeance from beneath the heavenly altar (6.9). Meanwhile the harlot Babylon, seated on the seven-headed beast, who for most commentators represents the indulgence and oppression of the city of Rome, built on seven hills, is revealed as 'drunk with the blood of the saints and the blood of the witnesses to Jesus' (17.6). All this, it could plausibly be argued, fits what Melito and Eusebius tell us about the Domitianic era. Indeed, many see in the designation of Rome as Babylon (Rev. 17.1–6), the first destroyer of Jerusalem and its Temple, conclusive evidence that Revelation was written after 70, i.e. after the destruction of the Second Temple by the forces of Rome.

Moreover, until relatively recently, New Testament scholars have generally appealed to Roman historical sources, some of which portray Domitian in a highly negative light, as confirmatory evidence for this Christian perception of Domitian as a 'second Nero'. According to Suetonius, for example, Domitian allowed himself to be called *Dominus et Deus noster*, 'our Lord and God' (*Domitian* 13), an expression used in Revelation of 'the one who sits upon the throne' (Rev. 4.11; 19.6 etc.; cf. 19.5). In line with this desire for worship, it has been claimed that Domitian particularly encouraged the development of the emperor cult, which was especially popular in the eastern provinces, not least Asia, and served a useful purpose in promoting provincial loyalty to the centre. Much is made, for example, of the fact that Ephesus received a new imperial temple during his reign. Finally, Roman sources relating the 'cruelty' of his later years have also been appealed to in support of the later Christian claim that Domitian, like Nero, was a persecutor of the Church.

Two episodes have been given particular attention. The first concerns the *fiscus iudaicus*, the replacement for the Jewish Temple tax, traditionally paid by Jews throughout the world to the Jerusalem Temple. With the destruction of the Temple under Domitian's father Vespasian, this tax was replaced by a 'Jewish head tax' paid into the coffers of the Temple of Jupiter Capitolinus in Rome. According to Suetonius, Domitian extended this to include those who 'without publicly acknowledging that faith yet lived as Jews, as well as those who concealed their origin and did not pay the tribute levied upon their people' (*Domitian* 12).[5] Such could have included Jewish Christians, and the *fiscus iudaicus* is thus often seen as a potential opportunity for state action against Christians. The second is an incident occurring in 96 CE, when members of the imperial household, including Domitian's own cousin Flavius Clemens and his wife Domitilla, were charged with 'atheism' or violation of the state religion, which Cassius Dio connected with Judaism (67.14.2). As a result, Clemens was executed and Domitilla exiled to the island of Pontia. Eusebius later explicitly claims that Domitilla, whom he believes to be Clemens' niece rather than his wife, was a Christian (*H.E.* 3.18.4).

However, a significant number of recent scholars, working in both classical and New Testament fields, have expressed dissatisfaction with the received view, both in terms of its dating and its setting at a time of persecution. While the Domitianic dating retains many staunch adherents, others have revived a view often espoused in the nineteenth century, which proposes a much earlier date for Revelation, namely the late 60s (Robinson, 1976, 221–53; Rowland, 1982, 403–13). This was a politically turbulent period for the empire at large (the year 69 saw no fewer than four emperors), and for Jews and Judaeo-Christians in particular (66 saw the beginnings of the Jewish revolt against Rome in Palestine). Moreover, even those who continue to hold to the traditional Domitianic dating have suggested other possible settings besides one of persecution.

An Alternative Dating

Let us turn, first, to the evidence for dating the book. The tradition that connects the writing of Revelation to the latter years of Domitian's reign is very early and very strong, but is largely based on external evidence (such as the testimony of Irenaeus), and is not unassailable. Even in the ancient world, alternative datings were espoused, even if none of these have gained much support in the subsequent history of interpretation. Two early Syriac versions date John's banishment, and therefore his visions, to the reign of Nero (54–68), while Epiphanius, fourth-century Bishop of Salamis, attributes the writing of the Apocalypse even earlier, to the time of the Emperor Claudius (41–54), a dating also found in a late medieval Ethiopian commentary on the book. Theophylact, writing in the eleventh century, testifies to a tradition which dates Revelation to the even later reign of Trajan (98–117), a dating which is not impossible given Irenaeus' claim that John was still alive at this time. It is likely that one or other of these suggestions (probably that of Epiphanius) is mistaken, given that both Claudius and Nero were known, rather confusingly, as Claudius Nero. Yet the widespread patristic preference for Domitian's reign should not necessarily be taken as more trustworthy because of its numerical strength, for it may simply reflect the repetition of Irenaeus' view rather than a number of independent witnesses for this late dating.

Before turning to the internal evidence of Revelation itself, a closer look at Irenaeus' words, and the context in which he wrote them, is called for. First of all, it should be noted that Irenaeus does not claim that the Apocalypse was *written* during the latter years of Domitian's reign. In the usual translation of the passage (preserved in Greek by Eusebius), Irenaeus claims only that John *saw* his apocalyptic vision then: Irenaeus is therefore no stronger a supporter for a Domitianic dating of the book than for one of the alternative proposals, namely that John wrote in the later reign of Trajan. But in fact, the Greek verb used (ἑωράθη) is ambiguous: it could either mean 'it [i.e. the Apocalypse] was seen' at the end of Domitian's reign, or alternatively 'he was seen'. If the latter, then Irenaeus is not speaking about the book at all, but rather making a point about the longevity of John. In the Latin version of Irenaeus, things are even more obscure, given that the phrase is clearly neuter: 'it was seen' (*visum est*). A reference to John would have required the masculine, to the Apocalypse the feminine (*apocalypsis*). The neuter *visum est* may rather refer to the 'name', *nomen*, of Antichrist.

Second, even if one concludes, with the majority of commentators since Irenaeus' day, that Irenaeus does indeed date John's visions to the end of Domitian's reign, and the writing of the book to the same period, one might still question his motives for doing so. On a more general point, scholars who feel quite at liberty to disregard Irenaeus' testimony on a host of other issues (e.g. the apostolic authorship of Matthew's Gospel) suddenly suffer pangs of conscience when it comes to his testimony about John's Apocalypse. This is all the more surprising given the ambiguity of Irenaeus' words here, and his chronological distance from the event he describes (he was not born until *c.* 130 CE). More specifically, in Book 5 of *Adversus Haereses* Irenaeus is concerned to discourage speculation about the identity of the Antichrist, and has a vested interest in dating John's non-announcement of Antichrist's name as late as possible, so that it may still apply to Irenaeus' own day. Indeed,

Alan Garrow has suggested a further reason why this Domitianic dating supports Irenaeus' concerns: namely, his dependence upon Polycarp, his direct link with John. Elsewhere, Irenaeus speaks of John being present with his disciples such as Polycarp into the reign of Trajan (indeed, Polycarp would have been little more than a lad in the reign of Domitian). Closing the gap between Polycarp and the Apocalypse would have strengthened Irenaeus' claim that the name of Antichrist had never been announced publicly (Garrow, 1997, 67–9).

None of this, of course, disproves Irenaeus' dating. What it does do, however, is to raise questions as to how solid Irenaeus' testimony here is, not least because of the ambiguity of what he actually says. This is all the more significant if the consensus view of the patristic period (and indeed the modern scholarly consensus) is simply the result of the repetition of Irenaeus' words, not always read particularly carefully. Moreover, when one turns to the internal evidence of Revelation, the case for an alternative dating becomes even stronger. It is to the various pieces of this internal evidence that we shall now turn.

The Seven Heads of the Beast

A crucial piece of internal evidence for dating Revelation is the explanation provided for the seven heads of the beast in Revelation 17. But it is precisely this passage which causes most embarrassment for the traditional dating, and raises the distinct possibility that this book should be dated much earlier, to the late 60s. Whatever further allusions and identifications have been found in the history of Christian commentary on and iconography of this vision, the primary referent for its original first-century hearers is clarified by a rare interpretation offered in verses 9–10:

> This calls for a mind that has wisdom: the seven heads are seven mountains on which the woman is seated; also, they are seven kings, of whom five have fallen, one is living, and the other has not yet come; and when he comes, he must remain only a little while.
>
> (Rev. 17.9–10)

The reference to Rome (the city built on seven hills), and to seven of its emperors (seven kings) could not be clearer, particularly in the light of v. 18, which states that the woman is 'the great city that rules over the kings of the earth' (this seems to rule out the alternative interpretation which views Babylon as Jerusalem). According to the interpretation offered in 17.9–10, the reader, and the hearers, are led to expect that the seer is writing in the reign of the sixth king, five having already reigned, and with the expectation (due perhaps to turmoil in the world) that the seventh yet to come would have only a short reign.

Figure 7. Roman emperors

[Julius Caesar]	d. 44 BCE
Augustus	27 BCE–14 CE
Tiberius	14–37
Gaius Caligula	37–41
Claudius	41–54
Nero	54–68
Galba	68–69
Otho	69
Vitellius	69
Vespasian	69–79
Titus	79–81
Domitian	81–96
Nerva	96–98
Trajan	98–117

Yet it is precisely this interpretation which poses the problem for Irenaeus' dating. Only a great deal of mathematical juggling enables commentators to arrive at Domitian as the sixth king presently reigning, and one cannot but wonder whether this tortuous exegesis arises out of a desire to uphold Irenaeus' Domitianic dating at all costs. Among such approaches are the following: that a passage originally written in the 60s has been incorporated into Revelation written at a later date; that one should begin counting not with the first (Julius Caesar or Augustus) but with a later emperor, such as Caligula, or Nero as the first 'antichrist' figure, and that one should omit from the equation the short-lived figures of Galba, Otho and Vitellius (see Figure 7); that the seer actually wrote during Domitian's reign, but 'antedated' his prophecy in order to make it look as if it had been received at an earlier stage (just as older Jewish apocalypses claim to have been seen by figures of the distant past), or that the vision is merely symbolic, with no reference to historical figures, which seems to run counter to the clear import of v. 10 (Robinson, 1976, 244–5; Yarbro Collins, 1984, 58–64). There is, however, a much more straightforward solution: to begin with the first emperor and count each succeeding emperor in turn.

There may be some reasonable debate over whether to begin counting with Julius Caesar or Augustus, since Suetonius does include the former in his *Lives of the Twelve Caesars*, although strictly speaking the empire began with Augustus (Octavian). However, there would appear to be little reason for disregarding the three emperors who reigned briefly in 69 (Galba, Otho and Vitellius). Suetonius writes lives of these three, even if he does speak rather disparagingly of the *rebellio trium principum* (*Vespasian* 1). Moreover, they are also included by Tacitus (*Hist.* 1.49), Josephus (*War* 4.491–6), *Sibylline Oracles* 5.12 and *4 Ezra* 12.13. Beginning with Julius Caesar, the sixth emperor reigning at the time the Apocalypse was written would be Nero (54–68), in line with one alternative early dating; beginning with Augustus, Galba, thus dating the Apocalypse to the turbulent years 68 or 69. In the face of this evidence, attempts to justify the position of Domitian as the sixth king presently reigning seem like special pleading.

Nero redivivus
Given the early Syriac tradition, one might wish to prefer the former of these two alternative datings. But in fact, a second piece of evidence is generally considered as ruling out Nero as the king presently reigning, and thus favouring Galba: apparent allusions to the so-called *Nero redivivus* myth. Already in the vision of the beast from the sea, mention has been made of one of the seven heads as possessing a mortal wound which was healed (Rev. 13.3), a demonic parody of the slain Lamb. That a specific historical allusion is implied, however, is confirmed by a precise statement of the manner of its death, 'by the sword' (13.14), and by the complex interpretation of the beast in Revelation 17, which suggests that it represents not only Rome, but also one of its emperors. In 17.8 we are told that the beast 'was, and is not, and is about to ascend from the bottomless pit and go to destruction', a phrase which is further clarified in v. 11: 'As for the beast that was and is not, it is an eighth but it belongs to the seven, and it goes to destruction.' Who is this eighth, who is also one of the seven (i.e. a new king considered the new manifestation of an old king)? The answer is provided by a variety of stories which gathered round the memory of Nero on his death in 68, and developed into a potent myth proclaiming that Nero would come again (for early Christians, the blasphemous echoes of the Second Coming of Christ would have been startling).

Already in 68, stories began circulating that Nero had not died:

> Yet there were some who for a long time decorated his tomb with spring and summer flowers, and now produced his statues on the rostra in the fringed toga, and now his edicts, as if he were still alive and would shortly return and deal destruction to his enemies.
>
> (Suetonius, *Nero* 57)

That the myth developed in the following decades of the century, and Neronian pretenders could arise as late as 90, is undisputed (e.g. *Sib. Or.* 5.361–85; *Asc. Isa.* 4.1–13; Dio Chrysostom, *Or.* 21). However, this does not mean that the sinister form in which it seems to appear in Revelation must be dated to the end of the century, as is often claimed. Tacitus tells us that in 69, prior to the murder of Galba, both Achaia and John's own Asia were terrified by rumours of Nero's return, spawned by doubts about his death, and an initially successful pretender seized the opportunity (Tacitus, *Hist.* 2.8). The allusions to this myth in Revelation, while ruling out a dating in Nero's reign, are not a difficulty for the alternative dating during the relatively brief and turbulent reign of Galba.

That the deceased Nero is on the mind of the seer of Revelation is confirmed by the allusion to the number of the beast (666 in most manuscripts), which is described as 'the number of a person' (13.18). Despite the protestations of Irenaeus, the text encourages its audience to identify this figure, and we seem here to have a good example of the ancient practice of *gematria*, popular among Jews. Given that letters of the Hebrew and Greek alphabets had their equivalent numbers, the 'number' of a word, or of somebody's name, could be calculated by adding together the numbers of the individual letters (e.g. the number of the name Παῦλος, Paul, is 80 + 1 + 400 + 30 + 70 + 200 = 781). The consensus view (recognizing that the author of Revelation comes from a bilingual milieu) is that 666 is the number of the Greek for 'Emperor Nero', Νέρων Καῖσαρ, written in and calculated from Hebrew letters. Though this bilingual explanation might appear rather too sophisticated, it seems to be confirmed by the variant reading 616, known as early as the late second century, which is the number of the Latin form *Nero Caesar*, again written in Hebrew characters.

Rome as Babylon

We now turn to a piece of internal evidence which is often regarded as conclusive evidence for a post-70 dating for Revelation, and thus regularly cited in support of a dating in Domitian's reign: the identification of Babylon in Revelation 17 with the city and empire of Rome. The claim is frequently made that Rome was only known as Babylon *after* the fall of Jerusalem (once Rome was remembered as the destroyer of Jerusalem and its Temple, like Babylon of old). For those concerned to explore the potential of an earlier dating, implied by the most obvious reading of the 'seven heads' vision and not undermined by the *Nero redivivus* myth, two responses are possible.

One is to question the identification of Babylon with Rome in Revelation. A small but significant minority of scholars has argued that John's 'Babylon' is a designation not for pagan Rome, but for unfaithful Jerusalem (Barker, 2000, 279–301). They point, for example, to the prophetic charge of harlotry laid against the holy city (e.g. Isa. 1.21ff.; Ezek. 16; 23) and the land of Judah (Jer. 3.6–10). They are sensitive to the fact that the vision differentiates between the woman and the beast upon which she sits, claiming that, even if the beast is to be identified as Rome, the same does not necessarily hold true for Babylon herself. Some, indeed, point to visions such as *1 Enoch* 24 as evidence that Jerusalem could be viewed as a city built on seven mountains.[6] They also highlight the literary parallels between present Babylon and the heavenly Jerusalem, arguing that the latter vision is the key to interpreting the former. This, however, is not a view which has

Figure 8. The number of the beast

Alphabetic numbers in Greek

α	1	ι	10	ρ	100
β	2	κ	20	σ	200
γ	3	λ	30	τ	300
δ	4	μ	40	υ	400
ε	5	ν	50	φ	500
ζ	7	ξ	60	χ	600
η	8	ο	70	ψ	700
θ	9	π	80	ω	800

Irenaeus' reckoning:
Τειταν (*Teitan*, 'Titan') = 300 + 5 + 10 + 300 + 1 + 50 = 666
Λατεινος (*Lateinos*, 'Latin') = 30 + 1 + 300 + 5 + 10 + 50 + 70 + 200 = 666

Alphabetic numbers in Hebrew

א	1	י	10	ק	100
ב	2	כ	20	ר	200
ג	3	ל	30	שׁ	300
ד	4	מ	40	ת	400
ה	5	נ	50	תק	500
ו	6	ס	60	תר	600
ז	7	ע	70	תש	700
ח	8	פ	80	תת	800
ט	9	צ	90	תתק	900

The number of 'Nero Caesar':
קסר נרון (*NRWN QSR – Greek form*) = 50 + 200 + 6 + 50 + 100 + 60 + 200 = 666
קסר נרו (*NRW QSR – Latin form*) = 50 + 200 + 6 + 100 + 60 + 200 = 616

commended itself to many. Better parallels can be found with the city and empire of Rome. Indeed, if Jerusalem were envisaged, it is surprising that this left no mark on the earliest interpretation of this passage, which seems to have been unanimous in viewing Babylon as Rome.

The second is to challenge the widespread claim that a Roman identification necessitates a post-70 dating. Eugene Boring is typical of many proponents of the Domitianic dating when he asserts: 'This practice [of describing Rome as 'Babylon'] did not become common until after the destruction of the city and would not have been appropriate before' (Boring, 1989, 10). Yet one wonders whether a certain amount of circular reasoning is not going on here, for Boring cites 1 Peter 5.13 as evidence that Jews and Christians only used

Babylon as a symbol for Rome after the Jewish war. However, commentators on this latter text often point to Revelation's use of Babylon, no less than that of *2 Baruch* and *4 Ezra*, as evidence for a post-70 dating of 1 Peter! This is all the more surprising a claim, given that a significant number of scholars are quite happy to attribute 1 Peter to a pre-70 situation.

A general point is pertinent here. The name of Babylon was not simply associated with the destruction of the First Temple in the Old Testament, such that it could only become an appropriate designation for Rome in light of the destruction of the Second Temple. Babylon's historical role as a place of exile for the Judaeans (cf. Ps. 137.1) may well underlie the use of that term for the author of 1 Peter. Deutero-Isaiah's image of Babylon as arrogant oppressor (Isa. 47; cf. Rev. 18) could have provided the raw materials for a pre-70 Judaeo-Christian description of Rome, particularly in the aftermath of the Neronian persecution in that city and in the light of events in Palestine from 66. Already in the second century BCE Babylon and its kings had become a symbol for Jews of other foreign oppressors (Dan. 5), not least Antiochus Epiphanes, even though he did not destroy the Temple or lead the people into exile (though he did set up a pagan altar and defile the sanctuary). At Qumran, the Chaldeans (i.e. the Babylonians) of Habakkuk 1.6 were already identified as the 'Kittim', i.e. the Romans, by the turn of the Christian era (1QpHab 2.10–14). Similarly, the *Psalms of Solomon*, dating from the first century BCE, seem to have made a connection between the arrival of Pompey 'from the end of the earth' and the coming of the Babylonians centuries before (ἀπ’ ἐσχάτου τῆς γῆς: Jer. 6.22 LXX; *Pss. Sol.* 8.15).

But more specifically, the insistence upon a post-70 provenance for Rome's identification with Babylon also ignores the prophetic claims for this book. While it is the case that prophecy is misunderstood if equated with telling the future (as in popular perception), prophets in the Israelite and Christian traditions have frequently been gifted with a particular sensibility for reading the signs of the times and warning their contemporaries of the likely outcome of contemporary events. Is it so impossible that a Jewish-Christian prophet, particularly one who had witnessed some of the events in Palestine in the first years of the Jewish revolt again Rome, would have been able to see the 'writing on the wall' (as did the author of Daniel in relation to the downfall of Antiochus Epiphanes)? Is it not conceivable that a work such as John's Apocalypse, which seeks to shape people's perceptions, rather than simply respond to what has already taken place, could have taken the bold step of portraying Rome in the colours of another great and idolatrous empire, long remembered as a dangerous enemy of God's people?

Temple
Up to this point, the evidence has been shown to be equally susceptible to a pre- and post-70 dating for the book, with the exception of the identification

of the seven heads, which seems to point most obviously to a period soon after Nero's demise in 68. This general ambiguity seems particularly pronounced in our final piece of evidence, the description of the measuring of the Temple in Revelation 11. Having swallowed the little scroll given him by the angel, John is given a measuring rod and told to measure the temple, its altar and its worshippers, but to omit the outer court, which is to be given to the Gentiles, who will trample the holy city for forty-two months. He is further told by the heavenly voice of the fate of the 'two witnesses'. For some, this provides clear evidence for a pre-70 date, assuming as it appears to that the Temple is still standing. For others, it provides equally clear evidence for a post-70 dating. Either they detect a close correspondence between the details of the vision and what is known of the last stages of the fall of Jerusalem, when the Jewish rebels sheltered in the inner Temple courts (Josephus, War 6.3.12), or traces of an earlier prophetic oracle, reworked symbolically, so that the Temple now refers not to an architectural structure in Jerusalem but to the new Temple which is the Christian community (e.g. 1 Cor. 3.16–17; Eph. 2.21).

A number of scholars view 11.1–2 as a fragment of a zealot oracle, spoken in Jerusalem during the last days of the war against Rome, before the Romans had entered the temple itself, and now incorporated, somewhat awkwardly, into John's description of the two witnesses. In its present context, the measuring is understood to be for the protection, not of Herod's temple pre-70, but of the Church post-70, sent to witness before a hostile world, even to the point of laying down her life. But is this interpretation so clearly the case?

As George Caird has written of this thesis, which goes back to Wellhausen, it is based on the underlying assumption that 'John could not have intended these words to be taken figuratively unless someone else had previously used them in their literal sense' (Caird, 1984, 131). Yet the opening verses, no less than the rest of the chapter, make good symbolic sense, and do not require a hypothetical prophetic oracle as their source. The expectation that the Gentiles would oppress God's people, as they had done again and again throughout history, including recently in Rome during the reign of Nero, would have been quite possible for a Christian apocalyptic seer, even before Rome's destruction of the physical Temple in Jerusalem. Indeed, the language echoes that of Daniel 8.10–14, which speaks of the trampling of God's sanctuary for 'two thousand and three hundred evenings and mornings' (i.e. about three and a half years or forty-two months; cf. Isa. 63.18; Ps. 79.1); Daniel is a book which, as we have seen, played a crucial role in John's visionary awareness. It may well be that events in Jerusalem in the late 60s had some impact upon what John (rather than a hypothetical zealot prophet) saw; but this need not require us to date his finished symbolic product to a much later date. Indeed, if Revelation 11 as a whole were written after the destruction of Jerusalem, why is the reader told in John's visionary account, contrary to historical fact, that only 'a tenth of the city fell' (11.13)?

All in all, then, the evidence for dating, leaving aside the external testimony of Irenaeus, is relatively ambiguous, not allowing us to pronounce clearly one way or the other. Nevertheless, the most obvious interpretation of the complex 'seven heads' vision would appear to tip the balance somewhat in the direction of the earlier dating, in the late 60s, certainly after Nero's death in 68, and possibly in the reign of Galba between June 68 and January 69. Yet there remains an apparent problem: Revelation has seemed to many to have a particular focus on Roman persecution of Christians. Can an earlier dating, in the turbulent years of the late 60s for which there is no evidence for Roman persecution of Christians, make adequate sense of this book?

An Alternative Setting

The whole question of Revelation and persecution is currently facing re-examination. It is true that the dating of the book to the reign of Domitian has often (though not always) been tied to the belief that Revelation is a response to persecution. The reasoning has often seemed to be as follows: (1) Revelation presupposes state persecution; (2) only Nero and Domitian were remembered as persecutors of the Church during the first century; (3) therefore, given that the *Nero redivivus* myth rules out the former, Irenaeus' dating to Domitian's reign is well established. Remove the equation of persecution, however, and one has removed one of the main planks of the Domitianic dating theory. But in fact, the tradition that Domitian was a fanatical tyrant and fierce persecutor of Christians has been challenged by recent classical historians (Bell, 1978–9; Thompson, 1990, 95–115), while the claim that Revelation presupposes actual state persecution has been revisited by New Testament scholars.

Let us begin with the traditional portrayal of Domitian as a mad megalomaniac eager to condemn those who did not worship him. As Thompson and others have shown, this is a portrait derived largely from authors writing after the emperor's death, with a vested interest in denigrating the Flavian dynasty in favour of the new emperor Trajan, and needs to be balanced by sources contemporary with his reign. The later sources consistently attribute malicious motives to him, even to his good deeds, and compare him unfavourably with his imperial successor. Whereas Dio Cassius claims that Domitian regarded praise of his predecessors as reviling himself, contrary evidence shows that the emperor dedicated a temple to the cult of his immediate predecessors Vespasian and Titus, and contemporary poets Statius and Martial wrote in praise of these two emperors, quite unhindered by Domitian himself (Thompson, 1990, 101–3).

With regard to the emperor cult, Suetonius' claim that Domitian demanded the title *dominus et deus noster* finds no echo in writings of his reign, not even those of Statius and Quintilian, commissioned by Domitian himself. This is surprising, if such a title reflected the emperor's own wishes. But in fact, such a self-designation is not to be found on inscriptions, coins or medallions from the Domitianic era. Indeed, according to Statius, when Domitian was acclaimed as 'Lord' at one of his Saturnalia, the emperor forbade such a designation (Statius, *Silv.* 1.6.81–4). On the other hand, another contemporary poet, Martial, does use *dominus* and *deus* of Domitian, and the 'crowd' are described as calling the emperor *dominus deusque*, which reveals something of the popular mood (Martial, *Epigrams* 7.34). But there is no contemporary evidence that Domitian himself claimed that title nor that he demanded it of others. This is not to deny that Domitian became increasingly ruthless and paranoid towards the end of his reign, in the light of conspiracies against him: one recent judicious assessment of his reign can still speak of his later years as a 'reign of terror' (Goodman, 1997, 65). Nevertheless, there are good grounds for questioning the frequently repeated claim that Domitian's reign witnessed a marked development in the imperial cult, spurred on by the arrogant pretensions of the emperor himself.

Turning to the tradition of an official persecution of Christians during Domitian's reign, this has also been shown to rest upon slender and highly ambiguous evidence (Bell, 1978–9, 94). A substantial plank of this thesis is the identification of Flavius Clemens (whom Domitian had executed) and his wife Domitilla (who was exiled) as Christians, an identification certainly made, in the case of Domitilla, by Eusebius (*H.E.* 3.18.4), who seems to be echoing an earlier tradition.[7] Yet this may be little more than a conclusion drawn from the statement of Cassius Dio that Clemens was put to death and his wife exiled on a charge of 'atheism', which Dio equates with the customs of the Jews (Dio 67.14.2).

Bell posits two difficulties with this: first, Dio lived late enough (*c.* 150–235) for the split between church and synagogue to have become universal knowledge, even among pagans, being, as he was, contemporary with Justin Martyr and Irenaeus. If this were an issue of targeting Christians, then Dio would certainly have been able to make the distinction. Second, the alternative account of Clemens' death found in Suetonius suggests a non-religious motive for the execution. Even allowing for Suetonius' partiality, one must admit some truth in his claim that Domitian became paranoid about his death towards the end of his reign (a trait not unique to him among Roman emperors!). Clemens would then have been killed under suspicion of complicity in a plot to kill the emperor (Bell, 95); Suetonius, indeed, claims that the execution was sudden and based on very slight suspicion (*Domitian* 15.1). A further problem with the 'Christian persecution' hypothesis should also be mentioned here: Suetonius explicitly praises Nero for his persecution of Christians; if those executed under Domitian had also been Christians, surely Suetonius would have mentioned the fact.

Other evidence cited in favour of a persecution under Domitian remains ambiguous. Eusebius, dependent here upon the second-century church historian Hegesippus, describes action taken by Domitian against members of the Davidic family, including blood relatives of Christ (*H.E.* 3.19–20). Eusebius' interpretation is that the emperor ordered their execution. Yet the actual episode is rather more tame, for, as Eusebius is forced to admit, on learning that they were simple workers who expected an otherworldly kingdom and thus posed no political threat, Domitian released them unharmed, and took no more action against Christians. This is echoed by some words of Tertullian, also cited by Eusebius: 'Domitian also once tried to do the same as he, for he was a Nero in cruelty, but, I believe, inasmuch as he had some sense, he stopped at once and recalled those whom he had banished' (*H.E.* 3.20.7). At most this evidence allows that Domitian took short-lived action against the Church (and presumably only in the city of Rome), but quickly relented. Yet it is difficult to know the historical worth of these distinctly Christian traditions, and how far their perception of Domitian of a second Nero is dependent upon the negative portrayal of this emperor as a cruel megalomaniac derived from historians of the Trajanic era and beyond.

Equally ambiguous is the statement at the beginning of the First Epistle of Clement, translated in the Loeb version as 'Owing to the sudden and repeated misfortunes and calamities which have befallen us' (*1 Clem.* 1.1).[8] Often interpreted as a reference to persecution under Domitian, this has been used to date *1 Clement* to the end of the first century. Yet 'misfortunes and calamities' may well be an overly negative translation of Clement's Greek, which could simply mean 'events and experiences'. It is true that the author, in reminding his addressees of the examples of the martyr-apostles Peter and Paul, states: 'for we are in the same arena, and the same struggle is before us' (*1 Clem.* 7.1). But the reference here is too vague to be defined more closely, and moreover would appear to describe the localized situation of Clement in Rome; it can hardly be cited as evidence for imperial hostility towards Christians in Asia during the reign of Domitian. All in all, the evidence for a persecution of Christians under Domitian would appear decidedly shaky, even though one cannot rule out more localized social antagonism towards Christians from time to time. Yet we have already suggested grounds for challenging the dating of the Apocalypse to Domitian's reign. We shall now turn to evidence from the book itself, which suggests that a background of official state persecution may not in fact be required by internal evidence.

The so-called 'Letters to the Seven Churches', which form chapters 2—3 of Revelation, are widely recognized as an important internal source for gleaning evidence about the social setting of the Christian communities to whom the Apocalypse was first addressed. Sir William Ramsay early in the twentieth century, and subsequently Colin Hemer, have shown through their detailed study of the history, geography and archaeology of first-century proconsular Asia how intimate was the seer's knowledge of these seven communities and the cities to which they belonged (Ramsay, 1904; Hemer, 1986). An analysis of these 'seven letters' confirms the paucity of evidence for actual hostility towards Christians within these cities. Only two actual martyrs are mentioned by name in the seven letters, namely, Antipas of Pergamum, whose death seems to have been at some time in the past (2.13), and Jesus Christ, the 'faithful and true witness' (3.14). The other martyrs mentioned in the visions in the later part of the book, whether the souls crying out under the altar (6.9–11), the great multitude who have passed through the Great Tribulation (7.14), or those on whose blood Babylon the Great is drunk (17.6) are not further specified, and the nature of apocalyptic vision makes it unclear whether we are given an insight into the past (including the Neronian persecution), the present (actual persecution), or the future (that which John expects to happen). Indeed, the language used of the souls under the altar suggests strongly that John has been influenced by Jewish traditions about the blood of Abel (cf. *Targum Neofiti* on Gen. 4.10; *1 Enoch* 47; Matt. 23.35). This may therefore be a vision of all God's righteous ones slain from the beginning of time to the present, or even into the visionary future, and not simply of Christian martyrs of John's generation. That some of the visions describe a future rather than past or present aspect may be implied by the letter to Philadelphia, which speaks of 'the hour of trial that is coming on the whole world' (Rev. 3.10; cf. Matt. 6.13). Either way, the allusions to actual hostility are surprisingly small.

From the perspective of many within these churches, on the contrary, the situation appears rather to be one of prosperity. The Laodiceans, for example, are boasting of their riches (3.17), suggesting that their own understanding of Christianity involves playing a full part within contemporary society, not least its economic aspect. Later in the Apocalypse, imperial commerce will be explicitly linked to the mark of the beast, and the Laodiceans are therefore implicated in it (13.17). The author also makes fierce criticism of Christians who hold to the teaching of the Nicolaitans (in Pergamum, 2.15, where it may correspond to the 'teaching of Balaam'; on the fringes in Ephesus, 2.6) and those at Thyatira who follow the prophetess whom John rather cuttingly names 'Jezebel' (2.20). Both of these groups are encouraging other Christians to 'practice fornication and to eat food sacrificed to idols': again, the issue concerns the extent to which Christians can participate in the life of their respective cities, in which aspects of pagan cults would influence every aspect of urban life, political, religious and commercial. John's revelation comes down firmly on the side of uncompromising Judaeo-Christian tradition, and, if Theissen is correct (Theissen, 1982, 121ff.), of the poor, criticizing those who have accommodated themselves too readily to pagan society, with at least implicit acceptance of its cultic (idolatrous) aspects. Other Christians, including 'Jezebel' and those who held to the teaching of 'Balaam' and the Nicolaitans, would obviously not agree with this assessment (Boxall, 1998).

Thus from one Christian perspective there is a situation of relative prosperity within the churches of the province of Asia: from this viewpoint, talk of 'crisis' or persecution would appear largely inappropriate. On the other hand, Revelation, through its use of apocalyptic imagery to shed light on the social situation, offers a challenge to many Christians to reconsider their own position as regards Graeco-Roman society and its perception of 'the way the world is'. The prophetess 'Jezebel' shares some of the traits of the great harlot (e.g. compare 2.20 with 17.2), and 'beguiles' or 'leads astray', as does the false prophet at 13.14. The dividing line between the harlot and the bride of the Lamb is a fine one, as a heavenly voice warns (18.4). The real danger for many of John's first hearers is not so much persecution as complacency and accommodation. Only two churches of the seven, those at Smyrna and Philadelphia, are found worthy. Viewed from this perspective, then, the Apocalypse would appear to be written not so much to console the persecuted, as has so often been thought, as to challenge the complacent. It is a call to martyrdom, a challenge to (perhaps unwittingly) complacent Christians to put themselves in a position where they might find themselves facing martyrdom, a position of challenge to the prevailing *Pax Romana*, revealed in this apocalypse as Satanic.

Nevertheless, the older view cannot be ruled out entirely. The very mention of the two 'worthy' churches, Smyrna and Philadelphia, does indicate that, while we cannot speak of widespread persecution, some limited hostility towards and action against certain Christians has already taken place. Smyrna, for example, has had 'affliction' (2.9), and is poor, perhaps reflecting its refusal to accommodate itself to pagan society, in contrast to Laodicea which boasts of its riches. Philadelphia has 'little power', but has not 'denied my name' (3.8). But in both these cities there are indications that hostility may have been provoked, not by Roman officials or even by pagan neighbours, but by the synagogue, or a rival synagogue. At Smyrna, they have endured blasphemy from 'those who say that they are Jews' but are a 'synagogue of Satan' (2.9), words which reveal the painful and bitter relationship between the diverging sibling communities in this period. John hears that they are about to suffer, and that some will be thrown into prison, albeit for a limited period; some, indeed, may be called upon to be faithful unto death (2.10), raising the possibility (though not the certainty) of actual martyrdom in the near future.

The New Testament writings provide ample testimony to the often bitter 'family feuds' within the first-century Jewish community over allegiance to Jesus Christ. The Acts of the Apostles preserves traditions in which Paul and his companions frequently provoke the ire of the leaders of diaspora synagogues (e.g. Acts 14.1–7, 19), who sometimes bring them before the city authorities (e.g. Acts 17.1–9; 18.12–17). While this is something of a Lucan motif, one should not dismiss these stories as without any historical basis. The Gospel of Matthew testifies to persecution of Jewish-Christian missionaries, probably by the leaders of Pharisaic synagogues (e.g. Matt. 10.17–23), while the Fourth Gospel is written at a time when some Jewish disciples of Jesus have been forced out of the synagogue community (John 9.22). John of Patmos likewise knows of antagonism in some of the cities of Asia from other Jewish groups. Judging by the phrase he uses for them ('those who say that they are Jews and are not'), he continues to claim for himself and other Christians of Jewish origin membership of the covenant people, true Jews as opposed to 'false Jews'. This is confirmed by his rather conservative Jewish attitude to 'food sacrificed to idols', and his describing Christian opponents as 'Balaam' and 'Jezebel', pagan outsiders who compromised the purity of the holy people of Israel. Given his further description of them as 'a synagogue of Satan', he may well regard his Jewish opponents as too closely associated with the satanic empire of Rome.

The situation in Philadelphia is less clear, but again there may be hostility from the 'synagogue of Satan' (3.9): the church has already had to endure, and is praised by Christ for not denying his name (3.8). We know from the account of the martyrdom of Polycarp that there was virulent bitterness towards Christians on the part of the Jews in second-century Smyrna; Polycarp's contemporary Melito of Sardis reveals tensions between Jews and Christians in his city. Revelation suggests a similar situation, in Smyrna and Philadelphia, already in the first century. Whatever reason we posit for such hostility, it seems clear that it is local and not initiated by Roman officials.

There is also the possibility that limited action has been taken with regard to Christian refusal to participate in the emperor cult (perhaps linked to Jewish disowning of Christians). The imperial cult had been firmly established in Asia as early as the first century BCE, apparently with popular local support, and there is no need to link it specifically with Domitian's reign. Some have suggested, for example, that the death of Antipas in Pergamum was connected with this issue, interpreting the phrase 'the throne of Satan' as a reference to the emperor cult in which Pergamum played an important role. It is equally likely, however, that reference is made here to one of the city's other great shrines, perhaps the throne-altar to Zeus or the shrine of Asklepios Soter, both associated with the serpent, Revelation's image for Satan (Rev. 12), or possibly to the whole acropolis which rises up from the lower city to a height of nearly 1,300 feet. But what is important is Antipas' death. Although, for John the prophet, the real time of testing is yet to come, there is a precedent, however small,[9] and however long ago, for Christian martyrdom in Asia. The possibility is there, for those who can see the heavenly realities which John sees, and who have the faith and the endurance to keep the commandments of God and hold the testimony of Jesus.

Concluding Thoughts

The attempt to locate this book, and its author, on the plane of human history, is, as we have seen, both a fascinating and a frustrating task. There are good grounds both for challenging the traditional setting of the work in the reign of Domitian (as a number of nineteenth-century scholars already did), and for reassessing the relationship between this text and Roman persecution of Christians. The possibility that the seer wrote during the turbulent period in the life of the empire as a whole, and of Jews and Jewish Christians in particular, which followed the death of Nero in 68, is an attractive one. The likelihood that he understood the visions he described as challenging Christians who had compromised too readily with the great empire of Rome, rather than comforting those in the throes of bitter persecution from that empire, adds a particular edge to the historical understanding of this book. Not least, it forces us to take much more seriously than commentators have sometimes done that this is an apocalypse, a work of 'unveiling' or 'revelation', which forces the reader, and the hearer, to view reality in a new and often shocking light, and change their allegiance accordingly. The shocking nature of this 'unveiling' is a stark reminder that this text is not simply, or even primarily, a source for historical reconstruction, however. Indeed, for much of its history, no less than today, it has been read not for what it can tell us about the past, but rather for what it is believed to reveal about the future. It is to this future aspect of interpretation that we shall turn in the next chapter.

NOTES

1.   This would account for the omission of other known first-century Christian communities in this area: Colossae and Hierapolis, for example, near Laodicea in the Lycus valley (cf. Col. 1.2; 4.13). At the beginning of the second century, Ignatius of Antioch can write to two others, Magnesia-on-the-Meander and Tralles.

2.   Translation from A. Roberts and J. Donaldson (eds), *The Ante-Nicene Fathers* (Hendrickson, Peabody, MA, 1994), vol. 1, pp. 559–60.

3.   Translation from K. Lake, *Eusebius: The Ecclesiastical History*, Loeb Classical Library (William Heinemann, London, 1953), vol. 1, p. 235.

4.   *Ante-Nicene Fathers*, vol. 3, p. 22.

5.   Translation from J. C. Rolfe, *Suetonius*, Loeb Classical Library (William Heinemann, London, 1950), vol. 2, pp. 365f.

6. Though in fact in Enoch's vision Jerusalem is built on one mountain, surrounded by the other six.
7. One of the Christian catacombs in Rome is named after a certain 'Domitilla', traditionally identified with Flavia Domitilla. But this could be an erroneous conclusion, given the popularity of the name in the Roman world.
8. Translation by K. Lake, *The Apostolic Fathers*, Loeb Classical Library (William Heinemann, London and New York, 1925), vol. 1, p. 9.
9. Ignatius, fixated on martyrdom, is apparently unaware of martyrs in the churches of Ephesus, Smyrna and Philadelphia; Polycarp, martyred about the year 155, is only the twelfth Christian to be martyred in Smyrna and Philadelphia together (*Mart. Pol.* 19.1).

REFERENCES

Barker, M. (2000), *The Revelation of Jesus Christ.* T. & T. Clark, Edinburgh.

Bell, A. A. (1978–9), 'The Date of John's Apocalypse: The Evidence of Some Roman Historians Reconsidered', *New Testament Studies* 25, pp. 93–102.

Boring, M. E. (1989), *Revelation.* Interpretation Commentary; John Knox Press, Louisville.

Boxall, I. (1998), '"For Paul" or "For Cephas"? The Book of Revelation and Early Asian Christianity' in C. Rowland and C. H. T. Fletcher-Louis (eds), *Understanding, Studying and Reading.* Sheffield Academic Press, Sheffield, pp. 198–218.

Caird, G. B. (1984), *The Revelation of St John the Divine*, 2nd edn. A. & C. Black, London.

Garrow, A. J. P. (1997), *Revelation.* New Testament Readings; Routledge, London and New York, pp. 66–79.

Goodman, M. (1997), *The Roman World 44 BC–AD 180.* Routledge History of the Ancient World; Routledge, London and New York, pp. 58–66.

Hemer, C. J. (1986), *The Letters to the Seven Churches of Asia in their Local Setting,* JSNT Supplement Series 11; Sheffield Academic Press, Sheffield.

Ramsay, W. M. (1904), *The Letters to the Seven Churches of Asia.* Hodder & Stoughton, London.

Robinson, J. A. T. (1976), *Redating the New Testament.* SCM Press, London, pp. 221–53.

Rowland, C. C. (1982), *The Open Heaven.* SPCK, London, pp. 403–13.

Saffrey, H. D. (1975), 'Relire L'Apocalypse à Patmos', *Revue Biblique*, pp. 385–417.

Theissen, G. (1982), *The Social Setting of Pauline Christianity.* ET T. & T. Clark, Edinburgh.

Thompson, L. L. (1990), *The Book of Revelation: Apocalypse and Empire.* Oxford University Press, Oxford.

Yarbro Collins, A. (1984), *Crisis and Catharsis.* Westminster Press, Philadelphia.

5

Looking into the Future

Brothers, this Lord Jesus shall return again,
With his Father's glory, with his angel train;
For all wreaths of empire meet upon his brow,
And our hearts confess him, King of glory now.

(Caroline M. Noel, 1817–77)

What Must Happen Hereafter

The events which took place at the wooden compound known as Mount Carmel, near Waco, Texas, in the fifty-one days leading up to 19 April 1993, have become as legendary as the details of them are obscure. The FBI siege of this outpost of the Branch Davidians, an offshoot of the Seventh-day Adventists, meant posthumous fame for its leader Vernon Howell, alias David Koresh, even as it ended in a tragic fire and the deaths of both Davidians, Koresh among them, and federal agents. Claims and counterclaims abound: Mount Carmel under Koresh was a hotbed of sexual immorality; Koresh's followers practised voluntary celibacy. Koresh was stockpiling weapon parts in preparation for an armed conflict with the federal government; Koresh could have been persuaded to surrender if the authorities had paid more attention to the group's millenarian beliefs. What can be known for sure is that the Branch Davidians were a fervently millenarian group, inspired not least by the theology and imagery of the book of Revelation, as interpreted by their leader. Koresh was particularly influenced by the sequence of the seven seals in Revelation 6.1—8.1, and believed, by the time of his death, that the contents of the fifth seal (the beginnings of the final martyrdom of the saints) had begun to be fulfilled.

The tragedy of the Waco episode is a timely reminder of the potency of the Apocalypse to inspire and fire millenarian groups of all kinds, who read the book as a collection of future prophecies relating to their own times. Similar groups can be found at virtually every stage of Christian history, some peaceable but threatened minorities, others prepared to take up arms to hasten their religious destiny. What they have in common is their fervent belief that Revelation is a gift for God's people of the last days, not a historical relic of a bygone age. In short, it is a text about the eschatological future, which threatens at any time to break into the present, and therefore calls for an urgent response on the part of its readers.

Clearly there are passages in this book which speak, at least in part, of events still to come in the future. Our limited knowledge of the Apocalypse interpretation of the earliest centuries (associated with figures such as Papias of Hierapolis, Justin Martyr, Hippolytus of Rome and Irenaeus of Lyons) suggests that they placed particular emphasis upon the future establishment of a thousand-year reign of Christ, understanding Revelation 20 in a literal and this-worldly sense. Even those like Augustine who offered a non-literal interpretation of the 'Millennium', as a metaphor for the period of the Church inaugurated by the first coming of Christ, believed that it had still not come to an end in their own time. The final consummation of the 'new heavens and new earth', and the appearing of the New Jerusalem in whatever form that is to take, are still to be fully realized. But widespread popular readings of this book pose a more specific question: how central is this future aspect to the book as a whole? How far is the whole Apocalypse a work of eschatology, teaching its readers about the End-times? Moreover, where does the twenty-first-century reader stand chronologically in relation to these eschatological events?

The view that John of Patmos was given a vision of future events is one shared by a wide variety of approaches to the Apocalypse, therefore, and not simply the full-blooded 'Futurist' approach of popular millenarianism. Even those who insist on the importance of John's first-century context for understanding his visions do not necessarily deny that he saw some things still to come. Those who interpret the visions as describing the broad sweep of world, or church, history would regard the bulk of the visions as relating to events after the seer's lifetime. An important distinction ought to be made between the perspective of John and the perspective of the reader. Even events which for the contemporary reader belong to ancient history (such as the fall of Babylon/Rome) would still have been in the future for the visionary John, even if he may have glimpsed something of the significance of what was to take place.

But many popular readings of Revelation today do not simply regard John as an astute commentator on the world of his own generation (as does the kind of historical or 'preterist' interpretation common among scholars, and tackled in the previous chapter). Nor do they regard him as a prophet granted insight into the stages of history from his day to the present, a line of interpretation particularly inspired by the twelfth-century Abbot Joachim of Fiore, which flourished in Western Europe during the later Middle Ages. Rather, they view him as gazing far into the distant future, describing events to come to pass many centuries after his own demise, and indeed many of them still unfulfilled in our present day. Given the wide dissemination of this kind of eschatological interpretation, and the popular belief that it is the only way in which this book is to be read, this chapter will pay it particular, though not exclusive, attention.

Plotting the Course of History

Before we turn to this, however, it seems prudent to devote some attention to a somewhat different type of future interpretation of the Apocalypse, which nevertheless helped lay the foundations for the thoroughgoing eschatology of Futurist readings that flood contemporary bookshops, both Christian and secular. This approach regards the book of Revelation as a series of visions which plot the successive stages of the history of the world, or of the Church (and is commonly known as the 'world-historical' or 'church-historical' approach). Emerging out of, and as a reaction to, more spiritualized readings of the Apocalypse in the Augustinian-Tyconian tradition, it takes seriously the claim that this book has something quite profound to say, prophetically speaking, about the unfolding shape of human history, in which the Church of Christ has been granted a key role. It is rooted in the conviction that there is a divine plan for the historical process, not least in its final consummation. On the one hand, it accepts that at least some of John's visions would have had particular relevance for readers of his own day (hence allusions may be detected to imperial Rome in the earlier visions). On the other hand, it recognizes that the Apocalypse is a vision, a gift to John, whose meaning cannot simply be reduced to any sense subsequently made of it by the seer himself (an assumption of the historical-critical or preterist approach).

Revelation is a prophetic text, whose deeper meaning unfolds in parallel with human history, and with the hindsight of later, more privileged interpreters. Interestingly, this historical approach is not confined to any one geographical area. Though it has been particularly associated with Western Christendom of the first half of the second millennium, it also appears, in a somewhat different form, in Apocalypse interpretation of the Ethiopian Orthodox Church. In medieval Ethiopian exegesis, the visions of Revelation have been regarded variously as describing the whole sweep of human history from the beginning (in a similar way to the *Animal Apocalypse* of *1 Enoch*, a text highly influential among Ethiopian Christians), the period between the coming of Christ and the rise of Islam (reflecting the particular political circumstances of that part of the world), the 'times of the Muslims', and the 'three and a half years' of the reign of the false Messiah (Cowley, 1983, 53).

In the more widely known Western tradition, the towering figure is the twelfth-century abbot and mystic Joachim of Fiore (*c.* 1135–1202), recognized as the originator of a new line of Apocalypse exegesis which became increasingly dominant in the Middle Ages and beyond. Though Joachim has received increasing attention, both scholarly and popular, in recent decades as a prophet of the End-time, it is important to note that underlying his whole Apocalypse exegesis is a philosophy of history, derived from his distinctive reading of Scripture as a whole (Reeves, 1999). It is a highly complex reading of history, a combination of different patterns found in Scripture, including a double set of seven periods plotting the course of Old and New Testaments, and three overlapping *status*, attributed to Father, Son and Spirit respectively. This broad perspective is important to hold on to, even though it is true that

Joachim regarded his generation as standing on the threshold of the third *status* of the Holy Spirit, the seeds of which had been sown centuries before by St Benedict.

In his fascination with the scroll with seven seals, for example, Joachim saw Revelation primarily as a unveiling of the broad sweep of human history, even if he did see himself as living at or close to the time of crisis, with signs all around him of the coming of the final Antichrist. Similarly, in his *Book of Figures*, Joachim identified the seven heads of the dragon of Revelation 12 (and the beast of Rev. 13 and 17) with seven major persecutors of God's people throughout history from the incarnation to the present: five of these (Herod, Nero, Constantius, Mohammed, Mesemoth) belonged to the past, one (Saladin, to whom Jerusalem fell in 1187) to Joachim's present, and the seventh, Antichrist, was still to come (McGinn, 1979, 135–41). The resurgence of Islam was for Joachim one of the potent signs that the time of Antichrist was imminent.

Attention to Joachim's interpretation reveals how crucial structural analyses often are to interpretations of the book as a whole. The Abbot of Fiore's division of Revelation into eight parts (1.1—3.22; 4.1—8.1; 8.2—11.18; 11.19—14.20; 15.1—16.17; 16.18—19.21; 20.1–10; 20.11—22.21) corresponds to seven periods of church history (the eighth symbolizing eternity); so also do the individual series of seven (letters, seals, trumpets, bowls), in a pattern of recapitulation reminiscent of Victorinus. Particular attention is devoted in Joachim's interpretation, and in exegesis dependent upon him, to the sixth period in each septet, the penultimate period, generally identified as the commentator's own day, the period of Antichrist which precedes the final consummation of history. Our literary analysis of the text in Chapter 3 above also highlights the key role of the penultimate sixth in the various cycles of the book.

Joachim's interpretation dominated medieval and early Reformation approaches to the Apocalypse, inspiring writers as diverse as Peter Olivi, Dante, Savonarola, the early Jesuits and the Reformer John Knox. He inspired no less artists such as Sandro Botticelli, who appended this inscription to his famous *Mystic Nativity*:

> I Sandro painted this picture at the end of the year 1500 in the troubles of Italy in the half time after the time according to the xith chapter of St John in the second woe of the Apocalypse in the loosing of the devil for three and a half years. Then he will be chained in the xiith chapter and we shall see him trodden down as in this picture.
>
> (Reeves, 1999, 93)

Joachim's insight into the Apocalypse was attractive not least because it enabled the book to speak in particularly acute ways to the contemporary reader, while not completely losing touch with the historical context of its original composition. Thus Joachim could identify at least two of the heads with historical figures – Herod and Nero – who had already died by the time John wrote, while shifting the focus of the later visions to his own age and his immediate future. In particular, the Joachite division of history into seven successive ages – with the fifth period marked by the decline of the Church prior to the appearance of Antichrist and subsequent renewal in the sixth period – enabled the use of the Apocalypse to challenge and critique the contemporary Church and individual church leaders. Though John of Patmos could speak harsh words of judgement against several of the churches of Asia, his vision offered an even greater challenge to the dominant ideology of first-century imperial Rome. But in the centuries following the reign of Constantine, the situation had altered radically. The Church of Christ, far from being a threatened minority, had taken the place of the Empire as the dominant ideology. How could the Apocalypse continue to speak in such a situation of role reversal? Joachite exegesis provided the key, as followers of Joachim went far beyond their master in their condemnation of the 'carnal church' of the fifth period, including the papacy. This novelty can be found in the writings of the Franciscan Spirituals such as Peter Olivi (d. 1298), who saw St Francis as angelic herald of the expected renewal in the sixth period (Burr, 1993). Ultimately it would be used, with increasing anti-Catholic abandon, by the Protestant Reformers, who illustrated their woodcuts of Revelation with harlots and beasts wearing the papal triple tiara.

Herein, of course, lies the danger of such interpretations. Just as the progress of history, and the place of the little Church of Christ within it, required a fresh reading of the challenge of John's book in the late Middle Ages and Renaissance, so too subsequent developments within both Church and State rendered even these new interpretations inappropriate. A Spanish Jesuit counterblast to the increasingly anti-papal readings of the Reformers largely spawned the Futurist approach, which undercut the Protestant polemic by claiming that the bulk of John's visions, including those supposedly referring to contemporary popes, in fact still remained to be fulfilled in the future. This approach is particularly associated with Francisco Ribeira (1537–91), confessor to and biographer of Teresa of Avila, and was taken up by Robert Bellarmine and the Dominican Thomas Malvenda. Ironically, at least over the past two centuries, this Futurist approach has been more commonly associated with Protestant exegesis, and coupled with the very anti-papal interpretation that it was designed to refute. It is to this different kind of 'looking into the future' that we shall now turn.

A Guidebook to the Last Days

Anyone familiar with the political rhetoric of the religious Right in the United States in recent decades, particularly in the final stages of the cold war, will be under no illusion as to its profound indebtedness to the Judaeo-

Christian apocalyptic tradition, and the book of Revelation specifically. Ronald Reagan's description of the Soviet Union as the 'evil empire' was a clear allusion to the last of Daniel's four beasts (Dan. 7), which underwent historical transformation in Revelation's beast from the sea (Rev. 13). The centrality of the name of Armageddon as a description of the great cosmic battle of the End likewise reveals the pervasive influence of John's Revelation for the politico-religious tradition within which Reagan and many of his administration stood (Rev. 16.16). This apocalyptic mindset and its accompanying mode of discourse reflects a pervasive tradition within one politically powerful strand of American Protestantism, which views the Apocalypse as the interpretative key to events on the contemporary global stage, and is prepared to put its votes, and its money, where its religious convictions are.

Perhaps the most well-known version of this interpretative approach, popular among the Christian masses in the USA especially, is a premillennial interpretation known as Dispensationalism.[1] This is generally attributed to John Nelson Darby (1800–82), a Church of Ireland priest who subsequently became a prominent leader of the Plymouth Brethren, though it was popularized in the Scofield Reference Bible, an edition of the King James Bible with annotations by C. I. Scofield, first published in 1909. This line of interpretation regards the book as largely a series of prophecies yet to be fulfilled from the modern reader's own temporal perspective. In a manner reminiscent of the Joachite tradition, history is to be divided into seven dispensations or epochs from the time of Noah onwards, leading up to the ultimate eschatological events at the end of the seventh epoch, the Millennium. Hence, one should distinguish carefully between biblical prophecies made to Israel and those to the Church. On the one hand, therefore, Dispensationalism has little place for the 'replacement theology' of the mainstream churches which has often been used to disastrous effect in Christian dealings with the Jewish people. On the other hand, the establishment of the modern state of Israel in 1948, and other events in the Middle East, have come to be regarded by modern Dispensationalists as the clear fulfilment of biblical prophecy to the chosen people of the First Covenant.

Both Darby and Scofield believed that the Bible offered a clear and systematic pattern of these events: biblical passages (notably from Revelation and its predecessors Ezekiel and Daniel), combined in a certain way and mutually interpreting each other, will make this clear. Through Scofield, this pattern has come to be widely accepted by several generations of careful Christian readers. Typical of this is the treatment of the so-called 'Rapture', a promised taking up of believers to 'meet the Lord in the air', which is not explicitly mentioned in Revelation, but is found at 1 Thessalonians 4.17. Most commentators would regard this passage as dealing with the fate of those still alive at the general resurrection of the dead on the Last Day (though they would disagree among themselves as to how literally this language of meeting Christ 'in the clouds' is to be taken). Moreover, most would probably accept that 1 Thessalonians represents but one stage, and an early stage at that, in the development of Paul's eschatological teaching as he attempted to grapple with the unexpected deaths of Thessalonian Christians prior to the return of the Lord. For Darby, however, the 'Rapture' describes an event prior to the final resurrection, to be followed by the final week (seven-year period) of tribulation described in Daniel 9, which in his Dispensationalist scheme will itself precede the Millennium of Revelation 20. He saw an allusion to this at Revelation 3.10, 'I will keep you from the hour of trial that is coming on the whole world.'

The Rapture, understood in a highly literalist way, exercises a centrality in Dispensationalist belief far beyond its actual importance in the biblical writings as a whole. Indeed, it is not restricted to Dispensationalist Christians, though other premillennialists locate the Rapture chronologically at a later stage, whether halfway through the final seven-year tribulation period, just before Armageddon or immediately prior to the Second Coming. Popular American commentaries often provide vivid visual warnings of the need to be prepared for this event, with pictures of apparently clean-living middle-class suburban families, mother 'raptured' into the clouds while hanging out the washing, little boy taken up while riding his tricycle in the garden, father left behind with the lawnmower to face the impending doom. What is distinctive about Dispensationalism is the claim that this Rapture will preserve the Christian elect from participation in the tribulation to come: they will be 'raptured' out of this evil and hopeless world before any of this begins.

Given the influence of the Scofield Reference Bible, some attention to the features of its exegesis of Revelation is called for. As for Joachim, so for Scofield the key lies in the structure of the book as a whole, and Revelation 1.19 is the crucial verse in this regard. The Greek of 1.19 suggests that it ought to be translated along the following lines: 'Write what you see,[2] namely the things that are now and the things which are to happen after this.' The visions in the book, therefore, describe both present reality and future event (and there is no clear indication that we should expect a neat division between the two). Scofield, however, interprets these words in a threefold rather than twofold sense, arguing that such a division of the book is crucial 'if the interpretation is to be sane and coherent' (Scofield, 1330):

1 the past, 'the things you have seen', i.e. the Patmos vision of 1.1–20;
2 the present, 'the things which are now', i.e. the letters to the churches (Rev. 2—3), who have taken the place of the Jews in the present, given the fall of Jerusalem in 70 (Scofield follows Irenaeus in dating Revelation to 96 CE);
3 the future, 'the things which are to happen after this', i.e. the remaining visions of the rest of the book (Rev. 4—22).

This third section (dealing with future events, at least from John's perspective) is therefore the most substantial, and has received the greatest attention in attempts to understand the meaning of this book. For Scofield and others in his tradition of interpretation, the events it describes are not simply future from the point of view of John and first-century Christians: they are largely future also for the contemporary reader. There is a certain irony here, given the generally anti-papal and anti-Catholic tinges of Dispensationalist interpretation, in that the father of modern Futurist readings of the Apocalypse is generally thought to be the sixteenth-century Spanish Jesuit Ribeira, reacting as he was to the equally anti-papal church-historical readings of his own day.

But how are these visions of the future to be interpreted? The answer is to be found in Scripture as a whole, albeit Scripture read within a particular framework. Careful study, it is claimed, will reveal greater precision as to the relationship of these End-time events to one another and to similar events described in other biblical writings, chief among them Daniel's description of the 'seventieth week' of years, marking the end of the desolations of Jerusalem (Dan. 9.24–27). Gabriel's revelation to Daniel speaks of the desolation to be expected in the latter half of this last 'week' (three and a half years) prior to the messianic kingdom, almost certainly referring to the contemporary defilement of the city of Jerusalem by Antiochus Epiphanes in the second century BCE. For Scofield, this 'time, times and half a time' (or thirty-six months, or one thousand two hundred and sixty days, cf. Dan. 7.25; Rev. 11.2–3; 12.6, 14) is to be correlated with the 'Great Tribulation' referred to at Revelation 7.14, understood as still in the future. Dispensationalist writings provide often detailed diagrams outlining the various stages of this and subsequent events (such as the battle of Armageddon, the Millennium and the second resurrection), and how the Pauline 'rapture', the 'man of lawlessness' (2 Thess. 2.3) and the Johannine 'Antichrist' (1 John 4.3; 2 John 7) fit into the overarching scheme.

Revelation's third section, describing events 'which are to happen hereafter' is itself to be subdivided according to the widely recognized pattern of sevens, describing in chronological order various stages associated with eschatological events. Scofield's notes identify six sets of seven within these chapters which, together with the letters to the churches, make seven septets.

Like other commentators, however, whatever approach they take to the book as a whole, Scofield has also recognized that there are substantial sections which seem to interrupt the flow of the narrative, such as the sealing of the 144,000 and the vision of the great multitude in Revelation 7. These he calls 'parenthetical passages', in that they are inserted into the text to provide interludes in which to take stock. In Scofield's own words: 'These passages do not advance the prophetic narrative. Looking backward and forward they sum up results accomplished, and speak of results yet to come as if they had already come' (Scofield, 1330). He identifies five such parenthetical passages (7.1–17; 10.1—11.14; 14.1–13; 16.13–16; 19.1–6). What he fails to explain is how such Janus-like interruptions can be reconciled with the claim that Revelation presents a coherent chronological timetable from beginning to end. That is an objection to which we shall return.

Two aspects of this Dispensationalist interpretation are particularly worthy of note. First, like Joachite interpreters of previous centuries, Scofield identified two evil eschatological figures or powers, one religious, the other political. Whether such a neat division between political authority and cultic activity would have been intelligible to the ancients is disputed. Nevertheless, these two aspects can be seen together in Revelation 13, in the imperial beast from the sea and the beast from the earth who orchestrates the worship of the former, and in Revelation 17, where the goddess Roma sits astride the political beast in the guise of a Roman prostitute, Babylon. In continuity with a long exegetical tradition, Scofield saw these as historical figures or movements of the penultimate dispensation, heralding the Great Tribulation and the final consummation of all things. Subsequent Dispensationalists have paid careful attention to developments in the religious and politico-economic spheres in order to identify the present or impending activity of these figures. Hence, from a religious perspective, they have tended to dismiss the Ecumenical Movement as a syncretistic endeavour inspired by the Antichrist. Similarly, they have attempted to locate prophetic fulfilment of these visions in developments in the political realm. The proposed establishment of the European Community in the early 1970s by the six member states of the existing EEC, plus Britain, Ireland, Denmark and Norway, seemed to many such observers an indisputable sign of the arrival of the ten-horned beast (Rev. 13.1; 17.3), until the machinations of the beast were foiled by a 'No' vote in the Norwegian referendum!

A second distinctive and immensely influential aspect of Scofield's reading, as for Darby before him, was the role given to the Jewish people in the divine plan (a role heightened by reading Revelation in the light of Paul's discussion of Israel in Rom. 9—11). The woman clothed with the sun is regarded as the personification of the nation of Israel, side-stepping the centuries-old ecclesiological and mariological interpretations of this vision. Similarly, the 144,000 sealed in Revelation 7 are not the Church, or Christian martyrs, or specifically Jewish Christians, but non-Christian Jews of the End-time, who 'will have returned to Palestine in unbelief', a remnant of whom will eventually be saved. Disciples of Scofield since 1948 have viewed the establishment of the state of Israel as evidence for the fulfilment of biblical prophecy in our own day, and a sign that the bulk of what this book foresees is only now coming to fruition. Such an approach has potential for good, in that it runs counter to the sad history of anti-Semitic readings of Revelation and other New Testament texts throughout the Christian centuries. In practice, however, it has generally resulted in a naively uncritical attitude towards political Zionism. Moreover, given the size of the Christian Dispensationalist vote in the USA, it has exercised a powerful influence upon US foreign policy in the Middle East, which has spelt disaster for the rights and aspirations of the Palestinian people, Christian no less than Muslim. It is one of the ironies of history that a book which speaks from the perspective of the exiled and vulnerable has so readily been used by the powerful for contrary purposes.

Futurist Insights

What is the contemporary reader to make of such Futurist interpretations of the Apocalypse? Certainly the impact of Dispensationalism on the politics of the Middle East raises profound questions about the ethical status of some of its readings. But a Futurist interpretation (even a Dispensationalist one) is not necessarily tied to an uncritical stance vis-à-vis Zionism and the government of the state of Israel. A careful assessment of this overall approach to Revelation is called for. This brings with it a word of warning. Those who would regard themselves as 'mainstream Christians' should beware of too readily dismissing the eschatological concerns of this approach as the misguided ramblings of biblical fundamentalists.

First of all, there are indications that they have a good deal in common with the interpretations found in early Christian writers such as Justin and Papias, who believed firmly that Christ would soon return to inaugurate a millennial reign centred on the city of Jerusalem. Revelation itself is full of warnings to stay awake, to be watchful, to repent in the light of the imminent coming of Christ. It is an urgent text, which calls for an urgent response. Moreover, its concern for the imminent end has much in common with the bulk of New Testament Christianity, which not only had a decidedly eschatological bent, but made sense of what had happened after Christ's death, and the expected fulfilment of his promises, in terms drawn from Jewish apocalyptic. There is a sense in which such readings appear more in tune with the New Testament writers than the findings of the American Jesus Seminar, with its decidedly non-eschatological Jesus, drawn largely from a hypothetical earlier layer of a hypothetical sayings source ('Q') rather than the canonical Gospels. It is understandable that the scholars of the Jesus Seminar have reacted sharply to the extreme, otherworldly eschatology of Dispensationalist Christians and their influence on the North American religious and political scene. What is much less clear is whether they have uncovered a 'Jesus' more at home in the world of Second Temple Palestinian Judaism than the late twentieth- or early twenty-first-century United States. Can a Jesus who emerged on the stage of history as a disciple of the thoroughly eschatological John the Baptist, and whose followers subsequently proclaimed his imminent return from heaven to bring in the Kingdom in its fullness, be divested of all End-time clothing, except by a case of special pleading? The eschatological urgency of Futurism may in some ways be far closer to the source.

Second, Futuristic readings also take more seriously than many the claim that Revelation is a prophetic book. For all its merits in highlighting the essential strangeness of the Apocalypse, and showing something of the book's impact on the stage of first-century history, the historical-critical approach of most contemporary scholars often fails to bridge the huge gulf between the first-century context of the seven churches and the very different contexts of contemporary readers. Its reading of the book frequently has little to say to the modern world, concerned as it is to locate the book within first-century proconsular Asia. Futurists refuse to leave Revelation there: many, indeed, would say that it has nothing at all to say about the historical setting of its author and first hearers, though progressive Dispensationalists at least do not ignore the first-century background (Pate, 1998, 135–75). But whatever allusions to John's own day may be detected, the main emphasis of Futurist interpreters is upon John's insight into history yet to unfold. In such a view, the Apocalypse was written not primarily for John's own contemporaries, but for generations yet to come, in the distant future. It is not a book whose meaning is immediately obvious, or exhausted by events and personages of the late first century, but one whose meaning unfolds gradually in parallel with the unfolding historical process.

Third, Futurist readings, with their emphasis upon the contemporary challenge to the present world order, and even to those within the Christian churches, take seriously the presence of evil in the universe and the necessity of divine judgement and human repentance. A theology which side-steps such issues, or dismisses them in Marcionite fashion as belonging to the 'religion of the Old Testament', appears hopelessly naive in the face of the numerous genocides and human capacity for mass destruction which have marred the twentieth century, and indeed political totalitarianism and economic exploitation in any age. Our reading of the Apocalypse as a whole in Chapters 3 and 4 has suggested that its literary strategy was to challenge as much as to comfort, to protest against the dominant ideology where that had succumbed to blasphemous and idolatrous arrogance. Whatever else it should do, the Apocalypse should shock and unnerve contemporary readers no less than their ancient counterparts. Futurist readings certainly have the potential to do that.

Cut Loose from the Source?

Yet Futurist readings are not without their shortcomings, even dangers. While they may avoid some of the pitfalls of preterist or historical-critical interpreters in allowing the text to speak to succeeding generations, they can easily succumb to another, the tendency to cut the book loose completely from its first-century source. If (as Dispensationalists claim) the book is almost exclusively concerned with the last stages of human history rather than the dilemmas confronted by Christians within the Roman world, then it would have had little interest to the fledgling Christian communities of first-century Asia, whether in Ephesus, Smyrna, Pergamum, Thyatira, Sardis, Philadelphia or Laodicea. Historical approaches at least provide some parameters within which interpretation can take place. Cut off from these historical parameters, there are few criteria against which to assess competing Futurist claims as to what the book actually intends. How can one decide whether the events of the last decade are any closer to the eschatological visions of the book than the events of 1914 (a crucial date for Jehovah's Witnesses), or of the French Revolution, or what may be the case in fifty years from now? How can one be sure that one's identification of Babylon the Great, or 'Jezebel' of the Thyatiran church, is not hopelessly misguided and simply confirming one's own prejudices? The imagery of John's visions of judgement – wars, earthquakes, stars falling to earth, plagues of locusts etc. – are drawn from a very ancient well of tradition, such that drawing precise correspondences between them and events of our own time, if such is required, is highly precarious.

Moreover, the definition of biblical prophecy with which Futurist interpreters often work is open to some criticism. Dispensationalists generally use the term 'prophecy' to mean telling the future, often the distant eschatological future, with no place allowed for what biblical scholars call *vaticinium ex eventu*, and little for the seer's present or immediate future. Thus, for example, Isaiah's prophecy of a young woman bearing a son has nothing in his mind to do with the birth of the future king Hezekiah, and everything to do with the birth of Jesus of Nazareth some seven hundred years later. Yet biblical scholarship has long argued that prophets – both Israelite and early Christian – should be regarded less as clairvoyants than as those who spoke of God's imminent intervention to their contemporaries, whether that meant salvation or judgement. They are, in other words, primarily *forthtellers* rather than *foretellers*. That is not to say that prophets could not on occasion foretell future events (e.g. Mal. 4.5–6; Acts 11.28), but that is not their main function. Thus there is something suspect about a line of interpretation which claims that the prophetic John had little specific to say to his own contemporaries about their situation, and much to say to an unknown people in centuries yet to come. This is all the more surprising given that Revelation explicitly forbids the sealing up of its message, claiming that the time is at hand (22.10).

Linear Chronology or Recapitulation?

A further question mark against the Futurist, particularly Dispensationalist, approach is related to the chronological framework it presupposes. On the one hand, the timetable of eschatological events with which it works is arguably imposed upon the book from outside, rather than being derived from Revelation itself. On the other, the tendency to see the visions from chapter 4 onwards as describing events of the End presupposes a sequential development throughout the book, rather than the schema of recapitulation (that is, describing the same events in different ways and with ever-increasing intensity).

We have already noted the parallels between the various septets of visions in the Apocalypse of John, especially the seals, trumpets and bowls. Dispensationalist and some other Futurist readings must find a linear chronology running throughout these visions, given that they regard everything from chapter 4 onwards as a prediction of 'the things which are to happen after this'. On an initial reading, such a linear progression seems to be justified: the distinction between 'a third' being destroyed in the trumpets sequence and the more universal judgement in the sequence of bowls implies that the former plagues are chronologically antecedent to the latter. But further readings may lead one to conclude that things are not so simple.

First, there is a considerable amount of overlap between the consequences of the various seals, trumpets and bowls, which causes difficulty if they are taken as literal descriptions of a sequence of events. The opening of the sixth seal, for example, issues in the virtual collapse of the cosmos: sun becoming black as sackcloth, moon turning to blood, the stars falling to earth, heaven being rolled up like a scroll and 'every mountain and island' being removed from their places (6.12–17). Yet stars manage to fall again at the sounding of the third and fifth trumpets (8.10; 9.1), a third of the sun is darkened again at the fourth trumpet, along with the moon and stars (8.12; cf. 9.2; 16.10), and the islands and mountains reappear in time to be dispersed by the pouring out of the seventh bowl (16.20). Likewise, the sea turns to blood twice (a third at 8.9; all of it at 16.3), the great city suffers from an earthquake on two occasions (a tenth falls at 11.13; the city is divided in three at 16.19), and its destruction is either announced, or described, at 14.8, 16.19, and more extensively in chapters 17—18. A more satisfactory explanation may well be that John presents, in three different ways, the same spiral of human history into degeneracy, and the resulting divine judgement. This is a reading noted as early as the third century by Victorinus of Pettau in what is the earliest surviving Latin commentary on the book. The sequences of seals, trumpets and bowls are not describing different chronological stages in the eschatological process, but one and the same process of judgement and vindication. The increasingly dramatic employment of apocalyptic imagery may well be a literary strategy designed to lead people to repentance, a theme already dominant in the letters to the seven churches (note how the refusal of humanity to repent is highlighted in all three sequences: 6.16–17; 9.20–21; 16.9, 11, 21).

Second, 'historical' allusions to the biblical story, and to the story of Jesus Christ, also confound attempts to detect a linear progression throughout the book. The vision of the woman and the dragon in Revelation 12, after the judgement sequences of seals and trumpets, contains allusions to events which from John's perspective are clearly past. The birth of the woman's male child and his being 'snatched up' to God refer to the birth of Jesus of Nazareth, and his exaltation after death. There may also be allusions in this chapter to the struggle between Eve and the serpent in the garden of Eden, or the mythological fall of the Watchers in primeval times. It is perhaps significant that the Scofield Reference Bible is virtually lacking in interpretative notes on Revelation 12. Similarly, the vision of the Lamb that was slain (5.6), and the reference to the treading of the winepress outside the city (14.20; cf. 19.13–15; Heb. 13.12), look back to the historical death of Christ outside Jerusalem. The polyvalent vision of the two witnesses (Rev. 11.3ff.) contains some echoes of the stories of Moses and Elijah, or Elijah and Enoch, as well as possible allusions to the Neronian martyrdoms of the early 60s. Other visions blur the distinctions between past, present and future still further. John's initial glimpse of the heavenly throne-room, for example, contains a curious mixture of aorist, imperfect, present and future tenses, giving the impression that he has laid aside our own earthly time and entered into God's time. The greater attention to detail, and to the broad sweep of the apocalyptic drama, the more difficult it is to plot the kind of neat chronology which Futurist readings demand.

This is no less the case for that section of the book which even preterists and world-historical interpreters would acknowledge to be concerned with events of the last days, Revelation 19—22. The Dispensationalist reading understands the final sequence of events to begin with the appearance of the rider on the white horse (19.11–16), interpreted as the Parousia or Second Coming of Christ. There then follows (according to Scofield's notes): the destruction of the beast, his armies and the false prophet; the judgement of the nations; the thousand-year reign of Christ or 'kingdom-age'; the release of Satan and his end; the second resurrection and final judgement; the purging of the earth by fire in preparation for the new heavens and new earth. Into this sequence must also be fitted the 'Rapture' of 1 Thessalonians 4.17, at some point prior to the Millennium or 'kingdom-age' (as the premillenarian view dictates).

But there are difficulties with this. First, as Jack McKelvey has shown, there are reasons for questioning whether the appearance of the rider on the white horse refers to the Parousia (McKelvey, 1999, 77–80). Features of undisputed New Testament Parousia texts (e.g. Matt. 24.30–31; Luke 21.27; 1 Thess. 4.16–17), such as the coming on clouds, accompanying angels, and the gathering of the elect are lacking here. His elect are already with him, clothed in white robes, as he comes, and the focus is upon the battle of truth over falsehood which, as we have already been told, was won on the cross and replayed again and again by his faithful witnesses upon earth (Rev. 12.11).

But even if we accept this vision as a distinctly Johannine description of Christ's final coming, other difficulties remain. The apparent repetition within these chapters has led commentators to advocate the combination of different sources here, or to detect the hand of a rather clumsy redactor who has destroyed an originally clear chronology. There would seem to be two accounts of the final judgement (20.4–6; 20.11–15), and two battles (19.17–21; 20.7–9). There is nothing to suggest that the dead at the second judgement exclude the martyrs of Christ, yet they have already been raised, and judged worthy, at the first assize. The armies of the nations are destroyed at 19.21, only to reappear at 20.8–9. Likewise, John has two visions of the New Jerusalem, one as a bride (21.1–2), the other as a great city (21.9—22.5). An alternative to the source-critical and reordering solutions would be to accept the fluidity of visionary experience: John describes here what he saw, visions which confronted him with different aspects of the ultimate victory of Christ, but in such a way as to evade strict chronological sequence.

This difficulty with finding sequence and structure in the final visions of Revelation is confirmed by Scofield's analysis of chapters 21—22, which he calls the 'seven new things'. This seems somewhat arbitrary, not least because not all these seven have the adjective 'new' (καινός) attached to them. The word in fact only appears four times in Revelation 21, to describe heaven, earth, the holy city and God making 'all things new' (21.1, 2, 5; cf. 3.12). Moreover, the word has already been used on several occasions in earlier sections of the book. One could equally speak of the 'new name' which Christians bear (2.17; 3.12), and the 'new song' sung by the four living creatures and twenty-four elders (5.9), and later by the 144,000 on Mount Zion (14.3). If the song and the name are related to the new age (as the promises to the victors in Pergamum and Philadelphia suggest), then not only do they disrupt any neat chronology one might have hoped for in this book, they also either increase Scofield's list of last 'new things' to nine, or (if one pays attention to the actual use of the word 'new') reduce it to six. Moreover, the double phrase 'new heaven and new earth' (21.1) seems to describe one event of renewal, not two. The septet, and therefore the chronological progression, is not quite as obvious as Scofield claims.

It is in these final visions that one major criticism of the Dispensationalist view comes particularly to the fore. As Scofield's notes on Revelation's final visions reveal, it is derived from a piecing together of a variety of biblical passages, to create a supposedly 'biblical' eschatological framework which is not always quite so obvious to other readers of the Bible. An important role is given to certain passages from Daniel, a book which certainly seems to have been an important source for the seer of Patmos, though the so-called 'Rapture' passage from 1 Thessalonians and the so-called 'Little Apocalypse' of Mark 13 and parallels are also crucial. Moreover, these passages, and the schema derived from them, are understood as referring only to events of the eschatological future. Yet scholarship has wanted to argue that the visions of Daniel address the dire situation of Jews in Palestine during the reign of Antiochus IV Epiphanes in the second century BCE, and that the words of Jesus regarding future cataclysm were regarded by at least some of the evangelists as finding partial fulfilment during the first Jewish Revolt against Rome (e.g. Luke 21).

Let us take as an example Revelation's use of Daniel. It is certainly the case that the latter's eschatological timescale has influenced the former: hence, the 'time, times and half a time' of Daniel 7.25 and 12.7 has influenced Revelation's expectation of a time of hostility lasting 1,260 days, or forty-two months (11.2–3; 12.6; 13.5; cf. 12.14). In the light of Daniel 9, this is to be interpreted as half of the last, seventieth week of the 490 years of the desolation of Jerusalem (according to Daniel's interpretation of the prophecy of Jer. 25.12): i.e. three and a half years of particular trauma prior to the restoration of the holy city. Yet there appears to be a different focus in the Apocalypse. Daniel clearly has historical Jerusalem in mind (and, in the eyes of most commentators, its specific restoration by Judas Maccabeus after the onslaughts of Antiochus Epiphanes). John, however, seems to envisage a wider, ecclesiological context. The woman, the heavenly counterpart of God's people, is taken into the wilderness for 'a time, times, and half a time' (12.14). The prophetic witness of the Church described in Revelation 11 will last for the same period of forty-two months as the 'times of the Gentiles'. The beast's power to wage war with the saints is also granted only for this limited period (13.5–7). In other words, earlier traditions and language have taken on new shapes in John's visions, enabling him to understand the role of the followers of Christ in what is yet to come. That this expected hostility is not related to some unspecified distant future, but involves in a particular way his own generation, is implied by Revelation 1.1: for John the mysteries revealed are to happen not simply in the last days, but 'soon' (ἐν τάχει).[3] One cannot simply interpret Revelation in the light of Daniel and its chronological framework, while ignoring the particular interests and circumstances of each.

What of those other planks of the Dispensationalist chronology, the Rapture and the Millennium? Criticisms may be made of both. First, there is no clear reference to the 'rapturing' of Christians in the Apocalypse, and thus it strikes many commentators as an alien concept imposed upon the book from outside. Indeed, the only figure who can be said to be 'raptured' (from the verb ἁρπάζειν) is Christ, the male child who is 'snatched up' or 'raptured' to God and to his throne at 12.5. This, however, is almost certainly a reference to Christ's exaltation to the Father's right hand following his historical death on the cross. Nor is it evident that even the famous Rapture passage of 1 Thessalonians 4.17 belongs chronologically to its Dispensationalist location. Most commentators would regard the text as referring to the resurrection of the dead rather than to a separate eschatological event prior to it: the context, after all, is the fate of Christian Thessalonians who have unexpectedly died prior to the return of the Lord. Paul reassures the community that their loved ones will not be at a disadvantage when it comes to participation in the Kingdom. The dead in Christ will rise *first*, and *only then* will those who remain alive be caught up with Christ 'in the air'. Even a literal reading of this passage makes it difficult to locate the Rapture where Dispensationalists often wish to do so.

Second, the Dispensationalist chronological schema also devotes a disproportionate amount of attention to the 'Millennium'. This 'thousand-year reign' in fact takes up only three verses in the 404 verses of the whole book. Moreover, we have found good reason elsewhere to take the numbers in this book as symbolic rather than literal. To insist upon an over-literal interpretation of this theme may actually be to miss something of its potency as a symbol of Christ's royal rule, shared with his own people, and related in some way to the binding of Satan which, according to the Gospels, began already during his earthly ministry (cf. Mark 3.27).

One final question mark remains over this chronological framework. How far does it produce a reading out of conformity with the New Testament as a whole (and indeed, ironically, with the overall outlook of the Apocalypse itself)? Dispensationalism has frequently advocated a Christian flight from this world, and its doctrine of the Rapture in particular has taught its advocates to expect exemption from the Great Tribulation to befall humanity. There is little here of the Christian passion for justice, the challenge to enter into the political struggle in order to facilitate change in God's world. One searches in vain for the profound involvement with the poor, oppressed and suffering which typified the ministry not only of Jesus but of countless of his disciples in every succeeding generation. Yet such a stance, one might reasonably protest, is far from alien to the challenge of Revelation. From the messages to the seven churches onwards, the theme of faithful witness, even to the point of death, has been a constant one. Far from being urged to flee from this wicked world, or to expect some miraculous rapture from its tribulations, Christ's people are prepared for a prophetic ministry within it, and a bloody one at that (e.g. Rev. 2.10; 11.7–9; 12.11). The overall theme is not one of removal from suffering, but rather victory through it. It is this which has shaped its distinctive Christology of the slain Lamb, who died but now lives for ever and ever, who has conquered the dragon by confronting the powers and being slain in the process. Equally it is this which has shaped the book's distinctive demands of discipleship. Followers of Jesus receive not the reassurance of exemption from military service, but a place in the front line of battle, as they are described in terms derived from the Jewish Holy War tradition (e.g. Rev. 14.1-5). Can any reading which overlooks such overarching themes claim to be in continuity with the prophetic message of John of Patmos?

The Precarious Nature of Decoding

A final issue raised by Futurist readings (though one not unknown in preterist readings also) is the legitimacy of decoding particular aspects of the visions. Is the imagery sufficiently precise as to allow for one-to-one correspondences which exhaust the meaning of specific visionary passages? This is particularly the case with Futurist readings, given that they cannot be tested against what is known of John's first-century context. The student of ecclesiastical and secular history might well conclude that both interpretations in the tradition of Joachim, and the more recent Dispensationalist approach, have been rendered obsolete by non-fulfilment. These diverse 'future' readings of John's Apocalypse, with their almost perverse tendency to use the book, and other biblical prophetic writings, to plot the chronology of the End, have resulted in a history of embarrassing miscalculations.

The Montanists famously expected the New Jerusalem to descend on the city of Pepuza in Phrygia, at some point in the second century, but to no avail. In fifteenth-century Bohemia, a group known as the Taborites believed that the Lord would return between 10 and 14 February 1420, and made extensive preparations to escape the conflagration which would accompany it. Far from community disillusion when 14 February came and went, the story began to circulate that Christ had in fact returned, but secretly. Attempts to calculate the timing of the End are no less associated with interpreters of more recent centuries who have regarded the Apocalypse as concerned almost exclusively with the future climax of history, and themselves as standing upon its threshold. William Miller (1782–1849), the man regarded as the forefather of the Seventh-day Adventists, calculated the date of the Second Coming to the period between 21 March 1843 and 21 March 1844, only to be devastated by its non-arrival. This did not prevent one of his followers, Samuel Snow, offering an alternative date of 22 October in that year. A similar ability to cope with miscalculations of the End is to be found among Jehovah's Witnesses. Their founder, Charles Russell, taught that Christ would return to establish his thousand-year reign in 1914, and Witnesses were consequently encouraged by the outbreak of the Great War, as one of the expected signs of the End. The year 1914 came and went, however, without the anticipated appearance of Christ, leading Russell's successor to offer a new dating of 1926. Even more recently than this, some groups in the United States were spurred into anticipation of the End by the calculations of another Middle East watcher, Edgar C. Whisenant. Working forwards from the establishment of the state of Israel in 1948, he announced that battle would be engaged at Armageddon on 5 October 1995, to be followed on 23 December by the inauguration of the Millennium. Yet again, disappointment ensued, at least temporarily, but recovered in time for the widespread Millennium fever which accompanied the dawn of the year 2000 (and, for those who more accurately calculated the beginning of the twenty-first century, the year 2001).

This obsession with timetables of the End is surprising for its tenacity, not only despite this long history of miscalculation, but even more so given the gospel warning of Jesus that no one knows the day or hour, not even the Son (Mark 13.32 and parallels). In fairness, not all Dispensationalists by any means attempt to calculate the hour, day, or even the year, though they do have a more general interest in the sequence of eschatological events and their duration.

A similar kind of objection could be made to the attempt to relate specific aspects of Revelation's visions to historical and political events in the contemporary world, often driven by the conviction that the commentator is living on the verge of the crucial End-time events. Typical of this procedure is Hal Lindsey, who in his hugely popular *The Late Great Planet Earth* (Lindsey, 1970) and a series of other publications, interpreted visions from the book as detailed predictions of twentieth-century upheavals, from the cold war in Europe to events in the Middle East, from the emergence of the European Community to the looming military threat from the People's Republic of China (the 200 million cavalry of 9.16). Less than thirty years later, Lindsey's decoding of the book appears hopelessly dated, as old enemies have fallen and new interpretative possibilities have arisen. Why should Lindsey's identifications be any more reliable than those made by interpreters in the eleventh or sixteenth centuries?

A similar example is the continual obsession with the number of the beast, 666. Attempts to identify the referent of this number are almost as numerous as the interpreters themselves. We have already seen how many contemporary commentators see here an identification with the Emperor Nero (an identification also implied in the variant reading of 616, known already to Irenaeus). Irenaeus himself, keen to play down attempts to identify Antichrist with particular figures of the past, prefers a more general interpretation, which nevertheless recognizes Revelation's critique of the empire of Rome. His suggestions are three: ΕΥΑΝΘΑΣ, ΛΑΤΕΙΝΟΣ (Latin), and ΤΕΙΤΑΝ (Titan), his preference being for the last. But commentators throughout history have regularly moved beyond imperial Rome, or one of its emperors, in their quest for the name of the beast. In the medieval struggle between Pope Innocent IV (1243–54) and the Emperor Frederick II, for example, a propagandist of the latter calculated that the number of the name INNOCENTIUS PAPA was 666. Papal supporters were equally clear from their apocalyptic readings that Frederick was the beast from the sea of Revelation 13! Similar claims were made for Pope Benedict XI (1303–4), whose name in Greek, βενεδικτος, also contains the requisite number (2 + 5 + 50 + 5 + 4 + 10 + 20 + 300 + 70 + 200).

The papal office, indeed, has frequently been connected with the number of the beast, under its title *Vicarius Filii Dei*. Beatus of Liébana, whose Apocalypse commentary was immensely influential in the West during the Middle Ages, reasoned that 666 in Roman numerals (DCLXVI) was an anagram for DICLUX, one of the titles of Antichrist. Other candidates for the name of the beast have been Julian the Apostate, Napoleon, Patriarch Nikon of Moscow (by the Russian Old Believers), Margaret Thatcher and Saddam Hussein, ruler of the historical successor to Babylon. Some, like Adolf Hitler, have appeared to their contemporaries utterly deserving of the title, others less obviously so. With developments in computerization in recent decades, one ingenious solution has been to find the beastly number hidden on bar codes, highlighting the economic aspect of the mark of the beast at Revelation 13.16–18. Some have even argued that, in the numerical alphabet utilized by the World Bank, the letters of the word COMPUTER combine to make 666.[4] Given the apparently endless attempts to decode the number, some recent commentators have argued that a more symbolic interpretation is called for. In ancient Jewish numerology, six was a number of penultimacy, imperfection, being one less than the perfect number seven. Thus the repeated six hundred and sixty-six, it is argued, is nothing more and nothing less than the ultimate symbol of evil and imperfection, the appropriate number for the beast wherever it may be found in succeeding generations.

Rather more worrying, indeed morally objectionable, are the examples of this kind of interpretation provoking violence against fellow human beings. The fifteenth-century Taborites came to view themselves as God's eschatological army, commissioned with carrying out Revelation's promised plagues. Under Jan Bockelson, the Anabaptist 'New Jerusalem' of sixteenth-century Münster witnessed execution of religious opponents, famine and increasingly squalid conditions for townsfolk, before being relegated to the history books as yet another failed Utopian dream. It has even been claimed, not without some justification, that Hitler's Third Reich was in no small measure indebted to Joachim of Fiore's tripartite division of history. All these examples point to the dangerous uses to which this text can be put when its status as protest literature for vulnerable Christian communities is overlooked or forgotten, and it finds itself in the hands of those who currently hold the balance of power. Yet it remains the case that not a single passage of the book bids its readers to take up arms or resort to violence against their fellow human beings. Despite the dominance of the language of warfare, battle and victory, vengeance is firmly placed in the hands of the Creator and Judge of the world. The only route offered to those who hear the message of this book is that already taken by the Lamb, who gave his own life in order to give life to others. There is a battle to be won, but the sole weapon permitted is the word of truth (e.g. 12.11; 19.15), and the only blood shed is that of the Lamb and his martyr-band (e.g. 6.9–11; 7.14; 19.13).

Concluding Thoughts

What many of these essentially historical interpretations have in common (and this is true also of the 'contemporary historical' or 'preterist' approach outlined in the previous chapter) is the conviction that the Apocalypse is essentially a book written in code, which only the wise or privileged can unlock. But to decode it by translating it into a historical commentary, or a guide to the end of the world, is not only a precarious business, resulting in competing interpretations which are very difficult to assess. It also risks robbing its often elusive images and forceful rhetoric of their power. For Revelation, in a profounder sense than perhaps any other biblical book, the medium is the message. One needs to hear and visualize the relentless cycle of seals, trumpets and bowls, to be overwhelmed by the terrifying presence of the Son of Man, or touched by the pathos of Babylon's downfall, in order to gain true insight from this book. It is not some kind of apocalyptic nut whose husk can be discarded in order to reveal its inner kernel. To try and translate it into another genre is to do it a disservice. This is perhaps why Rudolf Bultmann, in his process of demythologization, was at a loss as to what to do with Revelation (Bultmann, 1955, 173–5).

But there is an alternative to decoding, and hints of it may be detected in that broader line of future interpretation discussed earlier in this chapter, associated with the name of Joachim of Fiore and his spiritual heirs. With its emphasis upon the broad sweep of history, the Joachite tradition did not reduce the meaning of John's visionary book to predictions about the future, even if Joachim and his successors believed themselves to be living at a crucial stage in the historical drama. Nor did it regard the book as one whose meaning was exhausted by events of the first century, though Joachim did not ignore John's own historical context, detecting echoes of both Herod and Nero in the heads of the dragon. Although Joachite exegesis was not immune from the temptation to decode, it recognized no less the prophetic nature of this book, and the open-ended nature of many of its visions which meant that they contained the potential to speak afresh in new contexts. A history of interpretation which refused to identify John's Babylon solely with the first-century Roman empire, but struggled to locate Babylon's presence in subsequent kingdoms, governments and ecclesiastical insti-tutions, is arguably more in tune with the seer of Patmos than readings which reduce the Apocalypse either to a source for ancient history or a hotbed of unbridled End-time speculation (Boxall, 2001).

The past few decades have witnessed, at least in certain parts of the globe, a revival of this insight. Readers of the Apocalypse have been increasingly concerned to relate its visions to the world of the contemporary reader, but not by identifying one-to-one correspondences in the manner of decoding. Such readings take seriously the prophetic nature of the book, not in the sense of telling the future (as Dispensationalism tends to do) but addressing a word of challenge to the world and God's people. But they also recognize Revelation's open-endedness, its paucity of specific interpretations of its visions that would tie them too closely to any particular age or situation. This approach will be the subject of the next chapter.

NOTES

1. 'Premillennialism' reflects the belief that the return of Christ will take place prior to the thousand-year reign of the saints described in Rev. 20, in contrast to 'postmillennialism', which regards the Millennium as a period of church growth preceding the Second Coming, and 'amillennialism', which rejects a literal, this-worldly understanding of the vision.
2. Literally 'what you have seen': an epistolary aorist, given that, though John is still seeing the vision of the Son of Man at 1.19, and is yet to see the other visions, from the perspective of the reader/hearers of the apocalypse they are past events.
3. Compare Dan. 2.28, which speaks less specifically of what must happen 'at the end of days'. Dispensationalists often read John's phrase as meaning that these things will happen 'swiftly', 'with rapidity', when they finally occur in the distant future.
4. C = 18, O = 90, M = 78, P = 96, U = 126, T = 120, E = 30, R = 108.

REFERENCES

Boxall, I. (2001), 'The Many Faces of Babylon the Great: *Wirkungsgeschichte* and the Interpretation of Revelation 17' in S. Moyise (ed.), *Studies in the Book of Revelation.* T. & T. Clark, Edinburgh, pp. 51–68.

Bultmann, R. (1955), *Theology of the New Testament: Volume Two.* ET SCM Press, London.

Burr, D. (1993), *Olivi's Peaceable Kingdom: A Reading of the Apocalypse Commentary.* University of Pennsylvania Press, Philadelphia.

Cowley, R. W. (1983), *The Traditional Interpretation of the Apocalypse of St John in the Ethiopian Orthodox Church.* Cambridge University Press, Cambridge.

Lindsey, H., with C. C. Carlson (1970), *The Late Great Planet Earth.* Zondervan, Grand Rapids.

McGinn, B. (1979), *Apocalyptic Spirituality.* Classics of Western Spirituality; Paulist Press, New York.

McKelvey, R. J. (1999), *The Millennium and the Book of Revelation.* Lutterworth Press, Cambridge.

Pate, C. M. (ed.) (1998), *Four Views on the Book of Revelation.* Zondervan, Grand Rapids, MI.

Reeves, M. (1999), *Joachim of Fiore and the Prophetic Future,* rev. edn. Sutton Publishing, Stroud.

Scofield, C. I. (no date given), *The King James Study Bible: Reference Edition.* Barbour, Uhrichsville, OH.

6

Looking into the Heart of the World

Yet saints their watch are keeping, their cry goes up, 'How long?' And soon the night of weeping shall be the morn of song.

(Samuel Stone, 1839–1900)

Mary and the Apocalyptic Battle

One of the most celebrated and loved Christian shrines in the continent of Latin America is the basilica of Our Lady of Guadalupe, at Tepeyac on the outskirts of Mexico City. It lies close to the site of apparitions of Mary to a local Indian, Juan Diego, in 1531. She appeared to Juan Diego clothed with the sun, standing upon the moon, with stars adorning her blue mantle. This apocalyptic image, so tradition has it, was miraculously transferred to Diego's cloak, and now hangs for veneration in the new basilica, a recognizable symbol of Mexican Christianity throughout the Catholic world. As a champion of the indigenous population, who spoke to Juan Diego in his own native dialect, Our Lady of Guadalupe is revered as patroness not only of Mexico but of all Latin America. Hers is a potent image dear to the hearts of countless Latin American Christians, not least to members of the many Christian base communities in their struggle for a more just society. For the apocalyptic vision of the woman clothed with the sun is ultimately a vision of the Church's struggle against, and victory over, the forces of evil, chaos and oppression symbolized by the satanic dragon. A Mass leaflet for the Marian month of May, emanating from a Brazilian base community, has as one of its illustrations a picture of Our Lady in the garb of the woman of Revelation 12, cradling her child against the venom of the seven-headed dragon. The accompanying caption leaves the worshipper in no doubt as to the contemporary relevance of the visionary battle: *Com Maria combateremos o dragão.* The apocalyptic combat between Mary and the dragon is the same struggle in which contemporary Christians are to be engaged; the challenge for the community is to identify, and subsequently overcome, the dragon in its own day. The overtly political identification of the contemporary dragon is hinted at in one of the explanatory notes for the Mass, which claims that Cuba and Nicaragua have already succeeded in expelling it from their midst.

Shocking though this highly politicized reading of the Apocalypse may be to the 'objective' Western interpreter (and we have seen already the dangers of using the Apocalypse to demonize one's political and religious opponents), it can legitimately claim to stand in a tradition of interpretation which goes back as far as John of Patmos himself. John's apocalyptic unmasking of the satanic nature of the great Empire of Rome surely calls forth in every age a similar unmasking of the godless and oppressive Empire, by a Church which continues to regard this text as Scripture rather than an obscure writing of merely antique curiosity. Indeed, some of the most powerful readings of this book have been those which have taken seriously the prophetic call to God's people to 'come out of Babylon'. They have regarded this book not simply as a window onto the situation of seven first-century Asian churches, or as a prophecy of the end of the world. Rather, they have treated it as a window into the very heart of the world, a world created in love by the One who sits upon the throne, yet a world which now appears hopelessly out of kilter, shot through with disorder, injustice and evil.

Voice from the Underside of History

One of the most challenging claims emerging out of recent biblical scholarship is that one's ability to hear and understand the biblical text is profoundly influenced by where one stands. No reader or interpreter comes to a text from a 'neutral' perspective, but stands within a particular interpretative community, or a variety of communities, whether those be ecclesial communities (which accord a text like Revelation a particular authoritative status), academic communities (of various kinds) or other social and political groupings. Those communities may well have long and cherished ways of reading the Apocalypse, which impinge consciously or unconsciously upon the reader or interpreter. Awareness of these is often recognized as a crucial first step in the hermeneutical task.

The influences upon us of our interpretative communities may have both positive and negative effects. Our particular context as interpreters may in certain cases give us a privileged standpoint from which to view things, in other cases it may blind us from seeing, or hearing, what the text has to offer. A Catholic Christian may, for example, be more susceptible to detecting Marian resonances in the vision of the woman clothed with the sun, or recognizing eucharistic allusions throughout the Apocalypse. A Protestant Christian, standing in a long tradition of challenge to the ecclesial status quo reaching as far back as the anti-papal exegesis of the Reformers, may well hear far more loudly Revelation's critique of the contemporary Church, and its implications for ecclesiology. But one's political stance, social and economic status, race, gender and sexual orientation will have an impact on one's reading of the text no less than one's ecclesial allegiance.

This is especially evident in the case of the Apocalypse, which deals explicitly with questions of wealth and power, viewed from the perspective of one who identifies with, and is himself to some extent among, the powerless. Might it be the case that those who, like John, are without political or economic power, are in a more privileged position to hear his message and announce it afresh to their own generation than those bound too closely into the structures of power? Are there aspects of John's Apocalypse which only God's 'little people' can adequately hear? This is a valid question, and one which has been answered in the affirmative again and again throughout human history, and in our own generation has found a resounding yes among Christians in Latin America and South Africa. But before we look at their ways of reading Revelation, we ought to think more carefully about the perspective of its author. What can be gleaned from the text about John's context, and how similar is this to the context of the engaged readings of Christians outside the northern hemisphere?

Our discussion in Chapter 4 concluded that Revelation should not be viewed against a background of violent state persecution and constant threat of Christian martyrdom, even if it does present the paradigm for the Christian martyr in the figure of the slain Lamb. Yet it is equally clear that John regards himself as having suffered hostility for bearing the name of Christ: he describes himself as 'your brother who share with you in Jesus the persecution and the kingdom and the patient endurance' (Rev. 1.9). Indeed, it is highly likely that his present sojourn on Patmos is the direct result of action taken by the secular authorities. Thus, even if not in prison or sentenced to work in the mines, he writes from the perspective of a reluctant exile, separated by sea from those communities over which he claims prophetic and pastoral oversight. The form of his punishment – exile rather than execution – may point to his relatively high social status, a possibility reflected in some early traditions about him. But whatever his socio-economic position, the prophetic message which he utters in the name of the risen Christ (Rev. 2—3) places him firmly on the side of those who find themselves vulnerable before the world: the Smyrneans, who in the Lord's eyes are rich though they experience tribulation and poverty, and suffer hostility from their Jewish brethren (2.9); the Christians of Pergamum who have held fast to Christ's name despite the memory of martyrdom in the person of their brother Antipas (2.13); the few in Sardis who have not defiled their garments through compromise with the world (3.4); the little ones in Philadelphia who despite their lack of power have kept Christ's word and have not denied his name (3.8).

John's status as one disengaged from the dominant ideology of Rome and granted insight into its demonic character is also reflected in his explicit attempts to interpret the vision of Babylon and the beast in Revelation 17—18, one of the few such interpretative passages in his whole apocalypse. The impressive and alluring city is revealed in the garb of a Roman prostitute, her true identity written on her forehead, and wearing the imperial colours which have already been revealed as the colours of war and bloodshed (17.4–5; cf. 6.4). These characteristics are important, and highlight her true nature, for in many other ways she resembles the New Jerusalem, the bride of the Lamb. Both are adorned in fine linen (18.16; 19.8), though the bright and pure linen of the Bride is contrasted with the purple and scarlet linen of the harlot. Likewise, Babylon does not have a monopoly on gold, precious stones and pearls (17.4), though their description in relation to this city exudes luxury and excess. The heavenly city will be made of 'pure gold', the foundations of its walls adorned with twelve precious stones, and each of its gates a whole pearl (21.18–21). What is wrong with the earthly city is not so much her association with wealth, as the means by which she has acquired it. The cup from which she drinks, and by which she has become intoxicated, contains not only 'the blood of the saints and the blood of the witnesses to Jesus' (17.6): she is equally held responsible for the blood of 'all who have been slaughtered on earth' (18.24). As an alluring and corrupting civilization, she rides on the back of the seven-headed beast, the seven heads being seven kings, the political and military might of the empire. The dirge over fallen Babylon which follows John's vision is a sustained critique of the exploitative manner by which this city has prospered. As Richard Bauckham has shown, the cargo list in the merchants' lament (18.12–13) accurately reflects the imports of the city of Rome in the first century (Bauckham, 1993, 350–71), a number of these being specifically mentioned in ancient critiques of Roman opulence. The last item on the list, shockingly, refers to Rome's transformation of human lives into mere commodities for the city and empire: 'slaves – and human lives' (18.13).

Elsewhere too, images of riches and power in the present world order are either debunked as counterfeit and illusory, or reinterpreted in terms of the truer, heavenly realm when true 'power and wealth' are ascribed to God and to the Lamb (5.12). The 'throne' of ultimate authority is not that of the dragon or his vicegerent the beast (2.13; 13.2; 16.10) but of God in his heavenly throne-room, shared by the Lamb.[1] The seven 'diadems' of the dragon (a perfect number, 12.3), and the ten of the beast from the sea (13.1) are revealed as mere demonic parodies of true kingship in the light of the 'many diadems' of the King of kings and Lord of lords (19.12). Similarly the crowns 'like gold' worn by the demonic army of locusts (9.7) are counterfeit in comparison to the golden crowns of the twenty-four elders (4.4, 10), the starry crown of the woman (12.1), or the crown of life promised to the victorious Christian (2.10). John's vision leaves the reader in no doubt as to where true wealth and kingship are to be found, and the privileged stance required in order for this to become evident.

With this in view, we return to some recent readings of this book, emanating from Christians who, like John, find themselves at a critical distance from the dominant political ideology of their society. The first, a commentary by a famous minister of the Dutch Reformed Mission Church, emerged out of South Africa during the period of apartheid, and was particularly shaped by the author's experience of solitary confinement in a Pretoria prison (Boesak, 1987). The second is a distinctive example of liberationist exegesis from a Chilean priest and theologian, the fruit of the author's study and reflection in two very different but converging contexts: the academic context of the National University of Costa Rica, and workshops with pastoral agents of Christian base communities throughout Latin America (Richard, 1995). Both commentaries share the belief that it is those 'on the underside of history' who have a privileged insight into the meaning and challenge of this apparently impenetrable book.

Allan Boesak draws a very clear parallel between the experience of black South Africans, and his own imprisonment, on the one hand, and that of John of Patmos on the other. Writing of the years of violence, protest and states of emergency, he has this to say: 'During these years, I believe, I have discovered the heart of that lonely, brave prophet on his island: with fear and trembling, yes, but also with a joy that no one can take away. For I know now what he knew then. Jesus Christ is Lord' (Boesak, 1987, 14). What is striking about Boesak's reading of Revelation is that it is totally lacking that First World embarrassment and unease with the book's language of violence, judgement and vindication. It is a sobering thought that the 'moral affront' which so many Christian readers experience in hearing the Apocalypse is regarded by other Christian readers as the misguided response of the privileged few, who have never been on the receiving end of suffering and oppression. When one has heard the cries of the poor, victimized and oppressed, when one has witnessed police brutality and known solitary confinement in a South African prison, when the cries of the oppressed have become one's own cries also, then the language and imagery of Revelation become the language and imagery of salvation. The 'how long?' of the souls under the altar (6.9–11), far from being the bloodthirsty cry for vengeance, is recognized as the cry of the martyrs and all victims of violence and bloodshed, convinced that ultimately God's true justice will prevail. Boesak may overstate his case about the tyranny of the Roman emperors of the first century, and the persecution and hostility which Christians had to face, in the light of his own experience of state brutality in South Africa during the period of apartheid. But his sensitive theological reading of the book has a profound authority and authenticity about it, as from one whose experiences as a disciple of Jesus Christ have enabled him to view the world from a similar perspective and through a similar lens to John the exile of Patmos.

For Pablo Richard, too, it is a particular stance which provides his Latin American commentary with its potency.

> I have sought to produce a work that is scholarly and exegetically well grounded, but from the standpoint of the oppressed: the poor, indigenous people, blacks, women, young people, the cosmos and nature, and all those who endure the discrimination of the oppressive and idolatrous system.
>
> (Richard, 1995, 3)

In particular, his work alongside members of base communities throughout Latin America has profoundly influenced his scholarly study of the Apocalypse. Thus, he views Revelation as arising not so much out of a situation of persecution, as out of one of 'oppression and exclusion' (Richard, 23), a situation which fits well the experience of many of his fellow Latin American Christians, as it does recent historical reassessments of the early empire and particularly the reign of Domitian. Indeed, he claims that the Latin American experience of oppression and the even more dehumanizing phenomenon of exclusion affords a privileged insight into the experience of John and those whom his Apocalypse describe as 'conquerors', those who have not polluted their garments.

Of course, there is a danger of anachronism here. The experience of the poor in Latin America may be very different from the experience of John of Patmos (particularly if his island exile is an indication of his higher social status), just as it is different in significant respects from the experience of those segregated and dehumanized for the colour of their skin in apartheid South Africa. Yet there are some common features, not least the experience of marginalization, the sense of powerlessness in the face of an overwhelming and apparently invincible political, economic, and in some cases religious, system. It is precisely this perspective of weakness in the face of power which is praised by the risen Christ through the lips of his servant John (e.g. 3.8), and which distinguishes readings of Revelation 'from the underside of history' from those more dangerous readings of the powerful, which demonize their weaker political and religious opponents, often with dire consequences. Ironically, both Adolf Hitler's millenarian vision of a Third Reich and the subversive preaching of the Confessing Church in the person of Dietrich Bonhoeffer can be traced to particular interpretations of the book of Revelation. Yet only one mediates the prophetic word of God, while the other is a demonic and blasphemous parody. The issue of perspective, of context, is one of the crucial checks and balances in assessing any reading of this book. Does it come from the mouth of those exercising power, from those consciously or unwittingly bound into the dominant ideology, or from the vulnerable people who, like John of Patmos, find themselves compelled to protest against those authorities which have left them excluded or disenfranchised?

Identifying the Great Empire

One of the recurring features of contemporary 'political' readings of Revelation, shared with a wide variety of readings of the book throughout the history of its interpretation, is the claim that the Great Empire, Babylon, finds new incarnations in every age. That is to say, they take seriously the text's claim to be a work of prophecy. This is very different from the understanding of prophecy in the popular mindset, or presupposed within Dispensationalist and other millenarian circles, which can often reduce the prophetic task to foretelling the distant future. The readings of interpreters such as Boesak and Richard do not regard the visions of the book as predictions of specific events to happen in the future. Nor, however, are they convinced, as historical-critical interpretations often assume, that the meaning of these visions can be reduced to events of the first century such as the demise of Nero or Domitian, the martyrdoms of Peter and Paul, or the flight of the Jerusalem church to Pella. Such events may well be alluded to, but they do not exhaust the meaning of the text. Rather, this approach claims that the symbols in John's visions are polyvalent, with a capacity to mediate God's word of judgement and salvation in every generation. They are prophetic not in the sense that they refer simply to specific historical events, whether in the first or twenty-first century, but in that they offer a profound insight into human history. In the words of Boesak: 'If the prophecy is the expression of an undeniable truth which comes from God, it will be fulfilled at different times and in different ways in the history of the world' (Boesak, 28f.).

There are indications in the Apocalypse itself that this is not a purely arbitrary approach. First, as we have already seen, John stands within an ongoing apocalyptic interpretative tradition, and is utilizing ancient figures and symbols which have had a fluidity of meaning. In the case of the beast from the sea of Revelation 13 (generally identified with the harlot's beast in Rev. 17), we are witnessing a metamorphosis of the four beasts of Daniel 7, representative of four pagan kings or kingdoms (the Babylonians, Medes, Persians and Greeks), into their present manifestation in the kingdom of Rome, which bears characteristics of all four. There is no indication in the text, however, that Rome is the last manifestation of the beast, only that it is its current manifestation from John's temporal perspective.

Second, the relative lack of explicit interpretation within Revelation, in marked contrast to the juxtaposition of vision and angelic interpretation in Daniel and 4 Ezra, militates against too close an identification between visionary elements and historical events. While some have seen allusions to the Parthian threat to Rome, or (on a Domitianic dating) the eruption of Vesuvius in 79 CE, in the visions describing the unsealing of the seven seals (6.1—8.1), these are only passing allusions, and cannot fully explain or exhaust the power of the whole sequence, which makes use of traditional apocalyptic imagery. In the third place, attention to specific visions, and the multiplicity of interpretations of them, seems to bear out the claim that they are polyvalent, that is, that they cannot be tied to any one particular referent, like a code to be cracked, but are made up of open-ended symbols. 'Babylon' is not a code-word for 'Rome', but a potent symbolic name, evoking a whole religious and cultural history in which the city and empire of Babylon has played a powerful role, which finds particular resonances at a particular point in history in the city and empire of Rome. That the application of this 'great city' to Rome is but one aspect of its meaning is implied already by its 'spiritual' or 'allegorical' naming as 'Sodom and Egypt, where also their Lord was crucified' (11.8).

Similarly, the woman clothed with the sun conjures up a whole host of images and impressions, such that her image loses something of its potency if it is reduced to a mere code, whether for Israel, or Mary, or the Church.

There are good grounds, therefore, for thinking that the contemporary reader is right to strive to interpret Revelation for his or her own day, or, more truthfully, to interpret his or her own day in the light of Revelation. But what are the 'ground rules' for identifying the great empire in subsequent generations? There has been no shortage of candidates over the Christian centuries: unfaithful Jerusalem, with all its anti-Semitic resonances, Islam, the renaissance papacy, the Soviet Empire, Saddam's Iraq. But can all such identifications be legitimate? Moreover, how can one justify the violence and bloodshed which has sometimes accompanied such identifications?

A number of rules suggest themselves. First of all, the issue of perspective comes to the fore again. Is the naming of Babylon or the beast being made from a similar perspective to John's, or does it come from a ruling and powerful elite? There are obvious differences between the prophetic challenge of Boesak to the South African regime, and the 'evil empire' rhetoric of cold war US foreign policy, or of the Western allies during the Gulf War. That is not to deny that the powerful may not on occasion correctly identify a beastly and oppressive regime; they are, however, more prone to self-deception in exonerating themselves from participation in Babylon. But some would want to claim that even the readings of allegedly 'neutral' and 'objective' interpreters are liable to be suspect, or wide of the mark, given their own implicit involvement in the dominant ideology.

Just one example of where perspective dramatically alters one's apprehension of a passage is the way in which commentators respond to the vision of Babylon, and the laments over her fall, in Revelation 17—18. George Caird is typical of many Western interpreters in his understanding of this passage:

> The cry, 'Was there ever a city like the great city?' is wrung from his own heart as he contemplates the obliteration of the grandeur that was Rome ... In the meantime it is with infinite pathos that John surveys the loss of so much wealth.
>
> (Caird, 1984, 227)

Such a reading of this passage is anathema to Boesak, who writes:

> It is so typically the viewpoint of those who do not know what it means to stand at the bottom of the list. No, the cries of the kings and merchants and shipmasters were *not* wrenched from John's heart. Their cries were the cries of those who benefitted from oppression and got rich from exploitation – the captains and barons of industry, the privileged, the owners of Rome.
>
> (Boesak, 121f.)

For Boesak and others like him, John's cry is rather the victory shout of the saints and apostles and prophets (18.20). However one adjudicates between the divergent readings of Boesak and Caird here, they have flagged up the crucial (if often unacknowledged) role of stance or perspective in every act of interpretation.

Second, careful attention to the characteristics of the beast within the text may assist the task of contemporary discernment. This is not as straightforward a task as might at first appear. Despite the polyvalence of many of John's symbols, there are clear allusions to the current empire of Rome in his two visions of the seven-headed beast in Revelation 13 and 17. The first beast of chapter 13 comes up 'out of the sea', almost certainly an allusion to the Roman proconsul of Asia, who would have arrived each year by sea at the harbour of Ephesus (13.1). It has a number, six hundred and sixty-six (or six hundred and sixteen in some ancient manuscripts, 13.18), which may imply a specific identification with a known human figure in the first century. References to the *Nero redivivus* myth, indeed, can be found in 13.3 and 17.8, 11. The interpretation of the seven heads (17.10–11) has been dominated by the evident allusion to seven Roman emperors of the first century. The ten horns are also interpreted as ten kings (17.12), though the lack of specificity as to their identity may suggest that they are simply borrowed from Daniel 7.

Nevertheless, there are more general traits, drawn from the living apocalyptic tradition, which suggest that the symbols of the beast and the great city have still more life within them. The clear commercial implications of bearing the mark of the beast (13.16–17), and the sustained critique of the arrogance and blasphemy of Babylon, lead us into the economic and political realm, and seem to warn against any ruler, authority or system of government which sets itself up in the place of God. Further, anxiety over the violence of which the apparently benevolent empire is capable, rears its head from time to time. The beast makes war on the saints and conquers them, if only for forty-two months (13.7). In Babylon is to be found not only the blood of prophets and saints, but of all the slain of the earth (18.24). Viewed in this light and in his own context, Boesak's reading can be understood as a particular fulfilment of John's prophetic vision:

> There is truth in the words we spoke to the apartheid regime on 16 June 1986: Your life shall be like the life of Ahab and the life of Jezebel. Your fate shall be the fate of Babylon, which is called Egypt, which is called Rome, which is called Pretoria.
>
> (Boesak, 116)

Third, any responsible attempt to contexualize the prophetic message of the Apocalypse must not fight shy of self-critique. The vision of Babylon, in the context of Revelation as a whole, does not exempt the reader or interpreter from the piercing light of divine judgement. On the contrary, the letters to the seven churches, with their unveiling of the compromised position of the Nicolaitans, 'Balaam' and 'Jezebel', place the Christian community, and the Christian interpreter, firmly under the spotlight. It is surely no coincidence that John's visionary description of Babylon bears an uncanny resemblance to the Jezebel of the Old Testament, as also to her counterpart in the city of Thyatira. A reading which criticizes and challenges only one's political, economic or religious opponents is likely to be suspect.

Vengeance or Justice?

It is now time to return to the troubling, even violent, language and imagery of the book. The writings of Boesak and Richard highlight the satanic nature of proud empires and institutions which the Apocalypse unveils. Yet the consequent emphasis upon divine judgement has been a particular difficulty for many modern readers. What has often been harder to deal with, even morally objectionable, is the implication that God wills the violent destruction of his own creation, and of a large section of humanity within it.

We briefly discussed in Chapter 1 various ways in which interpreters have grappled with the unnerving aspects of this book. It is possible simply to dismiss the whole book out of court as somehow sub-Christian and unworthy of the gospel of Christ. Many, indeed, will treat the theology of Revelation as a relic of a now defunct image of the Old Testament God. But this Neo-Marcionite response raises as many difficulties as it solves. Is it so simple to separate out the Old from the New Covenant? Is Revelation quite so unique within the New Testament in its conviction that there is an unfolding judgement, in which the world will be held to account before the Creator of all? More chillingly, isn't such an approach in danger of becoming hopelessly anti-Semitic, regarding the faith of Israel as a primitive and degenerate form of religion?

Other possibilities present themselves. The text can be treated as a mirror, reflecting back to us our own darker side, which for the most part remains unacknowledged, hidden below the surface. In this case, the Apocalypse reveals far more about the human condition, and its capacity for self-destruction, than about the divine will. But this approach, while containing part of an answer, might seem to be letting God 'off the hook' too easily. For it is indisputable that destructive forces seen by John are in some sense under divine control. This brings us to a third kind of approach, which goes to the heart of the Judaeo-Christian dilemma. It acknowledges that even evil in the world – or what appears to be evil – must come under the ultimate control and sovereignty of God; the alternative would be a hopeless dualism and a denial of the ultimate divine victory which for Christians is accomplished in and through Christ. Hence, theological weight is given to the repeated use of the verb ἐδόθη, 'it was permitted': the destructive visions speak of forces which, though not necessarily carrying out God's will directly, are understood to be under his ultimate control. Or, finally, it is possible that the destruction and violence viewed by John in his visions of judgement against the world is more apparent than real, that we should, along with Caird, read 'Lamb' instead of 'Lion'.

Attention to the commentaries of Boesak and Richard may be illuminating in discovering how, in their very different contexts, these so-called 'problematic' passages are regarded and dealt with. This shall be attempted in relation to the opening of the seven seals in 6.1—8.1, which includes that evocative vision of the four horsemen of the Apocalypse. For it is in passages such as this one, read within their respective contexts 'from the underside of history', that they claim to have rediscovered that biblical notion of 'justice' which is central to both Old and New Testaments.

In the four horsemen, Boesak sees not so much that divine thirst for vengeance which scandalizes so many modern readers, but rather the self-destructive nature of violence, concretized at a particular time in the empire of Rome. 'The erstwhile conquerors shall die in violence they themselves created and can now no longer control. Those who live by the sword shall perish by the sword' (Boesak, 63). This, of course, is no sub-Christian perspective to be found only on the margins of the New Testament, but a warning which lies at the very heart of the gospel (Matt. 26.52). What the horsemen reap on the earth are the lessons of history writ large; for John and fellow Christians, they are the voice of God, warning of the inevitable consequences of humanity's choices, and calling to repentance.

Pablo Richard is even more specific. Working from his own careful structural analysis of Revelation, which sees the seals sequence as the chiastic parallel to the fall of Babylon, the great empire, he views the horsemen vision as a revelation of the true nature of Rome, and of its impending destruction. Summoned by the four living creatures, who represent the cosmos, the horses and their riders speak eloquently from the four corners of the earth about this empire. The rider on the white horse, with its bow so characteristic of the Parthians (a constant threat on Rome's eastern borders) and other barbarian races, reveals how the universal victory of this apparently civilized empire is achieved in a manner no different from its barbarian enemies. In a similar manner, the red, black and pale green horses respectively reveal the ultimate violence of the so-called *Pax Romana*, its economic oppression and the empire's true status as an empire of death. These are all themes which are picked up again in the vision of Babylon in Revelation 17—18 (Richard, 68–71).

Moreover, the vision accompanying the opening of the fifth seal (the souls of the martyrs under the heavenly altar) is particularly crucial for understanding all Revelation's language and imagery of justice and judgement. For it highlights that the cry for justice and vengeance is the cry of the martyrs, who echo the cry of the Israelites in Egypt, or the cry of the despairing Psalmist. The cry only makes sense when viewed from the perspective of the victim; indeed, viewed from that perspective, it represents the only possible cry. Arising out of a biblical tradition which proclaims that God is just and that he acts on behalf of those who suffer injustice, God would not be God if he ultimately ignored the empire's reign of injustice and impunity. The vision serves to place God's apparent inaction into a broader revelatory context: the struggle continues, for the time, there will be more resistance and more martyrs. But ultimately, justice will be done.

Yet paradoxically for Richard, the violence of these passages is 'more literary than real'. This becomes clear when one recognizes the perspective from which John views his visions and from which he expects faithful Christians to read his apocalypse: a situation of extreme oppression and anguish (Richard, 4, 31–2). The language is real enough, but it is the language of those in dire situations of this sort. Revelation calls forth from such a context all the anguish, despair – yes, and even hatred – brings awareness of the situation, and enables catharsis to take place by transferring these emotions and frustrations onto the just Judge, who alone has the authority to act. Nevertheless, even what God does in response to this outcry is surprising. The opening of the sixth seal, for example, appears to describe cosmic collapse and destruction: sun darkened and moon turned to blood, the stars falling from heaven, and the removal of mountain and island, and mass human panic at the wrath of the Lamb. But this is a 'mythical-symbolic figure' (Richard, 71–3), concerned in fact not with the devastation of the world and those in it, but describing in mythological language actual human catastrophes within history. These include, but are not exhausted by, the eventual decline and fall of the Roman Empire which bears within it the seeds of its own destruction. Other visions seem to bear out the claim that John's nightmarish visions do not ultimately proclaim a divinely ordained cosmic slaughter. In Richard's words, 'the risen Jesus appears as a lamb beheaded; his victory is on the cross; the martyrs defeat Satan with their witness; Jesus defeats the kings of the earth with his word' (Richard, 4). It is with the power of myth to inspire and encourage faithful endurance that Revelation is ultimately concerned.

The Feminist Critique

Revelation's language of violence, so disturbing to many in the First World, has been reclaimed in the name of justice by their fellow Christians in parts of the Third World. Yet at the same time, it is precisely this imagery of violence which has evoked protest from a group of interpreters as concerned for the process of human liberation as the commentators of South Africa and Latin America: namely, feminist critics, who approach biblical texts both to recover the (often silent or marginalized) role of women in these narratives, and to challenge their patriarchal and (hetero)sexist depictions of women. One of the Apocalypse's fiercest critics from this school is Tina Pippin, who has become increasingly uneasy with the book's apparent justification of violence and destruction on the grounds that the oppressed ultimately triumph (Pippin, 1992). This is typified for her in the vision of Babylon's fall, which prevents the Apocalypse being 'liberating for women readers', because it portrays the violent murder (for Pippin a sexual murder) of a female prostitute. She writes: 'Having studied the evils of Roman imperial policy in the colonies, I find the violent destruction of Babylon very cathartic. But when I looked into the face of Babylon, I saw a woman' (Pippin, 1992, 80).

One might object that such a critique ignores the traditional application of feminine imagery to cities in the ancient world (a practice which continues, to a lesser degree, to the present day). To describe a city in female terms is not an overtly negative stereotype, any more than to personify a river as 'Old Father Thames'. But a feminist response would be that this is irrelevant, as is the claim that such was not the intention of the author; rather, one needs to ask what effects the reading of this passage will have upon typical readers. Will it perpetuate misogynist stereotypes, and even, on occasion, be used to justify or excuse physical and sexual violence against individual women? Certainly, there are indications in the artistic portrayal of Babylon's demise that such is a possibility. The woodcuts illustrating Revelation 17 and 18 by the sixteenth-century French engraver Jean Duvet, for example, utilize the full power of feminine 'allurement' in the portrayal of the bare-breasted prostitute in seductive pose astride the beast, who is subsequently brutally killed (dare one say violated?) by this beast and her erstwhile lovers.

Yet it must be said that the portrayal of Babylon's fall – as opposed to her present status – in terms of the destruction of a woman is not the dominant one within the iconographical tradition. Generally, the metaphorical nature of the language is acknowledged, and the fall of Babylon is depicted as the destruction of a city, as in the tenth-century *Morgan Beatus*, the Angers Tapestry, and the woodcuts of Duvet's contemporaries Dürer and Cranach. It is this image, of an arrogant city and mighty empire tumbling to the ground – with no hint of the gang rape of a violated woman – which has inspired and continues to inspire interpreters like Richard and the base Christian communities with whom he works.

A more general feminist critique is directed towards the overall portrayal of women in Revelation. They are, it is claimed, all androcentric stereotypes of the female, women in so far as they are controlled by men. Hence, one is presented with the polar opposites of the whore and the good woman, whether virgin, bride or mother. The reader is urged to make a choice between Babylon and New Jerusalem, Jezebel and the woman clothed with the sun, the faithful mother of the Messiah. But these are the idealized alternatives of the male author and male interpreter, for they shun the one who breaks free from male sexual domination (the harlot) and praise the woman whose sexual potency is under male control (wife and mother). In this case, what possibilities does Revelation hold out for single women, in a book where the female desire for power (unlike that of the male) is punished? This is a valid and challenging question. Yet Pippin wants to go even further, exhibiting a literalism which is in danger of matching that of the Dispensationalists. The 144,000 are literally a band of male warriors (described as 'those who have not defiled themselves with women', 14.4), thereby effectively excluding women and children from the New Jerusalem. This leads her on to an idiosyncratic reading of the vision of New Jerusalem, who is the beautiful young bride. The 'entering' of the city/bride by the 144,000 all-male followers of the Lamb is interpreted as a sexual 'entering': i.e. mass intercourse (Pippin, 1994, 119). Yet surely such a reading does violence to the obvious meaning of the text, which provides a vivid and detailed description of what is obviously a city, with walls, gates, foundations and a street.

Indeed, not all feminist scholars share Pippin's overly negative assessment of the Apocalypse. Both Adela Yarbro Collins and Elisabeth Schüssler Fiorenza have written extensively on Revelation (e.g. Yarbro Collins, 1984; Schüssler Fiorenza, 1985 and 1991), and continue to see it as in some sense a liberating book. Schüssler Fiorenza, while acknowledging the patriarchal assumptions of the author, nevertheless believes that much of the grammatically masculine language of the book can be read as conventional generic language, and that sexual and female language and images must also be read within their traditional as well as their modern contexts. To overstress the role of sex/gender stereotypes is to fail to grapple with those other aspects which a truly liberating reading of Revelation demands, such as racism, classism and colonialism (Schüssler Fiorenza, 1991, 14). As many commentators (female as well as male) acknowledge, sexual imagery is used throughout the Bible as a metaphor for fidelity to the God of Israel and the abandonment of exclusive attachment to him which is idolatry. Though the language may be feminine (the devotion of the bride and the unfaithfulness of the prostitute), it is applicable throughout the Apocalypse to all humanity, male no less than female.

A similar claim may be made in relation to Thyatira's 'Jezebel'. Though John's negative 'name-calling' may have overshadowed the prominence of women's ministry in the Church of first-century Asia (Yarbro Collins, 1998, 405), his portrayal of this prophetess is not in itself an androcentric attack on women. Revelation knows nothing of 1 Timothy's ban on women exercising a teaching role within the Christian community (1 Tim. 2.12). The reason for the rejection of Thyatira's 'Jezebel' is not that she is a woman claiming a prophetic ministry, but that this ministry is a false one, leading people astray. Males no less than females can be false prophets: the Jewish tradition had already made this claim for Balaam, and the message John transmits to the angel of the church in Pergamum picks up on this link (Rev. 2.14). There is little difference between Revelation's treatment of the female 'Jezebel' and the male 'Balaam'. Indeed, the two beasts – the second of whom is later identified as the false prophet – are frequently portrayed in the history of this book's interpretation in male terms. Even John's Greek can use the masculine pronoun for the beast from the sea (13.8), despite the word for 'beast' (θηρίον) being neuter. This is reflected in English translations, which routinely use the pronoun 'he' for both beasts of Revelation 13 (e.g. King James Bible; NIV; Douai-Rheims). Moreover, the web of seduction and exploitation is complex in the vision of Babylon in Revelation 17—18, for she is the object of desire of the 'kings of the earth' (clearly male), and is ultimately dependent, and in some sense the victim of, the beast upon which she sits.

Further, there are more positive portrayals of the feminine in the Apocalypse which do not reduce woman to what she is for man. The woman clothed with the sun of Revelation 12 is not powerless any more than she is negative. On the contrary, she plays a crucial role in the defeat of the beast who is intent on destroying her no less than her child. Moreover, as Christopher Rowland has suggested (Rowland, 1998, 687), the central demand of the Apocalypse – the faithful endurance of God's people, which is far from a passive role – is an essentially feminine characteristic, exemplified in the prayerful presence of Anna in the Temple (Luke 2.37), or the faithful women at the foot of the cross (John 19.25–27; cf. John 16.20–22; Rev. 12.2). Yet it is a demand made upon all who would bear the testimony of Jesus, whatever their gender.

They Shall Reign on Earth

True power in the face of the powerful: that is not restricted to the woman clothed with the sun. One of the reasons for the popularity and potency of the Apocalypse amongst marginalized and vulnerable groups may well be its capacity to empower those who appear powerless. This is as true today as it was for the small assemblies of Christians which dotted the cities of Asia in John's own time. Contemporary readings of Revelation view it as a work which subverts some myths (oppressive ones, such as the myth of imperial dominance) by replacing them with others (liberating ones). Despite superficial differences, it shares with the canonical Gospels and Paul the gospel theme of reversal, that God's power is made perfect in weakness (2 Cor. 12.9), that God has 'brought down the powerful from their thrones, and lifted up the lowly' (Luke 1.52). In short, it removes the veil which obscures true reality, investing those despised in the world with their true significance.

Scholarly discussions of the seven heads of the beast in Revelation 17 generally focus upon the identity of the seven heads/kings, and of the eighth, the beast that was and is not. But while John surely does have particular Roman emperors in mind at this point (one of the few places in the Apocalypse where the author does consciously attempt to interpret elements of his visions), might it be that over-concentration on the emperors has diverted the exegete's attention away from a more fundamental aspect of the vision? The angelic interpretation of this vision begins in v. 7 with the promise that the seer will learn 'the mystery of the woman, and of the beast with seven heads and ten horns that carries her'. The mystery of the woman will be unveiled towards the end of this chapter, and in the unfolding laments over Babylon in chapter 18. But, as Boesak has noted, the 'mystery' of the beast who is also an eighth king and one of the seven (17.11), may well be more profound that his identification with Nero or any other emperor (Boesak, 114). Twice in this interpretative section, the angel speaks of the beast as the one that 'was, and is not', and goes 'to perdition'. Might this, rather than the beast's identity, be the true 'mystery'? The apparently indestructible beast, the mighty empire before which the tiny groups of Christians in the Asian cities are as insignificant drops in the ocean, is destined for destruction. Nero, the erstwhile persecutor of the Roman church, in fear of whose return the empire, and Christians within it, lived in dread, is divested of his power. In every age, and in every nation, the days of the beast are numbered. Christians are reassured that they themselves – not the emperor in Rome, or the proconsul in his residence overlooking Ephesus, or the Asiarchs (high priests of the imperial cult) throughout the province – are priests and rulers in the truer, heavenly realm. 'To him who loves us and freed us from our sins by his blood, and made us to be a kingdom, priests serving his God and Father, to him be glory and dominion for ever and ever. Amen' (Rev. 1.5b–6).

Even today, the excavations of the great city of Ephesus are impressive indeed. The great upper city of Roman Pergamum, with its Altar of Zeus, looms like the 'throne of Satan' above the modern city of Bergama. The now-ruined Temple of Artemis, incorporating the cult of Mother Cybele, still stands as maternal protector of the city of Sardis. Somewhere under the grass of largely unexcavated Laodicea lies the ruined temple to Zeus Laodicenus. How much more would first-century Christians have been bombarded in these cities with buildings and images which spoke of the established order of the gods and the power and dominance of the Roman empire.

Late first-century visitors to Ephesus, entering by the Magnesian Gate, would have been overwhelmed by the sanctuary dedicated to Dea Roma and Divus Julius, the deified Julius Caesar, in the vicinity of the agora, the civic centre of the city. Reaching the top of Curetes Street, they may have seen the temple, altar and colossal statue, now known as the 'Temple of Domitian', but probably originally constructed under Vespasian. The colonnaded marble streets, lined with statues, and the Roman theatre accommodating 25,000, would have been impressive in the extreme. As if guarding the city on a hill to the north, was the great Artemision, the Temple of Artemis-Diana, one of the seven wonders of the ancient world. The city bore the proud title of νεωκόρος ('temple warden', Acts 19.35) of the great goddess. Trappings of the emperor cult – bound up intimately with civic and commercial life – were everywhere to be seen, on coins as well as in statues and architecture. Moreover, if they had been standing near the harbour at the right time of year, they might well have seen the personification of Roman imperial power in this province, the proconsul of Asia, arrive by sea to take up his office.

What might it have been like for a Christian in Ephesus, or Sardis, or Philadelphia, to hear the Apocalypse read in their midst? One recent estimate for the size of the first-century Ephesian church is between fifty and a hundred people, in a population of something like two hundred thousand people (Howard-Brook and Gwyther, 1999, xxii), and Ephesus is likely to have been one of the more prominent of the Asian churches, given the missionary activity of other, non-Johannine Christian leaders, such as Paul, Aquila and Priscilla, and Apollos. The Christian gatherings in some other cities may well have been tiny.

In such circumstances, the pressure to conform would have been enormous, and the lure and seduction of empire compelling. Yet Revelation invites these tiny urban churches to enter another symbolic universe, where their true worth and true standing are acknowledged, and where the illusions of empire are debunked. The Apocalypse makes quite astounding promises to those who endure. They are designated as kings and priests for God (1.6), a claim which flies in the face of Rome's presentation of imperial rule and the power and prestige of priests of the imperial cult in proconsular Asia. Despite their small numbers, they are revealed as belonging to that 'great multitude that no one could count' (7.9), which is victorious through the Lamb. When they break bread together, they are participating already in the great marriage feast of that Lamb (19.9). The invisible God whom they worship in their houses and hired halls is one before whom all the nations will worship (15.4), who sustains the cosmos and has the passage of history under his control. It is no wonder that the book is so full of canticles, in which the people of God burst into song of their destiny, of the victory which has been won for them.

Concluding Thoughts

Christians in the northern hemisphere are frequently ill at ease with John's Apocalypse, though not for the same reasons as many of their forebears. They are confronted with profound moral objections to a book which appears to gloat at the destruction of the wicked on the day of the Lamb's wrath. From another perspective, feminist critics have warned of the potentially destructive and oppressive nature of some of Revelation's images and language. Both kinds of objection need to be taken seriously. Yet, as we have seen, such are not the only reactions to this book. Others throughout the centuries have found that this book has offered them a vision, and provided them with a voice, which have been sources of profound liberation. It is a book which, viewed prophetically, can enable a penetrating critique of institutions and societies in every age. In a very real sense, it offers divine insight into the heart of the world. But it allows no less a window into the heart of the Church, illuminating its darkness and challenging its compromise no less than comforting it in its trials and encouraging its faithful witness. The final chapter will consider the ambiguous relationship between this book and the Church of God, both in the past and for the future.

NOTES

1. Of 46 occurrences of θρόνος in Revelation, 39 refer to that of God (and the Lamb), another four to the thrones of the twenty-four elders, and only three to the throne of Satan or the beast.

REFERENCES

Bauckham, R. (1993), 'The Economic Critique of Rome in Revelation 18' in *The Climax of Prophecy*. T. & T. Clark, Edinburgh, pp. 338–83.

Boesak, A. A. (1987), *Comfort and Protest*. Saint Andrew Press, Edinburgh.

Caird, G. B. (1984), *A Commentary on the Revelation of St John the Divine*, 2nd edn. Black's New Testament Commentaries; A. & C. Black, London.

Howard-Brook, W. and Gwyther, A. (1999), *Unveiling Empire: Reading Revelation Then and Now*. Orbis, Maryknoll, NY.

Pippin, T. (1992), *Death and Desire: The Rhetoric of Gender in the Apocalypse of John*. Westminster/John Knox Press, Louisville.

Pippin, T. (1994), 'The Revelation to John' in E. Schüssler Fiorenza (ed.), *Searching the Scriptures, Volume Two: A Feminist Commentary*. SCM Press, London, pp. 109–30.

Richard, P. (1995), *Apocalypse: A People's Commentary on the Book of Revelation*. Orbis, Maryknoll, NY.

Rowland, C. C. (1998), 'The Book of Revelation' in *The New Interpreter's Bible*, Vol. XII. Abingdon Press, Nashville, pp. 503–736.

Schüssler Fiorenza, E. (1985), *The Book of Revelation: Justice and Judgment*. Fortress Press, Philadelphia.

Schüssler Fiorenza, E. (1991), *Revelation: Vision of a Just World*. Proclamation Commentaries; Fortress Press, Philadelphia.

Yarbro Collins, A. (1984), *Crisis and Catharsis: The Power of the Apocalypse*. Westminster Press, Philadelphia.

Yarbro Collins, A. (1998), 'The Book of Revelation' in J. J. Collins (ed.), *The Encyclopedia of Apocalypticism, Vol. I: The Origins of Apocalypticism in Judaism and Christianity*. Continuum, New York, pp. 384–414.

7

Revelation in the Life of the Church

Now 'tis come, and faith espies thee, like an eaglet in the morn,
One in steadfast worship eyes thee, thy beloved, thy latest born.
(John Keble, 1792–1866)

Pointing Beyond Itself

In a book on the Apocalypse, one almost feels the need to justify the inclusion of this seventh and final chapter! For our discussion of the book's structure in Chapter 3 led us to the conclusion that it is made up of six sets of seven, the penultimate number of septets. It points beyond itself to the final consummation of that eschatological salvation in Christ's final coming again. Yet equally the reader of Revelation will be struck by its liturgical overtones, which punctuate the text at strategic points. The context of John's vision is his being caught up in the spirit 'on the Lord's day' (1.10), and the Apocalypse ends with a liturgical prayer for the Lord to come, in which the reader and hearers are invited to participate in the song of the Spirit and the Bride (22.17). Given the early Christian parallels, this prayer seems to be eucharistic as much as it is eschatological (cf. 1 Cor. 16.22; *Didache* 10.6). It is the prayer of the Church on the verge of the seventh week, eagerly anticipating in its eucharistic liturgy the final coming of God's Kingdom. 'Thy Kingdom come! Thy will be done on earth as it is in heaven!' So it is perhaps appropriate that this final, seventh chapter considers the role of the book of Revelation in the life of the worshipping Christian community, in that 'in-between' time between the first and second comings of the Lord. This is a complex history, in which the Apocalypse has often suffered liturgical neglect, while at other times and in other places it has fired and challenged the vision of the people of God.

The Canonical Struggle

The battle for Revelation's inclusion within the New Testament canon was long and bitterly fought, despite the claims it makes for its own prophetic authority (1.3; 22.18–19). From the earliest decades of its existence, it is puzzling that there are no clear references to or echoes of the book in the letters of Ignatius of Antioch (d. *c.* 107), given that Ignatius visited both Laodicea and Smyrna, and wrote letters to the Ephesians, Smyrneans and Philadelphians. Equally surprising is the silence of Polycarp, the Bishop of

Smyrna who was martyred about the year 155. This is especially the case given the wide range of New Testament writings which both Ignatius and Polycarp seem to know. It is highly unlikely that this silence is due to ignorance, particularly in the case of Polycarp. Some view it as evidence that the Apocalypse was already a disputed text at this time; others argue that the prophetic ministry it presumes clashed with Ignatius' emphasis upon the (post-Pauline?) monepiscopate represented by Ignatius.[1]

Whatever the facts in relation to Polycarp and Ignatius, it seems that for the most part the Apocalypse was regarded favourably up to the third century. Bishop Papias of Hierapolis (c. 60–130), near Laodicea in the Lycus Valley, seems to have known and cited from the Apocalypse (at least according to Andreas of Caesarea). Later in the second century, Justin Martyr, Irenaeus and Hippolytus also spoke highly of the Apocalypse, and regarded it as apostolic. Their contemporary Melito of Sardis (d. c. 190) wrote a treatise on it, not surprisingly for a bishop of one of the seven Asian churches addressed by this book (unfortunately, this has not survived).

What these second-century writers seem to have had in common is that they were chiliasts, who looked forward to Christ's millennial kingdom being established upon earth. It is notable that the period in which such chiliastic interpretation flourished was a period of persecution, and that a number of those who held to this interpretation faced martyrdom. They believed, in line with the interpretation springing from Irenaeus' Domitianic dating, that the Apocalypse was a book for the martyrs. It presented Jesus Christ, the slain Lamb, as the archetypal martyr, and called for Christian steadfastness and faithful witness in the face of adversity. It promised, for those who endured, citizenship of Christ's earthly kingdom and the New Jerusalem.

Nevertheless, there are signs of a rather more negative attitude in some quarters. At least one major reason was what some felt were crudely materialistic interpretations of Revelation 20 on the part of the chiliasts. According to Epiphanius, the second-century Alogoi rejected the Johannine writings and attributed them to the Gnostic leader Cerinthus; whether this dispute included the Apocalypse is a debated question. We are on firmer ground in the case of Marcion. According to Tertullian (*Adv. Marc.* 4.5), Marcion rejected the Apocalypse, no doubt because of its profoundly Jewish expression of the Christian revelation which he would have regarded as antithetical to the pure Pauline gospel. Indeed, the Apocalypse would become an important text for those who wished to oppose Marcion and others who denigrated the Old Testament. This can be seen in the commentary of Victorinus, which interprets the twenty-four elders before the throne as the books of the prophets and the Law (*In Apoc.* 4.3), as well as twelve patriarchs and twelve apostles.

According to Eusebius (*H.E.* 3.28.1–2), Gaius of Rome in the early third century also attributed the authorship of the Apocalypse to the Gnostic leader Cerinthus rather than to any of the Johns. Objections to chiliasm seem to underlie Gaius' objections. But Gaius, like the Alogoi, appears not to have reflected the consensus view, and he was vehemently opposed by his Roman contemporary Hippolytus. Later in the third century, however, specific doubts were raised about the Apocalypse which were to have far-reaching consequences, at least in the East. Dionysius of Alexandria (d. *c.* 264) questioned the Johannine authorship of Revelation, primarily on literary grounds. It is important to note that Dionysius – unlike Gaius – did not reject the Apocalypse per se, though he attributed it to another John besides the apostle. Rather, he sought to salvage the book's reputation from the over-literal interpretations of many of his predecessors, using the Alexandrian allegorical tradition which had already turned to the interpretation of Revelation as early as Clement of Alexandria (d. *c.* 215).

Yet others in this period continued to regard the Apocalypse as an authoritative and prophetic text. Revelation may have been an important text for the Montanists of second-century Asia Minor (which had some links with the Phrygian city of Philadelphia, and expected the New Jerusalem to descend upon the nearby town of Pepuza). Indeed, it is possible that the suspicion with which some held the book may have been a specific reaction to its use by the Montanist movement. Hippolytus, as we have said, answered the critique of his Roman contemporary Gaius by vigorously reasserting the book's apostolic authorship. Tertullian, faced with the violent persecution of Christianity in North Africa at the beginning of the third century, found in John's vision inspiration for his own church and his own time. In their different ways, these found in this prophetic book inspiration and hope.

The picture in the fourth century is likewise rather mixed. Athanasius, one of Dionysius' successors as Patriarch of Alexandria, listed all 27 books of our New Testament, the Apocalypse of John among them, in his famous *Festal Letter* of 367. On the other hand, the canons of the Council of Laodicea (late fourth century?) listed only 26 books of the New Testament, Revelation excluded. There is also a reference in the canons to the 'Phrygians' (Montanists), which may hint at the reasons for this exclusion. A similar omission of the Apocalypse can be found in other fourth-century canonical lists: the *Constitutions of the Holy Apostles* (which included the letters of Clement of Rome), and Cyril of Jerusalem (*Cat.* 4.33–6), who seemed to relegate it to those books which are neither read in church nor to be read by the faithful. In other words, both in Syria-Palestine and, more surprisingly, in its home territory of Asia Minor, fourth-century reservations about the Apocalypse's canonical status can be detected. This picture is supported by Eusebius of Caesarea, who observed how some placed Revelation with the undisputed New Testament writings, others among the books to be rejected, such as the *Acts of Paul, Apocalypse of Peter* and *Shepherd of Hermas* (*H.E.* 3.25). A similar claim for the Apocalypses of John and Peter is found in the Muratorian Canon, dated to the late second century at the earliest.

Elsewhere, silence may point to the Apocalypse being unknown rather than rejected. It does not appear to have made an appearance in the Syriac New Testament until the fifth century (the oldest Syriac manuscript in the British Museum to contain the Apocalypse dates from 1088 – Westcott, 1889), and even after that point was not read in public. Ephrem the Syrian in the fourth century does cite from the book and attribute it to John the Apostle, though he may well be dependent upon a Greek rather than a Syriac version. Otherwise, Syriac Christians in the first four centuries appear to have been ignorant of its existence (Gwynn, 1897). In the case of the Armenian church, the period of ignorance was even longer. The earliest attested Armenian version is found in the late twelfth century (Wainwright, 1993, 33), attributed to Nerses of Lambron, Bishop of Tarsus, though at least one scholar has claimed that Nerses' translation was in fact a revision from a Greek manuscript of an already long-existent Armenian version (Conybeare, 1907, 78).

If Dionysius' reservations had a lasting impact in the East, the fortunes of the Apocalypse in the West fared much better. It was regarded as canonical by the Synod of Carthage in 397. Early Latin Fathers (Tertullian, Cyprian, Commodian, Lactantius) are united in their acceptance of the book. A number of Latin commentaries survive from the third century onwards (e.g. Victorinus, Tyconius, Primasius), whereas the earliest surviving Greek commentaries are those of Oecumenius and Andreas of Caesarea, both from the sixth century. Andreas' commentary was to become the standard commentary on Revelation in both Greece and Russia, given the lack of earlier material, and the fact that John Chrysostom wrote no homilies on the book. This Eastern reserve is also reflected in iconography: there are few representations of scenes from the Apocalypse in the East during the Byzantine period, with the notable exceptions of Egypt, Syria and Cappadocia (van der Meer, 1978, 31).

Yet, even when the Apocalypse had gained canonical status, it continued to be a thorn in the side of the ecclesiastical authorities, regularly regarded with suspicion or bemusement. The reservations of Eusebius – in contrast to the enthusiasm of figures like Justin and Tertullian – almost certainly reflect the sea-change brought about by the accession of Constantine and so-called 'Edict of Milan'. Revelation's fierce critique of empires and political institutions would hardly endear itself to supporters of the Emperor such as Eusebius, hence his at best ambivalent attitude towards the book. In the later Middle Ages, particularly in the wake of the Joachite school, Revelation came to be used by radical movements as a weapon against what they considered the corruption and compromise of the Church, its leaders, and Christian princes. Anxiety surfaced again at the Reformation over both apostolic authorship and canonicity. Martin Luther treated it as little more than an appendix to the New Testament, justifying this decision with the claim that Christ is neither taught nor known in it, unlike truly apostolic writings. This did not, however, prevent him using Cranach's woodcuts of the Apocalypse to good polemical effect, with their decidedly anti-papal interpretation of some of its visions (see especially the Babylon of his 1522 *September Testament*). None of this should surprise us, however. Christians today – no less than in generations past – are still at a loss as to what to do with this book. Is there a way forward?

The Apocalypse and Liturgy

We have already suggested that the profound liturgical aspects of the Apocalypse may point to a suitable context in which this book might be read and appropriated. From the opening vision of the One like a Son of Man (1.10ff.) to the concluding eucharistic call for the Lord to come (22.20), the book is saturated not only with echoes of biblical texts, but with explicit liturgical actions, implicit liturgical allusions, and bold liturgical canticles. A number of scholars argue that the garb of Christ in John's inaugural vision – long robe and golden sash – reveals him as the heavenly High Priest (Barker, 2000, 82–92), thus linking the Christology of this book with that of the Epistle to the Hebrews. That Christ stands in the midst of seven lampstands is an indication that a priestly, temple setting is not an inappropriate interpretation. When John is taken up and beholds a vision of the *Merkavah* (4.1), the scene has as many liturgical allusions as it has those of the imperial court. At strategic points in this book, liturgical actions take place in the heavenly sanctuary, or characters in the heavenly drama burst into song. The Hebrew liturgical refrains 'Amen!' and 'Alleluia!' occur eight times and four times respectively (in the case of the latter, Revelation is the only New Testament book to use the term). The whole Apocalypse cries out to be understood, and to be read, liturgically.

Moreover, eucharistic allusions abound. In the letters to the seven churches, references are made to eating from the tree of life (2.7), and being given some of the hidden manna (2.17), as well as an invitation to sit down and eat with Christ (3.20). The proclamation of the Lord's death (cf. 1 Cor. 11.26) permeates this book through its central symbol of the slain Lamb, culminating in the announcement of the Lamb's marriage feast, to which the faithful are invited (19.7, 9). The shedding of his blood is a recurrent theme (e.g. 1.5; 7.14; 12.11; 19.13–15; cf. 14.20), and beings in heaven render 'thanksgiving' ($\epsilon\mathring{\upsilon}\chi\alpha\rho\iota\sigma\tau\acute{\iota}\alpha$) to the one seated on the throne (4.9; 7.12; cf. 11.17). This makes it all the more probable that it was precisely within the context of eucharistic worship that the small Christian congregations of the seven Asian cities first heard this text read aloud.

Yet paradoxically, the history of the liturgical reading of the Apocalypse is not a very promising one. The Orthodox Church forbids the reading of the book during public worship, reserving the book for the spiritually mature, a policy which echoes strictures against the private reading of the early chapters of Ezekiel in Judaism. In the West, the picture is rather mixed. Rome and Canterbury admit Revelation to their lectionaries, though exposure to it during the Eucharist is limited to a small number of 'purple passages'. Yet in certain parts of Western Christendom too, in recent years, questions have been raised about the appropriateness or otherwise of this book being read by, or even to, the faithful. In the face of widespread world-renouncing Dispensationalist readings in the United States, some voices in the mainstream American churches have urged that the book ought to be taken out of the hands of the people, and expunged from the official Lectionary. Revelation, it is claimed, is just too dangerous a book to be allowed into the hands of the fundamentalist, impressionable or uninstructed.

Such a response is understandable, in the light of some of the excesses described in Chapter 5. But is it the most appropriate response? Should the Church omit from its Lectionary that which causes the contemporary world difficulty, or embarrassment, or which is open to misuse? Should ambiguous Pauline passages regarding husbands and wives be excluded from public worship (an issue which has recently exercised the Irish Catholic bishops)? Should Christians expunge from their Paschal Liturgy the reading from Exodus 14 celebrating the horrific drowning of several hundred Egyptians? Should the people of God be shielded from the shocking and disturbing visionary aspects of the book of Revelation? One difficulty with an affirmative answer is that the Christian sense of what is problematic or downright objectionable shifts from generation to generation and culture to culture. This can depend, moreover, as much upon hermeneutical presuppositions as upon the 'spirit of the age' (as in the very different readings of Revelation by the allegorist Dionysius of Alexandria and his more literalist contemporary Nepos). But perhaps history itself will reveal the more severe objection to a policy of exclusion: the bizarre and sometimes dangerous usage of the Apocalypse by particular groups over the centuries may be a direct consequence of the relative neglect of this book by the churches. The appropriate answer to a difficult and dangerous text is not to ignore it, but to face it head on, and engage in some solid teaching. To remove such texts from liturgical use (whether they concern how Christian husbands are to treat their wives, or what believers are to make theologically of violent death by natural disaster or genocide) will not necessarily mean that people will no longer read them, but that they will be read in a dangerously uninformed and unreflective manner.

A liturgical context for reading, however, can minimize these dangers in two ways. First, the eucharistic Liturgy of the Word provides a ready setting for grappling with difficult, obscure or worrying texts, in the homily where the word proclaimed is broken for the faithful. Second, the liturgy itself provides constraints on how the text is be understood and appropriated. To participate in the liturgy demands participation of the whole person, sight as well as hearing, smell as well as speech, bodily gesture no less than mental assent. It connects the worshippers – not as individuals but as a corporate entity – with the profound prostrations of the twenty-four elders (4.10), the movements of the angels in the sanctuary (8.3), and the chorus of the heavenly choirs. Moreover, it links the hearers imaginatively with those Christian assemblies in Smyrna, Sardis and the other Asian cities, who would also have heard, seen and smelt the Apocalypse. Further, at the heart of the liturgy lies the drama of salvation, of what God has done for humanity in Christ, the same drama which is acted out within the Apocalypse itself. This eucharistic emphasis upon the divine initiative is a crucial antidote to those readings of the book which urge people to take matters into their own hands, sometimes with dangerous consequences. Finally, the structure of the Eucharist provides profound checks and balances to those readings of Revelation which tend only to demonize one's opponents, whether political or ecclesiastical. For it calls God's people first to repentance of sins, and presents them with the dynamic and challenging divine word, before inviting them to share in the Lamb's high feast. Like the Apocalypse, so too the Eucharist confronts the Church with the reality of divine judgement.

Many, indeed, have noted how in the Eastern Churches the avoidance of public reading of the Apocalypse has been coupled with a 'living out' of the Apocalypse in the eucharistic liturgy itself. The Orthodox Divine Liturgy is an experience of the worship of heaven, in which God's people participate together with the angels and saints in that perfect liturgy beyond the veil. In this, it maintains a powerful link with the worship of the Jerusalem Temple, in which Jesus and almost certainly John also participated, and with those other Jewish groupings such as the Qumran community who believed that in their liturgical celebrations they were worshipping along with the angels. Similarly in the Western Church, the Mass has traditionally been understood as that crucial meeting point of heaven and earth, where the Lamb's once-for-all sacrifice is made present, and the faithful share with the great High Priest in rendering fitting praise and thanksgiving to the Father. Moreover, in both West and East, the essentially eschatological nature of the Eucharist has been central, for in and through it Christ comes to his people in judgement and salvation, foreshadowing the final great coming at the end of time. As Christians had come to recognize as early as the middle of the first century CE: 'For as often as you eat this bread and drink the cup, you proclaim the Lord's death until he comes' (1 Cor. 11.26).

What might this eucharistic appropriation of John's Apocalypse have meant in practice to its first hearers, and what might it mean for contemporary Christian hearers? First, it reminds us of that privileged 'space' which the

Liturgy provides, and which is essential for maintaining the glorious vision that John beholds. There is a world of imaginative difference between the sober, individual reading of the Apocalypse in a scholar's study or a believer's living room and the corporate hearing of it by the ecclesial body gathered in worship. Christians in some other parts of the contemporary world may well have a greater affinity than ourselves with those little Christian assemblies in Ephesus, Pergamum or Philadelphia, who realized that they were doing something politically subversive in their liturgical reading of this book. In the Liturgy, they (and we) join their feeble voices to the mighty chorus, numbering 'myriads of myriads and thousands of thousands', singing with full voice that the Lamb is worthy (5.11–12). In the Liturgy, the historical 'ditch' separating first and twenty-first centuries is temporarily removed. In the Liturgy, the veil is lifted, enabling a clear vision of what God's world is, and what it can become. The Liturgy provides that sacred space in which God's vulnerable people can receive assurance of salvation.

This liturgical apprehension of John's vision has both positive and negative aspects. Positively, it sheds new light upon what the Apocalypse might mean in its expectant prayer for the coming of Christ. As we have seen, the book has often been read as if it were speaking primarily about the final great coming of Christ in glory. While the book clearly does point the reader to the ultimate consummation of all things, a eucharistic reading sets this expectation in a broader context. There are indications in the New Testament that the early Christian communities understood sayings about the Lord's 'coming' in a variety of ways, particularly as time passed and they had to grapple with the deaths of fellow believers (e.g. 1 Thess. 4), the passing of the apostolic generation (e.g. John 21.19, 23), and the apparent slowness of the Lord's return (e.g. 2 Pet. 3.8–10). This is especially the case with the Farewell Discourses of the Fourth Gospel (John 13—17), with which the Apocalypse has traditionally and canonically been paired. Here the Lord's sayings about his 'coming' have been reinterpreted to refer to the present divine indwelling (14.18–20), the coming of the Paraclete (14.16; 15.26; 16.7), and the resurrection appearances (16.22) as well as to his Parousia (14.3). Moreover, in the light of John 6 (e.g. 6.56), it is difficult not also to see allusions to Christ's eucharistic coming in some of these verses (e.g. 14.18–20).

So too in the eucharistically charged Apocalypse, references to Christ's 'coming' seem to be far richer than a mere allusion to his coming again at the end of time. The seven letters speak of the Son of Man's 'coming' in judgement and salvation to his churches (e.g. 2.5, 16; 3.20 – the latter in a clear eucharistic allusion). The victory cry accompanying the fall of Satan from heaven declares that God's Kingdom and the authority of his Messiah have 'come' (12.10): the context connects this with the past death of Christ, recalled in the Eucharist. The eucharistic canticle at 19.7 declares that the Lamb's marriage feast has 'come'. At 22.17, the Spirit and the Bride utter a prayer for Christ to 'Come!' and issue an invitation to the thirsty to 'come' and drink freely from the water of life. Finally, the eschatological urgency is placed in a eucharistic context in the penultimate verse of the book, when the 'Surely I am coming soon' is met with the liturgical cry: 'Amen! Come, Lord Jesus!' (22.20). It is in the context of the Lord's 'coming' to his fledgling churches in the Eucharist that the urgency of his final coming 'with the clouds' (1.7) is kept alive, and with it the promised transformation of the cosmos.

Second, this liturgical encounter with the One who comes strengthens the churches in their ongoing battle with the beast. A careful reader of the Apocalypse will recognize that it actually describes two very different liturgies, one associated with the true, heavenly realm, the other with the earthly. The worship of the One on the throne and the Lamb (Rev. 4—5), in which John and his fellow Christians participate through the eucharistic liturgy, is paralleled and parodied by the worship of the dragon and the beast 'from the sea', orchestrated by the false prophet, the second beast 'from the earth' (Rev. 13). Those who dwell on the earth 'worship' the dragon and the beast, saying, 'Who is like the beast, and who can fight against it?' (13.4); they are bidden to make an image of this beast and worship it (13.14); they bear the mark of the beast, which is required for any commercial transaction (13.16–17). First-century Asian hearers may well have noted in this idolatrous liturgy echoes of the imperial cult and other religio-political aspects of Roman urban life. From a 'this-worldly' perspective, such liturgy would appear to have the upper hand. Yet something subversive would happen in their own rival liturgy, away from the temples and marketplaces of their cities. The beast would be named for what it really is, its power dethroned and its transitory nature unveiled. It is replaced by a heavenly liturgy in which those who refuse to compromise with the beast are praised, and receive assurance of their own ultimate victory. Seen from this perspective, neither the book of Revelation nor the Church's Liturgy represent a 'flight from the world' into some parallel universe, but they lead Christians into the very heart of the world, as witnesses both to the truth about that world, and its need for redemption.

One of the ways in which this vision is kept alive is through the canticles which punctuate the book at key points. These do not simply function like the choruses of ancient Greek plays, commenting upon the surrounding action (Le Moignan, 2000, 85). They are hymns of praise, which proclaim the mighty works of the one seated on the throne and his Messiah. They orient the hearers towards the truth about God, and the truth about the world, but, more importantly, urge the hearers to make them their own. Critical questions raised by scholars about the canticles of Luke's Infancy Narratives (Luke 1—2) may also be posed of these Johannine canticles. Whether they are hymns already in liturgical use within the churches of John's time, or represent his own compositions in line with his theological vision, is not easy to decide. Indeed, we cannot rule out the distinct possibility in this visionary text that these canticles contain something of what John himself heard while 'in the spirit' on Patmos. It was not unknown for Jewish and Christian mystics to hear 'things that are not to be told' (2 Cor. 12.4), even the tongues of angels as well as of humans (1 Cor. 13.1). But whatever their origin, what they proclaim is central to the vision which Christians are to keep alive not least in their liturgical worship. It is particularly through song that human beings have maintained political, religious and cultural identity in the face of hostility, persecution or indifference. Protest songs have sustained the souls of nations in settings as diverse as Husak's Czechoslovakia, Botha's South Africa and Pinochet's Chile. The liturgical chanting of the Beatitudes and the singing of Marian hymns kept the rumour of God alive in Russia and Poland during the Soviet era. Prisoners in every age, from Paul and Silas in first-century Philippi (Acts 16.25), have found renewed courage and vision in singing the wonders of God. Such is the power also of the canticles of praise and salvation which John hears in his apocalyptic vision.

But there is also a more negative aspect to the liturgical reading of the Apocalypse. It calls the Church, no less than the world before which it is to bear witness, to judgement. The letters to the angelic guardians of the seven churches reveal the spiritual state of those churches, praising some and exhorting them to faithful endurance while rebuking and challenging others. One approach to the interpretation of these letters (given the symbolic significance of the number seven) is to see them as glimpses of the variable state of the churches in any age: sometimes faithful and in need of consolation, sometimes in danger of compromise, sometimes lacking in love or lukewarm. While historical critics struggle to place the figures of 'Jezebel' and the Nicolaitans on the map of first-century Christianity, and Futurists point the finger at rival religious leaders and churches, a liturgical reading shines the spotlight on the attendant worshippers, forcing them to ask where they stand within the spectrum of the seven churches. Such a question remains as sequences of seals, trumpets and bowls are read out, and Babylon and the beasts rear their heads. For in every age, the Church has had to battle against the tendency to compromise: the vision of the two beasts in Revelation 13 remains a chilling warning to the churches that false worship is as much a possibility as true worship, and that the distinction between the two is not always crystal clear. This is all the more pressing, and all the harder to discern, where the churches have lost their minority position and find themselves closely bound up with the status quo. In such cases, a liturgical hearing of the Apocalypse, in the context of confession of sin, becomes all the more pressing.

Reliving the Exodus

The liturgical dimensions of this text should by now be obvious. But some would wish to go further, connecting the Apocalypse specifically with the Easter liturgy of the Church. It has even been claimed that the Paschal Liturgy of the first-century Asian churches suggested to the seer of Patmos the structure for his book (Shepherd, 1960, 77–84). It may be that such a proposal is rather too optimistic about our ability to reconstruct first-century liturgical worship. But even if we acknowledge these difficulties, what of the alternative, namely, that Revelation has fed into the subsequent liturgical celebration of the Paschal Mystery? And what might it mean for the ecclesial interpretation of the Apocalypse?

It is evident that John's vision is saturated with echoes of and allusions to the scriptures of Israel. But a sensitive reader of the whole tapestry of Revelation may detect one specific thread which runs throughout the whole, and, moreover, has been crucial from the beginning for a Christian understanding of the Easter events. It is the theme of the Exodus – that fundamental narrative for the self-definition of God's people – relived and reinterpreted in the light of Christ. Only a quarter of a century after the death of Jesus of Nazareth, Paul attests the Christian interpretation of that death in terms of the sacrifice of the paschal lamb (1 Cor. 5.7–9), an understanding echoed later by the author of 1 Peter (1 Pet. 1.19–20; cf. Rev. 13.8). The early chapters of Matthew's Gospel see in the events of Christ's infancy and early years a re-enactment of the story of Moses' and Israel's Exodus journey out of slavery in Egypt (Matt. 2.13—4.11). The Fourth Gospel is even more explicit in its presentation of the death of Jesus as the slaughter of the Passover Lamb (John 19.14, 29, 36; cf. 1.29, 36). But it is the Apocalypse which makes this Passover and Exodus motif a major theme.

The christological affirmation of Jesus as the Lamb who conquers by being slain runs throughout the book. That the Passover lamb is particularly in mind is clarified by other echoes of the biblical narrative. The sequences of trumpets and especially the bowls parallel the plagues of Egypt described in Exodus 7—12, heralding divine judgement on the oppressors of God's people. Prior to this second plague sequence, we are given a vision of the followers of the Lamb standing beside a 'sea of glass mixed with fire', singing 'the song of Moses, the servant of God, and the song of the Lamb' (15.2–3). The Israelites sang the song of Moses after passing through the Red Sea (Exod. 15.1–18), proclaiming God's glorious victory over their enemies; here too, those who have resisted the beast sing of God's justice and righteous deeds, although now the Lamb has entered into the equation (15.3–4). But this 'new Exodus' motif has been prepared for even earlier in this book. At 1.6, the hearers are told that by his blood Christ has made them 'a kingdom, priests serving his God and Father', echoing the promise made to the Exodus generation (Exod. 19.6). At 2.17 the 'hidden manna', first given at Exodus 16, is promised. Moreover, the woman clothed with the sun, the heavenly counterpart of God's people of both old and new covenants, relives the experience of the wilderness generation when she is given the 'two wings of the great eagle' to fly into the wilderness (12.14; cf. Exod. 19.4) and escape the wrath of the dragon. Jewish hearers would well recall that Ezekiel had already likened the Egyptian Pharaoh to the great dragon (Ezek. 29.3; 32.3).

In and through the liturgical reading of this text, the Christian community is invited to relive the experience of the Israelites in the Exodus. It is not surprising, therefore, to find echoes of the Apocalypse, however faint, in the Paschal Liturgy of the Western Church. The *Exsultet* sung by the deacon proclaims the events of Easter night to be another Passover feast, in which the true Lamb is slain (*in quibus verus ille agnus occiditur*), and recalls the first Exodus when our fathers were led out of Egypt and passed through the Red Sea dry shod. The language used of the slain Lamb echoes more strongly the Vulgate of Revelation (*dignus est agnus qui occisus est*, Rev. 5.12) than the paschal passage in Paul (*etenim pascha nostrum immolatus est Christus*, 1 Cor. 5.7), or its Old Testament antecedent Exodus 12, which also uses the verb *immolare*. Likewise, the *Exsultet*'s reference to Christ as our 'morning star' (*lucifer matutinus*), while partly dependent upon 2 Peter 1.19 ('the morning star rises in your hearts'; *lucifer oriatur in cordibus vestris*), appears also to echo the language of Revelation 2.28 (*stella matutina*; cf. 22.16). Moreover, this Easter hymn is followed by a succession of Old Testament readings, one of which recounts the saving events of the crossing of the Red Sea (Exod. 14).

But the Apocalypse's retelling of this ancient story, in a liturgical setting, has several implications. In common with the wider New Testament treatment of the Exodus, the Apocalypse has universalized the motif so that it is concerned no longer with the redemption of a particular nation from a specific slavery, but deals with the profounder human need for liberation from sin (1.5: according to the preferred manuscript reading, Christ has '*freed* us from our sins by his blood'). Further, the redemption has been achieved by the slaying of the Lamb alone, not accompanied by the slaughter of the firstborn, or the deaths of the armies in the sea. The christological dimension is central to understanding the story, and receives particular focus in the context of the Paschal Liturgy. Third, the New Exodus story certainly takes seriously the heartfelt cry of the oppressed for justice to be done, but its liturgical articulation in the song of Moses and the Lamb removes the execution of that justice firmly out of the hands of dangerous human beings and into the hands of God alone (15.3–4). Finally, the universalization of the biblical narrative also has implications for the identity of God's redeemed people. John's vision of the 144,000 from all the tribes of Israel (7.1–8) has them transformed into an innumerable multitude, 'from every nation, from all tribes and peoples and languages' (7.9), who have continued the testimony of Jesus and have washed their robes in the blood of the Lamb. The challenging aspect of this liturgical re-enactment again comes to the fore: the faithful are called to follow the Lamb wherever he goes (14.4), even if that takes them in the way of the cross.

Concluding Thoughts

The biblical canon opens with a liturgical text recounting the wonders of the first creation (the Priestly account of Gen. 1). It is equally fitting, canonically speaking, that the Christian canon concludes with another liturgical text, which proclaims a new creation through Christ, who is 'the firstborn of the dead' (Rev. 1.5). For many throughout the meandering history of its interpretation, the Apocalypse has been regarded as the fitting climax to the biblical revelation, and an urgent reminder that the same Word which was spoken by God in the beginning is to come again, like a Mighty Warrior, to bring the divine work to completion. As we have seen, however, such has not always been the reception of the book of Revelation, even within the churches, over the centuries. Some have grappled earnestly with it, only to find it ultimately impenetrable. Others still have washed their hands of it, as just too dangerous, or bizarre, or unworthy of the gospel of Christ. The intention of this book, however, has been to offer one possible path through the maze – however idiosyncratic – in the conviction that Revelation is a book ultimately worth grappling with. It is possible that the Apocalypse, far from being a book to obscure and conceal, is what it claims to be, a book of revelation. In its dynamic and polyvalent visions, it invites many different ways of seeing, and through seeing, the possibility of greater insight into the mystery of God. Many before have grasped this vision, glimpsed this insight, and in doing so have heard what the Spirit is saying to the churches.

NOTES

1. It is true that Ignatius urges that people 'give heed to the prophets' (*Smyrn.* 7.2); but this seems to be a reference to the Old Testament prophets, since he adds 'and especially to the Gospel'.

REFERENCES

Barker, M. (2000), *The Revelation of Jesus Christ.* T. & T. Clark, Edinburgh.

Conybeare, F. C. (1907), *The Armenian Version of Revelation and Cyril of Alexandria's Schola on the Incarnation and Epistle on Easter.* The Text and Translation Society, London.

Gwynn, J. (ed.) (1897), *The Apocalypse of St. John, in a Syriac Version Hitherto Unknown.* Hodges, Figgis & Co., Dublin.

Le Moignan, C. (2000), *Following the Lamb: A Reading of Revelation for the New Millennium.* Epworth Press, Peterborough.

Meer, F. van der (1978), *Apocalypse: Visions from the Book of Revelation in Western Art.* Thames & Hudson, London.

Shepherd, M. H. (1960), *The Paschal Liturgy and the Apocalypse.* Ecumenical Studies in Worship No. 6; Lutterworth Press, London.

Wainwright, A. W. (1993), *Mysterious Apocalypse.* Abingdon Press, Nashville.

Westcott, B. F. (1889), *A General Survey of the History of the Canon of the New Testament,* 6th edn. Macmillan, Cambridge and London.

Further Reading

Apocalyptic

Collins, J. J. (1992), *The Apocalyptic Imagination*. Crossroad, New York.
Collins, J. J., McGinn, B. and Stein, S. J. (eds) (2000), *The Encyclopedia of Apocalypticism*. 3 volumes; Continuum, New York and London.
Rowland, C. (1982), *The Open Heaven*. SPCK, London.
Russell, D. S. (1992), *Divine Disclosure*. SCM Press, London.

Introductions

Bauckham, R. (1993), *The Theology of the Book of Revelation*. Cambridge University Press, Cambridge.
Court, J. M. (1979), *Myth and History in the Book of Revelation*. SPCK, London.
Court, J. M. (1994), *Revelation*. New Testament Guides; Sheffield Academic Press, Sheffield.
Desrosiers, G. (2000), *An Introduction to Revelation*. Continuum, London and New York.
Garrow, A. J. P. (1997), *Revelation*. New Testament Readings; Routledge, London and New York.
Le Moignan, C. (2000), *Following the Lamb: A Reading of Revelation for the New Millennium*. Epworth Press, Peterborough.
Prévost, J.-P. (1993), *How to Read the Apocalypse*. ET SCM Press, London.
Smalley, S. S. (1994), *Thunder and Love: John's Revelation and John's Community*. Word Publishing, Milton Keynes.

Commentaries

Introductory

Boesak, A. A. (1987), *Comfort and Protest*. Saint Andrew Press, Edinburgh.
Faley, R. J. (1999), *Apocalypse Then and Now*. Paulist Press, Mahwah, NJ.
Metzger, B. M. (1993), *Breaking the Code: Understanding the Book of Revelation*. Abingdon Press, Nashville, TN.

Rowland, C. (1993), *Revelation*. Epworth Commentaries; Epworth, London.
Schüssler Fiorenza, E. (1991), *Revelation: Vision of a Just World*. Proclamation Commentaries; Fortress Press, Minneapolis, MN.

More Substantial
Boring, M. E. (1989), *Revelation*. Interpretation Commentary; John Knox Press, Louisville, KY.
Caird, G. B. (1984), *The Revelation of St John the Divine*, 2nd edn. Black's New Testament Commentaries; A. & C. Black, London.
Harrington, W. J. OP (1993), *Revelation*. Sacra Pagina; Liturgical Press, Collegeville, MN.
Murphy, F. J. (1998), *Fallen Is Babylon*. New Testament in Context; Trinity Press International, Harrisburg, PA.
Richard, P. (1995), *Apocalypse: A People's Commentary on the Book of Revelation*. ET Orbis, Maryknoll, NY.
Roloff, J. (1993), *The Revelation of John: A Continental Commentary*. ET Fortress Press, Minneapolis, MN.
Rowland, C. C. (1998), 'The Book of Revelation' in *The New Interpreter's Bible*, Vol. XII. Abingdon Press, Nashville, TN, pp. 501–736.
Sweet, J. (1990), *Revelation*. TPI New Testament Commentaries; SCM Press, London/Trinity Press International, Philadelphia, PA.
Swete, H. B. (1906), *The Apocalypse of St. John*. Macmillan, London.

Specialist
Aune, D. E. (1997), *Revelation 1—5*. Word Biblical Commentary 52a; Word, Dallas, TX.
Aune, D. E. (1998), *Revelation 6—16*, and *Revelation 17—22*. Word Biblical Commentary 52b and 52c; Thomas Nelson, Nashville, TN.
Beale, G. (1999), *The Book of Revelation*. New International Greek Testament Commentary; Eerdmans, Grand Rapids, MI/Paternoster Press, Carlisle.
Charles, R. H. (1920), *A Critical and Exegetical Commentary on the Revelation of St John*. International Critical Commentary; T. & T. Clark, Edinburgh.

Other Studies on the Apocalypse
Bauckham, R. (1993), *The Climax of Prophecy*. T. & T. Clark, Edinburgh.
Farrer, A. (1949), *A Rebirth of Images*. Dacre Press, Westminster.
Howard-Brook, W. and Gwyther, A. (1999), *Unveiling Empire: Reading Revelation Then and Now*. Orbis, Maryknoll, NY.
McKelvey, R. J. (1999), *The Millennium and the Book of Revelation*. Lutterworth Press, Cambridge.
Moyise, S. (1995), *The Old Testament in the Book of Revelation*. Sheffield Academic Press, Sheffield.

Moyise, S. (ed.) (2001), *Studies in the Book of Revelation*. T. & T. Clark, Edinburgh.

Pate, C. M. (ed.) (1998), *Four Views on the Book of Revelation*. Zondervan, Grand Rapids, MI.

Pippin, T. (1992), *Death and Desire: The Rhetoric of Gender in the Apocalypse of John*. Westminster/John Knox Press, Louisville, KY.

Schüssler Fiorenza, E. (1985), *The Book of Revelation: Justice and Judgement*. Fortress Press, Philadelphia, PA.

Yarbro Collins, A. (1976), *The Combat Myth in the Book of Revelation*. Scholars Press, Missoula, MT.

Yarbro Collins, A. (1984), *Crisis and Catharsis: The Power of the Apocalypse*. Westminster Press, Philadelphia, PA.

Revelation in Its First-Century Context

Hemer, C. M. (1986), *The Letters to the Seven Churches of Asia in their Local Setting*. JSNT Supplement Series 11; Sheffield Academic Press, Sheffield.

Ramsay, W. M. (1904), *The Letters to the Seven Churches of Asia*. Hodder & Stoughton, London.

Thompson, L. L. (1990), *The Book of Revelation: Apocalypse and Empire*. Oxford University Press, Oxford.

Wengst, K. (1987), *Pax Romana and the Peace of Jesus Christ*. SCM Press, London.

Worth, R. H. (1999), *The Seven Cities of the Apocalypse and Roman Culture*. Paulist Press, New York and Mahwah, NJ.

Yamauchi, E. (1980), *The Archaeology of New Testament Cities in Western Asia Minor*. Baker Books, Grand Rapids, MI.

History of Interpretation

Charles, R. H. (1913), *Studies in the Book of Revelation*. T. & T. Clark, Edinburgh, pp. 1–78.

Rowland, C. C. (1998), 'The Book of Revelation' in *The New Interpreter's Bible*, Vol. XII. Abingdon Press, Nashville, TN, pp. 528–56.

Wainwright, A. W. (1993), *Mysterious Apocalypse*. Abingdon Press, Nashville, TN.

The Apocalypse and Liturgy

Barker, M. (2000), *The Revelation of Jesus Christ*. T. &. T. Clark, Edinburgh.

Barr, D. L. (1986), 'The Apocalypse of John as Oral Enactment', *Interpretation*, pp. 243–56.

Prigent, P. (1964), *Apocalypse et Liturgie*. Cahiers Théologiques; Delachaux et Niestlé, Neuchatel.

Shepherd, M. H. (1960), *The Paschal Liturgy and the Apocalypse.* Ecumenical Studies in Worship No. 6; Lutterworth Press, London.

The Apocalypse in Art

Grubb, N. (1997), *Revelations: Art of the Apocalypse.* Abbeville Press, New York, London and Paris.

James, M. R. (1931), *The Apocalypse in Art.* Schweich Lectures in Biblical Archaeology, 1927; Oxford University Press for the British Academy, London.

Meer, F. van der (1978), *Apocalypse: Visions from the Book of Revelation in Western Art.* Thames & Hudson, London.

Paley, M. D. (1986), *The Apocalyptic Sublime.* Yale University Press, New Haven, CT and London.

Scribner, R. W. (1981), *For the Sake of Simple Folk: Popular Propaganda for the German Reformation.* Cambridge University Press, Cambridge.

Strand, K. A. (1968), *Woodcuts to the Apocalypse in Dürer's Time.* Ann Arbor Publishers, Ann Arbor, MI.

Wright, R. M. (1995), *Art and Antichrist in Medieval Europe.* Manchester University Press, Manchester.

Music Inspired by the Apocalypse

Françaix, Jean, *L'Apocalypse selon St Jean*
Messiaen, Olivier, *Quatuor pour la fin du temps*
Schmidt, Franz, *Das Buch mit sieben Siegeln*

Useful Websites

Apocalypse Then, Apocalypse Now: The Book of Revelation from Rome to Waco, by Robert M. Royalty
(http://persweb.wabash.edu/facstaff/royaltyr/apocalypse.htm)

Art, Images, Music, and Materials related to the Book of Revelation, by Felix Just SJ
(http://clawww.lmu.edu/faculty/fjust/Revelation-Art.htm)

Cities of Revelation, by Craig Koester
(http://www.luthersem.edu/ckoester/Revelation/main.htm)

Frontline: Apocalypse!
(http://www.pbs.org/wgbh/pages/frontline/shows/apocalypse)

Links to Revelation, Apocalyptic and Millennial Websites and Materials, by Felix Just SJ
(http://clawww.lmu.edu/faculty/fjust/Apocalyptic _Links.htm)

Revelation Resources, by Georg Adamsen
(http://sunsite.dk/Revelation)

Index

Aelius Aristides 40
Alogoi 16, 147
Anabaptists 125
Andreas of Caesarea 9, 149
angels 51, 53, 66, 71; of the winds
    60
Angers Apocalypse 48, 140
Antichrist 90
apocalypse, meaning of 2
Apocalypse of Abraham 15, 32
apocalypses 12–16, 32–3
Apollo 41–2
Armageddon 73, 111
art 7–8, 22, 27, 140; *see also*
    Angers Apocalypse; Botticelli;
    Vathas; Velázquez
Asia Minor 83; map 84
Athanasius 148
audition 27
Augustine 107
Augustus 39–40

Babylon 73–7, 133–7; Rome as 94–
    6, 130–1; *see also* woman seated
    on a beast
Barr, David 5
Bauckham, Richard 58–9, 131
beasts 44–5, 69, 93, 130–1, 134,
    135–6; *see also* heads of the
    beast; number of the beast
Beatus of Liébana 125
Bockelson, Jan 125
Boesak, Allan 131–2, 134, 135–6,
    138, 143
Bonhoeffer, Dietrich 133
Boring, Eugene 95

Botticelli, Sandro 109
bowls 71–3
Branch Davidians 106

Caird, George 23, 97, 135–6
canticles 154–5
Carthage, Synod of 149
Cerinthus 16, 147, 148
Charles, R. H. 11
chiliasm 147, 148
Christ 53, 57–8; earthly kingdom
    147; in Easter liturgy 157; John's
    vision 150; Second Coming 119,
    153–4; *see also* Lamb
'church-historical' interpretation
    108
Clemens, Flavius 99
1 Clement 100
Clement of Alexandria 148
Clement of Rome 148
Collins, Adela Yarbro 73–4, 141
Collins, John J. 14–15
colours 60
Commodian 149
Constitutions of the Holy Apostles
    148
Cranach, Lucas 140, 150
Cyprian 149
Cyril of Jerusalem 148

Daniel 13, 15, 28, 31, 34, 43–5,
    113, 121
Darby, John Nelson 111–12
Diego, Juan 128
Dio, Cassius 99
Dionysius of Alexandria 16–17

Dispensationalism 111–15, 118,
     119–23
Domitian 86–9, 98–100
Domitilla 99
Dürer, Albrecht 140
Duvet, Jean 140

Easter liturgy 155–7
Edict of Milan 149
1 Enoch 15
Ephesus 20, 143–4
Ephrem the Syrian 149
Epiphanius 89, 90, 147
eschatology 12–13
Ethiopian Orthodox Church 108
eucharist 150, 152
Eusebius 22, 87–8, 89, 100, 148,
     149
Eve 8
evil 24
Exodus 156
Ezekiel 32–3, 56
4 Ezra 28, 32

feminist critique 139–42
festivals 36
Futurist interpretation 107, 110,
     115–17, 118, 123

Gaius of Rome 16, 148
Galba 91, 93, 94
Garrow, Alan 63, 91
greetings 51

harlot see woman seated on a
     beast
heads of the beast 91–3, 143
hearing 3–5, 57
Hekhalot 32
Hemer, Colin 54, 101
Hippolytus 147, 148
historical criticism 83, 116

Hitler, Adolf 125, 133
horsemen 58–60, 138

iconography 8
Ignatius of Antioch 146–7
incense 63–4
Irenaeus 19, 20, 87, 90–1, 124,
     147
Islam 108, 109
Israel 8, 114–15

Jehovah's Witnesses 61, 123
Jesus Seminar 115–16
Jewish apocalypses 32–3, 37
Joachim of Fiore 107, 108–10,
     126
John, exile on Patmos 83–6, 130
John the apostle 16, 19–21
John's Gospel, authorship 19
judgement 24, 73, 137–9
Jung, Carl Gustav 22
justice 23, 137–9
Justin Martyr 19, 147

Koresh, David 106

Lactantius 149
Lamb, the 57–8, 156, 157
Laodicea, Council of 148
Latin America 128, 132–3
lectionaries 6, 22, 151
letters to the churches 37, 51–6,
     101, 137, 155
Lindsey, Hal 124
liturgy 150–6
Luther, Martin 150

McKelvie, Jack 119
Marcion 147
mark of the beast 136
martyrdom 102
martyrs 51, 63–4, 101, 139, 147

Mary 68–9, 128, 129
meat 37–9
Melito of Sardis 147
Mexico 128
Miletus 86
millennarian groups 106
Millennium 78, 107, 111, 122
Miller, William 123
Montanists 123, 148
Morgan Beatus 140
Moyise, Steve 43
Muratorian Canon 149
music 5

Nero 42, 93, 94, 136, 143
Nerses of Lambron 149
New Jerusalem 79–80
new things 120
number of the beast 69, 94, 95, 124–5, 136
numerology 61, 62, 67, 81; *see also* number of the beast; seven

Oecumenius 149
Olivi, Peter 110
Orthodox liturgy 152

Papias of Hierapolis 146–7
Parousia 119
Paschal Liturgy 155–7
Passover 156
Patmos 52, 83–6, 130
Pax Romana 138
Pergamum 103
persecution 14, 69, 86–9, 98–103, 147
Philadelphia 103
Pippin, Tina 140, 141
plagues 64–5, 72, 156
Polycarp of Smyrna 20, 91, 146–7
prayers of the saints 63–4
premillennial interpretation 111

preterist interpretation 107
Primasius of Hadrumetum 9, 149
prophecy 12, 67, 96, 117, 133–4

Ramsay, William 54, 101
Rapture 111–12, 121–2
reading, public 3–5
Reagan, Ronald 111
redemption 157
repentance 118, 151
resurrection of the dead 122
revelation 13
Revelation: audience 11, 14; authorship 16–21, 148; canonicity 146–50; chronological pattern 10–11; date 86–98, 104; divisions for public reading 74; genre 11; imagery 8, 22–4, 43–6, 118, 134, 137; interpretation 1, 7; Jewish parallels 31–4; liturgical context 6, 12; New Testament parallels 29; structure 9–10, 49–81; title ix, 49
Riberia, Francisco 110, 113
Richard, Pablo 132–3, 138–9
Roloff, J. 15
Roma 40–1, 114
Roman Empire 37–42, 75, 139; emperors 92
Rome 75, 91, 130–1; as Babylon 94–6, 134; as beast from the sea 134
Rowland, Christopher 32, 33, 65, 142
Russell, Charles 123

Satan 75, 79
Schüssler Fiorenza, Elisabeth 17, 141

Scofield, C. I., Reference Bible 111–14, 119, 120
scrolls 57, 59, 66
seals 56–63
seeing 7, 57
seven, the number 9–10, 51; *see also* bowls; heads of the beast; letters to the churches; new things; seals; trumpets; visions, final; visions, of the church
silence 61
Smyrna 102, 103
Snow, Samuel 123
South Africa 131–2
Suetonius 88, 99–100
suffering 14, 69

Taborites 123, 125
Tacitus 40, 93
Temple 35, 36, 96–7
Tepeyac 128
Tertullian 88, 147, 148, 149
Theophylact 90

trumpets 63–8, 72
Tyconius 149

Vathas, Thomas 34
Velázquez, Diego 27, 28
Victorinus of Pettau 10, 64, 118, 147, 149
vision 27–36
visions 7, 30–5; final 77–80; of the church 68–70

Waco 106
Wellhausen, Julius 97
Whisenant, Edgar C. 123–4
woman clothed with the sun 68–9, 114, 128
woman seated on a beast 75, 88, 140, 143
women *see* feminist critique
word of truth 67
'world-historical' interpretation 108

Zionism 115

Printed in Great Britain
by Amazon

42319356R00104